Dear anny —

   Happy Birthday !
You are a surviver !
I love you.

        Debby

THE
SHERLOCK HOLMES
COOKBOOK

THE
SHERLOCK HOLMES
COOKBOOK

or
Mrs. Hudson's Stoveside Campanion
formed upon
principles of economy
and adapted to the use of private families

by
two gentlemen
and which contains in one volume

HOLMES COOKING
By
JOHN FARRELL

BAKER STREET
MEALS AND MENUS
By
SEAN M. WRIGHT

engravings
by F. DWIGHT SHUNDO

Bramhall House • NEW YORK

INTRODUCTION

For those who love Sherlock Holmes and the London of the 1890s, everything connected with that era has a special fascination. Gasogene and tantalus, coal scuttle and hansom cab, fog, and gaslit streets all charm away the spectres of the 1970s.

Sherlockians often attempt to recapture the charm of Sherlock Holmes' London in dress and in the furnishings of their homes. Victoria still reigns in the world, even if the television is blaring in the next room and the traffic is roaring in the street outside.

For those of us who try to live our dream lives at 221 Baker Street, nothing is too small or too unimportant. But until now, one major area of the London of just before the turn of the century has remained in the background, a part of that London that was as important and common as gaslight and the fog: food.

We know from the Canon some of the things Sherlock Holmes and Dr. Watson ate. Several meals are mentioned with what Poo-Bah called "affecting particulars." But beyond that, no one has really ventured, except in pleasant speculation. What we really know of the meals consumed on Baker Street boils down to a roast goose, a pâté de fois gras pie, and a couple of bottles of something choice (and tinned peaches on Dartmoor). Beyond that there is a great, unexplored void, a hungry void filled with meals that must have been eaten, cases of wine and whiskey, and seas of soda, tea, and coffee.

The late Victorian era, for all its image of tight-laced, tight-fisted men whose enjoyment was rather mundane, was a world that had not yet learned to be guilty about gustatory pleasure. Food and drink were indulged in, often to excess, by those who could afford the extravagance, and without fear of diets, cholesterol, and blood sugar levels. Fine food was dear, but large quantities of nourishing sustenance could still be hade for prices that weren't extravgant. Obesity was a sign of prosperity, and though both Holmes and Watson maintained themselves in fighting trim, those occasional steam baths must have reduced more than just the tensions of the day. The Master and his faithful amenuensis typify the age in which they lived. They ate and drank like men of their era. And if we can never know exactly what they ate and when, we can certainly try to eat as they might have eaten; in fact, as they must have eaten.

We can only glimpse the gaslight, only smell the foul, oppressive fog in our imaginations. But we can taste the food much as it was. We can sit down to meals that would have satisfied Watson after a long day following Holmes and Toby on the scent of a murderer. We can cook a meal that would have done Mrs. Hudson's reputation for breakfast proud. We can recreate a high tea in front of a roaring coal fire on an afternoon when the wind moans in the chimney pots at Baker Street.

This book, in part, is scholarly for those whose interests run to the historical and statistical. But it is mostly intended for pleasure. It will help you escape, in your kitchen and your dining room to that place where it is always 1895.

THE
SHERLOCK HOLMES
COOKBOOK

HOLMES COOKING

By
John Farrell

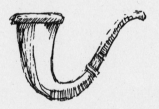

BREAKFAST

"...and we sat down together to the excellent breakfast which Mrs. Hudson had prepared."

Breakfast is the preeminent Sherlockian meal. It is also the triumph of the good Mrs. Hudson, who managed to tolerate the worst tenant in London for so many years. It was, after all, the one meal both her tenants could reasonably be relied upon to eat (barring Andaman Islanders with dart guns and other peculiarities she must have become inured to). And in England, breakfast has always been a national institution. Men and women of whatever business needed a satisfying meal to drive out the chill of bleak English mornings. And in Scotland, Mrs. Hudson's homeland, it can be even colder than London on a foggy morning when there is no case to brighten Sherlock Holmes' mood.

In present-day England, where modern-day rushing about has overtaken the slower life of Victorian London, a hearty breakfast is still appreciated. But in Sherlock Holmes' time, breakfast would have been even heartier. Cold joints of meat on the sideboard would have augmented the ham, bacon, grilled kidneys, kippers and eggs, porridge, toast, scones, and tea (or more likely, coffee). And for special occasions, even curried chicken might be offered (when Mrs. Hudson would rise to the occasion).

Mrs. Hudson must have had to rise for the occasion every day, getting up probably two hours before her lodgers to light the coal stove, boil water, and begin the meal. Watson, with his habit of rising late, might eat an hour or more later than Holmes. Mrs. Hudson must usually have had to prepare two breakfasts. But surely Holmes' "princely sums" must have made up to her, at least in some part, the patience she had to exercise with two such unusual gentlemen.

BACON

I have in my library a copy of *Mrs. Beeton's Cookery Book*, undated, but surely not too far removed from Victorian London. In it, a plate illustrates the various cuts of bacon. Collar, streaky, gammon, flank, long back, corner — all of these are foreign to me since I'm used to buying bacon in paper packages with glassine windows. And I'm not prepared to venture a guess as to which was the favorite on Baker Street.

The bacon that Holmes and Watson often ate was most probably grilled, rather than fried in the modern manner. Perhaps it came from Buckinghamshire, long noted as the source of the best English bacon, though little ever got to market since it was so popular amongst the country folk. In any case, bacon certainly figured large in the breakfast menu.

EGGS

We know that Holmes and Watson ate their eggs scrambled, at least on occasion, since Holmes, offering breakfast to Inspector Stanley Hopkins, warns him that the scrambled eggs are cold. And on another occasion (at tea, in "The Valley of Fear") Holmes talks of "polishing off" an egg. That egg may have been fried or boiled, (though it might have been a *Scotch Egg*, in which case Holmes must have been famished in order to finish four *Scotch Eggs* at one sitting. Soft-boiled eggs and their hard-boiled brothers each receive one Canonical mention. Mrs. Hudson was too good a cook to cook the breakfast eggs in only one manner, unless her lodgers had special preferences.

HAM

Both Sherlock Holmes and Dr. Watson are known to have liked ham and eggs. It appears that Watson was particularly fond of this breakfast dish.

Whether the ham was grilled, fried, or cut cold from the joint is a question that isn't answered in the Canon, though it is likely that it was served all three ways, and occasionally with a caper sauce.

The varieties of ham available to Holmes and Watson were many. The best hams in England come from Suffolk, thanks more to the way they are smoked than to the meat. Hams from Yorkshire are smoked with wet straw added to the wood and spices to produce great quantities of smoke. Holmes and Watson may have enjoyed either of these or other varieties, though if as some speculate, Holmes came from a farming background, he may have had his own home-grown hams provided.

Bacon and Egg Pie

Eggs, 3

Bacon, ½ lb.

Short crust pastry dough, 10
ounces

Salt and Pepper, to taste

Egg, beaten, 1 small

Grease a 7-inch pastry tin. Separate the dough into two pieces, one a little larger than the other. Roll out the larger piece and line the greased tin. Chop the bacon into small pieces, and season with pepper. Put the seasoned bacon into the pie shell, leaving spaces for the eggs. Drop an egg into each space, and season with pepper and salt. Using the beaten egg, brush the edge of the pie shell. Then roll out the smaller piece of dough, and use it to cover the pie. Decorate the edges, and cut a hole in the middle of the top. Bake at 400°F. for 40 minutes. (You may want to cover the top with foil or waxed paper after it browns.) Serve the pie cold with strong mustard. *Serves 3.*

KIPPERS

When fresh, kippers should be soaked for 1 or 2 minutes, then dried. You may fry them in butter or brush them with melted butter and grill.

Mutton and Tomatoes

Mutton, cooked and sliced,
½ lb.

Tomatoes, large, sliced, 3

Bread crumbs, 3 table-
spoons

Gravy, ½ cup

Butter, 2 tablespoons

Salt and pepper, to taste

In a greased baking dish, arrange a layer of tomato slices on the bottom; cover with bread crumbs. Season with salt and pepper, then arrange a layer of meat slices on top. Repeat until all the ingredients are used, making sure the last layer is tomato. Pour the gravy in, and sprinkle the top with the remaining bread crumbs. Place a few pats of butter on top. Bake for ½ hour at 300°F.

MARMALADE

Marmalade was invented just before the end of the eighteenth century by a Scotswoman, thus starting an English tradition. I've included two recipes here.

Breakfast Marmalade

Oranges, 2

Lemons, 2

Grapefruit, 2

Sugar

Wash the fruit and slice in very thin strips. Remove seeds and put slices in a cheesecloth sack. Measure the fruit, adding 2 cups of water for every cup of fruit. Soak overnight, or for 24 hours. Cook until the fruit is tender, cool, then measure and add an equal amount of sugar. Cook this mixture over a low fire until it is thick. Bottle in sterile jars.

Orange Marmalade

Oranges, 12

Sugar, equal weight of
oranges

Wash oranges and cut into sections, peeling and chopping the peel into small pieces. Remove the pulp and seeds and cover the orange section and peel with just over a quart of water for each pound of fruit and skin. Let the mixture stand for 24 hours; then boil it and simmer until reduced by half. Let this stand for an additional 24 hours; measure it and add an equal part of sugar. Bring this to a boil and simmer until mixture stiffens when cooled. Bottle in sterile jars.

Ham and Egg Pie

Mushrooms, sliced 4 oz.

Milk, 4 tablespoons

Salt and pepper, to taste

Ham, cooked, chopped,
6-8 oz.

Eggs, hard-boiled, chopped,
2

Green peas, cooked, 3 oz.

Mustard, prepared, 1 tea-
spoon

Flaky pastry dough, 10 oz.

Simmer mushrooms in milk with salt and pepper for 10 minutes. Add ham, eggs, peas, and mustard. Separate the pastry into a small and a larger piece. Roll the larger piece out to cover a greased baking dish, and trim the edges. Put in filling and cover the pie with remaining dough. Decorate as desired, brushing top with beaten egg for glaze. Bake at 450°F. until set, then at 325°F. for the remainder of 45-minute baking time. *Serves 2.*

Kidneys and Oysters

For each serving use 1 kidney, 3 oysters, and a small slice of toasted bread. Grill the kidney(s) and blanch oysters in their own juice, but don't overcook. Place 3 oysters on each one; serve on toast sprinkled with salt and pepper.

Jugged Kippers

Place kippers in a tall jug and boil for 10 minutes; drain and serve with butter.

Croquettes of Ham and Rice

Rice, cooked, 3 oz.	Sage, a pinch
Shallot, finely chopped, 1	Salt and pepper, to taste
Butter, 1 tablespoon	White sauce, 2 oz.
Ham, cooked, finely	Egg yolk, 1
chopped, 6 oz.	Egg, beaten, 1
	Breads crumbs, 1 cup

Cook the rice and pat dry; put it through a coarse sieve. Fry the shallot in the butter until brown, then add the ham, rice, sage, and salt and pepper. Stir over fire until hot. Mix together white sauce and egg yolk; add to other ingredients and stir until the preparation thickens. Spread on a plate until cool. Form into balls; coat each with egg and bread crumbs, and fry in deep fat until golden brown.

Ham and Tongue Soufflé

Butter, 1½ tablespoons	Ham, cooked, minced, 3 oz.
Flour, 1½ tablespoons	Tongue, cooked, minced,
Stock, 1 cup	3 oz.
Tomato puree, 1 cup	Egg whites, 3
Parsley, chopped, 2	
teaspoons	

Add stock, tomato pureé, and parsley and cook until boiling. Lightly sprinkle in the meat, season to taste, and cook for a few minutes. Cool mixture, then fold in stiffly-beaten egg whites, one at a time. Pour the mixture into a well-greased souffle pan and leave the mixture to rise. Bake at 350°F. for 30-45 minutes, until risen and browned. Serves 4-6.

Scotch Scones

Flour, 2 cups
Baking powder, 3
  teaspoons
Sugar, 2 tablespoons
Salt, ½ teaspoon
Shortening, 6 tablespoons
Buttermilk, 1½ cups

Sift the dry ingredients; cut in the shortening until mixture looks crumbly. Add buttermilk, mixing only enough to moisten flour. Turn the mixture onto a lightly-floured board and pat into a round about 1-inch thick. Cut into 12 pie-shaped pieces. Bake on greased cookie sheet for 20 minutes. *Makes 12 Scones.*

Potato Pasty

Beef, lean, diced, 4 oz.
Onion, finely chopped, 1 oz.
Potato, raw, diced, 4 oz.
Salt and pepper, to taste
Gravy or stock, 2-3
  tablespoons
Short crust pastry dough,
  10 oz.

Mix the meat with onion and potato. Season well; moisten with gravy or stock. Roll out dough to ¼ inch thick, keeping it as round as possible. Place mixture on one half of dough, moisten edge, and fold over, forming a semi-circle. Crimp the edges, and pierce with a fork. Bake at 425°F. for 10 minutes, then reduce heat to 325°F. and bake for another 35 minutes, until inside tests done. (Dough can form four smaller pasties, if desired.) *Serves 4.*

Sautéed Kidneys

Kidneys, sheep or pork,
  sliced thin
Shallot or small onion,
  finely chopped, 1
Butter, 2 tablespoons
Parsley, finely chopped, ½
  teaspoon
Salt and pepper, to taste
Brown sauce, 3-4
  tablespoons

Skin kidneys, removing core, and slice. Sauté shallot or onion in butter until lightly browned. Add kidneys and parsley. Season with salt and pepper, and toss over heat for 5-6 minutes. Add brown sauce; mix well with the kidneys. Heat and serve. *Makes 2 portions.*

Kidney Toast

Kidneys, sheep, 2 (½lb.)
Butter, 2 tablespoons
Lemon juice, ½ teaspoon

Cayenne, salt and black
pepper, to taste
Toast, buttered, 2 slices

Stew kidneys in water or stock until tender. Remove skin and gristle and pound with mortar until smooth. Add butter, lemon juice, pinch of cayenne pepper, salt, and black pepper. Pass mixture through wire sieve. Spread lightly on toast; heat in oven and then serve. *Makes 1-2 portions.*

Fish Pie

Cod or any white fish, ½lb.
Suet, finely chopped, 2 oz.
Potatoes, mashed, 2 tablespoons
Bread crumbs, white, 1
tablespoon

Salt and pepper
Egg, 1
Milk, 1 cup
Bread crumbs, brown, ¼
cup
Butter, 2 tablespoons

Skin and bone fish and chop it coarsley; add the suet, potato, white bread crumbs, and a good seasoning of salt and pepper. Now stir in egg with as much milk as will form a stiff batter, and turn into baking dish suitable for table. Cover surface lightly with brown bread crumbs and small bits of butter. Bake in 300°F. oven for 1 hour, or until mixture is set. Serve while hot. *Serves 2.*

Poached Eggs and Minced Beef

Butter, 1½ teaspoons
Onion, finely chopped, 1
Flour, ½ oz.
Gravy, ½ cup
Roast beef, underdone,
cubed, ½ lb.

Vinegar, salt and pepper, to
taste
Eggs, poached, 2
Toast, 2-3 slices

Melt the butter and fry the chopped onion until lightly done; sprinkle in the flour and brown lightly; Add the gravy and boil for a few minutes. Now add the meat and season with vinegar, salt, and pepper, and keep the mixture hot, but not boiling for 10-15 minutes. In the meantime, poach the eggs and trim the edges. Cut the toast into triangular shapes. When ready to serve, put the mixture in a hot plate, put the eggs on the top and surround the base with the toast. *Serves 2.*

Veal and Ham Patties

Veal, cooked, cold, cubed, ½ lb.

Ham, cooked, cubed, 2-4 oz.

Mixed herbs, to taste

Salt and pepper, to taste

Nutmeg, a pinch

Stock or water, 2 tablespoons

Flaky pastry dough, 10 oz.

Egg, beaten, 1

Parsley, for garnish

Add spices, salt, and pepper to cubed meats; moisten with stock or water. Roll out the dough thinly. Cut 12 circles of rolled dough slightly larger than cupcake mold. Reroll remaining dough and use to line the cupcake pan. Fill each pan with meat, and moisten edge of dough, then cover with circles. Decorate these to taste. Make a small hole in the center of each, and brush each with beaten egg. Cook at 450°F. until pastry dough sets, then lower heat and cook for total of 20 minutes. Garnish with the parsley. *Makes 12 patties.*

Toad in the Hole

Flour, 4 oz.

Milk, 1 cup

Salt, ¼ teaspoon

Egg, 1

Fat, 1 tablespoon

Sausages, 1 lb.

Make a batter from the flour, milk, salt, and egg and leave to stand for ½ hour. Heat the fat in a medium-sized baking dish. Skin the sausages and cook them in the fat; drain off the fat. Pour the batter over and bake at 425°F. for 30 minutes.

Sausage Croquettes

Pork sausages, 1 lb.

Butter, 1½ teaspoons

Milk, 1 teaspoon

Potatoes, mashed, ½ lb.

Nutmeg, salt and pepper, to taste

Egg yolk, 1

Egg, 1

Bread crumbs, ½ cup

Prick the sausages with a fork, put them into boiling water and cook for 10 minutes. When they are cold, remove the skins and cut them across in half. Melt butter in a saucepan; add milk and potatoes, seasoning well with nutmeg, salt, and pepper. Stir until hot; add the egg yolk and continue stirring and cooking for about 5 minutes longer. Let the potato mixture cool; then spread a thin layer over each sausage. Coat with egg and breadcrumbs and fry in oil until golden brown. *Serves 4.*

Oatmeal Porridge

Oatmeal can be prepared several ways, but the classic manner is the simplest and best. Into boiling, slightly salted water, pour the oatmeal while constantly stirring the mixture with a wooden spoon. Add oatmeal until the mixture is thick, then simmer for 20-30 minutes. Porridge should be served with cream, milk, or butter, with honey or syrup as a sweetener. But, if you don't like the oatmeal, here is a way to use it:

Oatmeal Scones

Cold oatmeal porridge
Flour

Into the cold oatmeal knead enough flour so that it can be rolled out to ¾ inch thickness. Cut into 3-cornered pieces and bake on a hot greased griddle or in the oven. Serve hot, split open, and buttered.

Fricassee of Eggs

Eggs, hard-boiled, 4   Parsley, chopped, for
White sauce, 1 cup   garnish
            Salt and pepper, to taste

Slice eggs thickly, reserving the yolk of one for a garnish. Put the sliced eggs in warmed white sauce and heat thoroughly. Arrange the eggs and sauce on a hot plate, and garnish with parsley and the remaining egg yolk, pushed through a sieve. *Serves 2.*

Egg Croquettes

Eggs, hard-boiled, 4   Butter, 2 tablespoons
Mushrooms, coarsely-   Flour, ½ oz.
    chopped, large, 6   Milk, 3 oz.

Salt and pepper, to taste   Bread crumbs, ½ cup
Nutmeg, a pinch   Parsley, fried

Chop eggs finely or push through sieve. Fry the mushrooms in the butter; stir in flour, add the milk, and boil well. Put in eggs, season to taste. Add a pinch of nutmeg, mix well over heat, then spread on a plate to cool. Shape mixture into balls, cover with batter of flour and milk mixed to consistency of cream, cover with bread crumbs, and fry in deep fat until golden brown. Drain and serve garnished with fried parsley. *Serves 2.*

Kippered Eggs

Kipper, cooked, 4   Cream, 1 tablespoon
  tablespoons   Eggs, lightly beaten, 4
Butter, 2 tablespoons   Toast buttered, 2 slices
Pepper, to taste   Parsley, for garnish

Warm the kipper meat in half the butter, seasoning with pepper. Stir until fish is well heated. Add remaining butter, cream, and eggs. Stir until eggs begin to set. Dish onto hot buttered toast and garnish with parsley. *Makes 2 portions.*

Eggs and Tomatoes

Take two ripe, firm tomatoes and cut a circular hole into the stalk ends. Remove seeds and pulp, leaving only the flesh adhering to the skin. Sprinkle inside of tomato with salt and pepper. Break 1 egg into each tomato. Lay a small piece of butter on top, and bake in a moderate (350°F.) oven until egg is set. Sprinkle with grated cheese. *Serves 2*

Scotch Woodcock

Eggs, 4   Anchovy fillets, 8
Toast, buttered, 4 slices   Capers, for garnish
Anchovy paste, 1½
  tablespoons

Scramble the eggs. Spread toast with anchovy paste and place eggs on top. Criss-cross each piece with 2 anchovy filets, and sprinkle with chopped capers. *Serves 2.*

Curried Chicken

I've saved this recipe until the end since it really doesn't belong here, but tradition and the Canon place it here. It was in "The Naval Treaty" where a most unusual breakfast dish was featured; that Holmes-praised, Mrs. Hudson's curried chicken.

Chicken, fryer, 1
Onion, minced, 1
Flour, 1 tablespoon
Curry powder, 1 tablespoon
Chicken stock, 1½ cups
Curry paste, 1 teaspoon
Coconut, chopped, 1
   teaspoon

Chutney, 1 teaspoon
Apple, sliced, 1
Lemon juice, 1 tablespoon
Salt, to taste
Cream or milk, 2
   tablespoons

Divide chicken into neat joints and fry lightly in hot butter. Remove chicken from frying pan and add minced onion, cook until soft but not brown. Add flour and curry powder and stir for a few minutes, pour in stock and stir until boiling. Replace chicken in pan, add curry paste, coconut, chutney, sliced apple, lemon juice, and salt to taste; cover and cook gently for ¾ of an hour or until flesh is tender. Arrange chicken neatly on a hot platter. Add cream or milk to sauce, stir, and pour over chicken. Serve with boiled, dried rice.

LUNCH

Lunch was not Mr. Holmes' favorite meal, although Watson seems at least to tolerate it. Holmes was always pocketing a sandwich or a piece of bread, or skipping the meal entirely in his haste. Lunch was easily dispensed with, and did not hold the same inviolable sanctity as breakfast.

Sometimes lunch at 221B must have been sumptuous, though. At one point in "The Sign of the Four," Dr. Watson admits that it might have been the Beaune he drank with lunch that bolstered his courage for a verbal attack on Holmes' drug habit.* If the meal featured a fine wine, it is safe to presume that it also featured at least two courses, one of which must have been either game or a strong flavored or red meat. Christopher Morley suggested that Watson was bracing himself for the arrival of Mary Morstan, whom he had married several months earlier. I personally believe that Watson would have sought his sure cure, brandy, for such an effect. In either case, a lunch with wine was more than just a sandwich or soup affair.

I believe that Holmes, if he used any drug, used marijuana, since his Asian connection and interests, and certain Canonical evidence seem to support this. The plugs and dottles collected on the mantlepiece, and a smoking herb dried in a Persian slipper seem to me to indicate something other than tobacco. I had the pleasure, at a meeting of the Non-Canonical Calabashes some two years back, of arguing the question with Mr. Nicholas Meyer, author of The Seven Percent Solution. While I admit his views have found a slightly larger audience than mine, I retain my opinions.

Watson, "thin as a lath and brown as a nut," and without funds besides, invites his friend and former dresser Stamford to lunch at the fashionable Holborn Restaurant. Lunch included wine, a favorite habit of Watson's, and the meal must have been the kind that befits a reunion of two old friends.*

In Elizabethan times, dinner was the midday meal, but it was eventually moved from noon to late afternoon, and finally to evening. Lunch replaced the early dinner, and by Sherlock Holmes' time, business in London had forced most of the working class to take lunch out, in pubs or restaurants, or from street-sellers. Pies, buns, eel soup, wine, and gingerbread were only part of the fair offered on the streets of London. Prepared meat shops finally put most of these vendors out of business, though a few survive even now, more as a curiosity than a necessity.

Many people bought their meals day after day from the street sellers, with a variety that may seem staggering to those raised in a world of hamburgers and French fries. Henry Mayhew, in London Labour and the London Poor, described in 1851 an institution that didn't finally vanish until the twentieth century: "The Coffee stall supplies a warm breakfast; shell fish of many kind tempt to a luncheon; hot eels or pea soup, flanked by a potato 'all hot,' serve for a dinner; and cakes and tarts, or nuts or oranges, with many varieties of pastry, confectionery, and fruit, woo to an indulgence in a dessert; while for supper there is a sandwich, a meat pudding, or a 'trotter.'" Holmes, tired and hungry from a morning's investigation, or Watson, exhausted from an emergency call to a patient, would have patronized these London institutions, or would have taken nourishment at a convenient pub, where hearty food and the "most stupendous" English beer Dickens mentions were to be had.

Despite the Canonical silence, Holmes and Watson must have often shared lunches like these and meals of a more sumptuous order. Even the ascetic Sherlock Holmes couldn't have survived on a daily diet of "some cold beef and a glass of beer."

*In the Footsteps of Sherlock Holmes, *Michael Harrison speculates that the meal included a "Pre−prandial sherry, and coffee and cigars afterwards, as well as the wine."*

Gravy Soup

Beef shin, chopped, 12 oz.	Bay leaf, ½
Butter, 1 tablespoon	Thyme, 1 sprig
Onions, sliced, 2	Parsley, 1 sprig
Carrots, small, sliced, 2	Salt and pepper, to taste
Celery, diced, 1 stalk	Flour, 1½ tablespoons
Beef stock, 3 pints	Butter, 1½ tablespoons

Sherry, ¼ cup

Cook meat until brown in a saucepan with a little butter. When meats begins to brown, add sliced vegetables and brown them. Add stock, bring to a boil and carefully skim. Add herbs and gently simmer for 2½-3 hours. Strain soup through cheesecloth and return to pot. Thicken with flour mixed with butter. Add sherry and simmer before serving. *Makes 5 cups.*

Shepherd's Pie

Mutton, cold, sliced thin,
 1 lb.
Mashed potatoes, 2 lbs.
Onion, chopped, 1
 tablespoon

Stock, 1 cup
Salt and pepper, to taste
Egg yolk, 1

Place meat in pie pan over mashed potatoes which have been mixed with butter. Sprinkle with chopped onion, add stock, season; and cover with another layer of potato. Smooth surface to look like pastry. Brush with egg yolk and bake in moderate (375°F.) oven until browned lightly. *Serves 4-6.*

Lancashire Hot-Pot

Mutton, neck end, best
 portion, 2 lbs.
Butter, 2-3 tablespoons
Kidneys, sheep, sliced, 3
Salt and pepper, to taste

Sugar, a pinch
Mushrooms, 3-4
Oysters, 18-20
Potatoes, thickly sliced,
 2 lbs.
Stock, 1½ cups

Divide the meat into cutlets and trim off skin and fat. Brown in butter, and place in a deep ovenproof baking dish. Season with salt, pepper and a pinch of sugar. Over the cutlets place the kidneys, mushrooms, and oysters in layers, covering completely with thickly sliced potatoes. Pour stock over this, cover, and bake in a moderate (375°F.) oven for 2 hours. About 15 minutes before serving, remove lid so potatoes will brown. *Serves 6-8.*

Marrow Bones

Marrow bones, cut to stand
 upright

Flour

Cover the top of each bone with a thick flour and water paste. Wrap each in a floured cloth, and boil for 1½-2 hours. When done, remove cloth and paste and serve wrapped in a napkin, with dry toast. (This was a favorite of Queen Victoria, one she had daily for lunch.)

Bubble and Squeak

Roast beef, rare, 1 lb. (or   Butter, 1½ tablespoons
    boiled salt beef)   Cabbage, 1 head
             Salt and pepper, to taste

Fry meat in butter until browned, but not hard. Set aside. Boil cabbage, squeeze it dry, chop it small, and fry, stirring. To serve, arrange cabbage in center of dish, circle with sliced beef. *Serves 4-6.*

Pork Pie

Pork, lean, without bone,   Salt and pepper, to taste
   1½ lbs.   Pie crust dough, about 1 lb.
Onion, 1   Eggs, hard-boiled, 3

Remove all bone and gristle from meat. Put pork in a saucepan and cover with water. Bring to a boil, skim, add onion, salt, and pepper. Simmer gently 2½-3 hours. Remove the meat from the saucepan, cube, and sprinkle with salt and pepper. Divide pie dough into 2 pieces, one larger than the other. Roll larger portion and form into a round or oval basin. Fill dough with meat and sliced eggs, and moisten with stock. Cover with rolled remainder of dough, and support and surround with extra dough scraps. Make hole in top, and brush the whole with egg yolk mixed with a little milk. Bake 2 hours in moderate (350°F.) oven. Pour in remaining warmed stock. *Serves 4.*

Scotch Fried Herrings

Herrings, cleaned and   Salt and pepper, to taste
   boned, 2   Oatmeal
           Butter

Dry fish in cloth with salt and pepper; coat with oatmeal. Fry in butter. Serve with lemon cut in quarters, and parsley.

Cock-a-leekie Soup

Prunes, 10-12
Chicken, stewing, 1
Salt, 2 teaspoons

Leeks, cut into small rings,
1 lb.

Soak prunes 12 hours in cold water. Put chicken in pot with sufficient cold water to cover it. Bring slowly to a simmering point and add salt. Add leeks to broth after 1 hour of cooking; simmer for 2-3 hours. Add prunes ½ hour before serving, and cook until just tender. Lift fowl out. Slice flesh and return to broth. Season carefully and serve. *Serves 4.*

Note: The prunes are a matter of taste and may be omitted.

Chestnuts au Jus

Chestnuts, 2 lbs.
Onion, small, 1
Cloves, whole, 2
Celery, 1 large stalk
Bay leaf, 1
Mace, 1 blade

Stock, brown, strong, 1 pint
Salt, to taste
Cayenne, a dash
Brown sugar glaze, 1
   teaspoon

Take a sharp knife and make an incision into each chestnut, in the shell only. Put in a saucepan and cover with water. Bring to a boil and cook for 2 minutes. Drain, peel, and skin chestnuts while hot. Put chestnuts, onion stuck with cloves, celery, bay leaf, and mace into the boiling stock. Season. Simmer about 1 hour, until the chestnuts are tender. Strain and keep the chestnuts hot. Return stock to pan, add glaze, and reduce to glazing consistency. Pile chestnuts in a hot vegetable dish and cover with glaze. *Serves 4.*

Country Style Braised Pork

Pork chops, 4
Oil, 2 tablespoons
Cider, 4 tablespoons
Bouquet garni, 1
Apples, baking, 2
Onions, chopped, 3

Cinnamon, a pinch
Salt and pepper, to taste
Mushrooms, large, thickly
   sliced, 3
Beets, 1 small can
Peas, 1 small can

Noodles, flat, 6-8 oz.

Trim chops and quickly fry in their trimmings until lightly browned. Place in casserole with cider and bouquet garni; cover and cook gently. Meanwhile, pour off excess fat from frying pan; peel, chop, and then fry apples and onions for a few minutes. Add cinnamon and water to cover them, and simmer until soft. Sieve, season to taste, and add to the chops. Cover and cook 1½-2 hours. Add thickly sliced mushrooms ½ hour before finish. Heat peas and beets seperately. Cook noodles in boiling salted water until just done. Serve pork chops on top of noodles, garnished with peas, beets, and mushrooms. *Serves 4.*

Irish Stew

Mutton, neck, 1½ lbs.
Onions, button, 6
Onion, small, 1
Potatoes, peeled, sliced,
   2 lbs.

Salt and pepper, to taste
Stock, 2 cups
Parsley, for garnish

Cut meat into serving size pieces and trim off some of the fat. Blanch the button onions. Put a layer of potatoes at the bottom of a stewpan, cover with a layer of meat and some sliced onions. Season with salt and pepper. Repeat until all ingredients are used. The top layer should be potatoes, and the button onions should be dispersed throughout. Add the stock, and bring to a boil. Skim it well. Cover stewpan and cook gently for about 1½ hours, or until the potatoes are thoroughly cooked and the stew is not watery. Pile in the center of a dish, sprinkle with chopped parsley, and serve. *Serves 4-5.*

Fried Lamb's Sweetbreads

Lamb's sweetbreads, 1 lb.
Salt, 1 teaspoon
Flour, seasoned, ¼ cup
Egg, 1

Bread crumbs, ¼ cup
Gravy, or tomato sauce, ¾ cup

Soak the sweetbreads in water for about 2 hours, changing the water 3 or 4 times. Drain well and place in a stewpan containing just enough cold water to cover. Add a little salt, bring to the boil, and simmer for about 15 minutes; then press between two dishes until cold. Roll lightly in flour seasoned with salt and pepper; coat carefully with egg and bread crumbs, and fry in deep fat until lightly browned. Serve gravy or sauce separately. *Serves 2-3.*

Liver Sausages

Calf's liver, chopped finely,
1 lb.

Bacon, fat, chopped finely,
¾ lb.

Bread crumbs, ½ lb.

Parsley, 1 teaspoon

Thyme, ¼ teaspoon

Lemon rind, grated, ¼ teaspoon

Nutmeg, ¼ teaspoon

Salt, 1 teaspoon

Pepper, ¼ teaspoon

Eggs, 2

Sausage skins

Mix together liver and bacon and add bread crumbs and the rest of the dry ingredients. Stir in the eggs (if too stiff, moisten with a little milk). Press mixture into sausage skins, leaving room for bread to swell. Put them aside 5-6 hours, then prick with a fork, fry in hot fat until well browned, and serve with mashed potatoes or on toast.

Apple and Beetroot Salad

Beet, large, cooked, diced, 1

Potatoes, large, cooked, diced, 2

Apples, large, peeled and cored, diced, 2

Salt and pepper, to taste

Mayonnaise, to bind

Capers, for garnish

Mix beet, potatoes, and apples. Season with salt and pepper, bind with mayonnaise, and sprinkle on a few capers. (This is good for those hot summer days when the sun is reflected from the street and windows of London.) *Serves 3-4.*

Rice and Tomato Pie

Rice, 4 oz.

Stock, strong, 2 cups

Salt and pepper, to taste

Curry powder, a dash

Tomatoes, chopped, 1 lb.

Bread crumbs, buttered, ½ cup

Cheese, grated, ½ cup (optional)

Cook the rice in stock; season with salt, pepper, and a little curry powder.

Put tomatoes in alternate layers with rice in casserole dish and season. Sprinkle top with buttered bread crumbs which have been mixed with melted butter. (If you like, grated cheese can be sprinkled over each tomato layer.) Bake for ½ hour in a moderate (350°F.) oven.

Potted Crab

Pick crab meat from 2 crabs, mix with salt, cayenne pepper, and mace to taste. Rub through a sieve. Press into small pots, cover with melted butter, and bake in a moderate (350°F.) oven for ½ hour. Cool and cover each pot with 1 tablespoon clarified butter. *Serves 2.*

Veal Pot Pie

Veal, lean, 1¼ lbs.	Stock, about 3-4 cups
Pork, pickled, ½ lb.	Potatoes, 1 lb.
Salt and pepper, to taste	Puff pastry dough, 8 oz.

Parsley, for garnish

Cut the meat into serving size portions, slicing the pork into thin slices. Place the meat and pork in alternating layers in a large casserole, seasoning each layer with salt and pepper. Fill the dish three-quarters full with stock. Cover and cook at 350°F. for 1½ hours. Meanwhile, parboil the potatoes and cut into thick slices. Remove meat and allow to cool slightly. Add more stock if necessary, place the potatoes on top, cover with the pastry, and make a hole on top. Bake in a hot (450°F.) oven until the pastry is set, then reduce the heat and cook slowly (300°F.) for 40-50 minutes. Add more hot stock through the hole in the top. Serve garnished with parsley.

Chicken Spatchcock

Chicken, 1	Salt and pepper, to taste
Butter, 2 tablespoons	Bacon rolls, for garnish

Split the chicken in half, cutting through only the back. Cut off the legs and wings at the first joint, flatten as much as you can and keep in place with skewers. Brush with melted butter, season lightly, to taste, and grill until flesh is cooked about 20 minutes. Brush the bird with more butter and turn frequently to ensure even browning. Remove the skewers, and serve garnished with bacon rolls. Serve with tartar sauce. *Serves 4.*

Celery and Chestnut Salad

Chestnuts, stewed, ½ lb.
Apple, sweet, small, 1
Celery hearts, 2

Mayonnaise or French
dressing, ¼ cup
Lettuce, several leaves

Cut the chestnuts into rather large pieces. Dice the apple and shred the celery. Mix all these lightly with the dressing. Serve on a bed of fresh lettuce leaves, decorated with celery stalks. *Serves 2.*

Beef Fritters

Roast beef, cold, chopped
  finely, ¼ lb.
Water, warm, ½ cup
Flour, 4 oz.
Butter, melted, 2
  tablespoons

Rind of ½ lemon
Nutmeg, a pinch
Salt and pepper, to taste
Egg white, 1

Mix the warm water, flour, and melted butter into a paste and add it to the meat, lemon rind, nutmeg, salt, and pepper. Stiffly whip the egg white and fold in. Drop the batter in tablespoonfuls into deep hot fat and fry until golden brown. Serve garnished with fried parsley.

Note: The mixture may be varied with the addition of ground onion and a pinch of sage, instead of the lemon rind and nutmeg.

Potted Game

Game, cooked, any kind
Butter, 2-3 oz. for each 1 lb.
  of game

Salt and pepper, to taste
Cayenne, a dash

Remove the meat from bones and gristle, and chop it finely or pass through a grinder. Pound in mortar until smooth, mixing in strong game stock or gravy, or clarified butter. Season well with salt, pepper, and cayenne pepper, then rub it through a fine sieve. Press into small pots and cover with clarified butter.

Fish Cakes

Fish, cold, cooked, ½ lb.   Milk, to moisten
Butter, 3 teaspoons   Egg, 1
Potatoes, mashed, ½ lb.   Bread crumbs, 2
Egg yolk, ½   tablespoons
Salt and pepper, to taste

Heat the butter in a saucepan and add the fish, potatoes, half the yolk of an egg, salt, pepper, and sufficient milk to moisten thoroughly. Sitr the ingredients over the fire for a few minutes, then turn onto a plate. When cold, shape into round, flat cakes, brush with beaten egg, cover with slightly browned bread crumbs, and bake in a fairly hot (400°F.) oven for about 20 minutes, or fry in deep fat until golden brown. *Serves 2.*

Note: *Fish Cakes* may be varied with the addition of forcemeat: made of 1 tablespoon finely chopped suet, 1 tablespoon bread crumbs, ½ teaspoon finely chopped parsley, salt, pepper, grated lemon rind, moistened with beaten egg. Or: 1 teaspoon coarsley-chopped shrimp, bread crumbs, ½ teaspoon finely chopped anchovy, a little melted butter, salt and pepper, cayenne pepper, and milk. When using either of these, make cake in three layers, with forcemeat sandwiched between two layers of fishcake mixture. Bake these in moderate (350°F.) oven for about 40 minutes.

Cod Pie

Oysters, 12   Butter, melted, 1 cup
Cod, cooked, cold, 1½ lbs.   Short crust pastry, ½ lb. (or
Salt and pepper, to taste   mashed potatoes, ½ lb.)
Nutmeg, a dash

Clean oysters and simmer them for a few minutes, then remove them from liquid and mix that liquid with the oyster liquor. Cut the oysters into 2 to 4 pieces, depending on size. Divide the fish into large flakes, put half of it into a pie dish, add the oysters, and season with salt, pepper, and nutmeg. Add the melted butter, and cover with the rest of the fish. Bake the whole about ½ hour in a moderate (350°F.) oven. *Serves 4.*

Scotch Collops

Roast veal, cold, 1½ lbs.   Lemon rind, 2-3 strips
Salt and pepper, to taste   Veal stock, about 1½ cups
Mace or nutmeg, ¼   Butter, 1 tablespoon
  teaspoon   Flour, 1 tablespoon
Onion, small, 1   Lemon juice, teaspoon
            Bacon strips, 3-4

Cut the veal into ½-inch slices, and trim into oval or round slices 2-3 inches in diameter. Score these on both sides with a sharp knife; sprinkle liberally with salt, pepper, powered mace or nutmeg, and put them aside. Place any bones and trimming there may be in a stewpan with the onion, lemon rind, a little mace or nutmeg, and a seasoning of salt and pepper. Cover with cold water, simmer gently for about 1 hour, strain and add stock or water to make 1 cup. Melt the butter in a stewpan, add the flour, and cook the mixture slowly until it acquires a nut-brown color; add the stock. Stir until boiling, season to taste, and simmer for about 20 minutes. Meanwhile dip the collops in a little flour seasoned with salt and pepper, fry them lightly in a little hot butter until golden-brown; drain and arrange neatly in a dish. Add the lemon juice to the prepared sauce, strain around the collops, garnish with crisply fried rounds of bacon, and serve hot. *Serves 4.*

Fish Pudding

Fish, white, cooked, 1 lb.   Salt and pepper, to taste
Suet, finely chopped, 4 oz.   Eggs, 2
Bread crumbs, 2 oz.   Milk, ½ cup
Parsley, finely chopped, 1
  teaspoon

Skin and bone the fish and pound it well with the suet, or, force fish and suet through a fine sieve. Add the bread crumbs, parsley, salt, and pepper and mix well. Beat the eggs slightly, add the milk and mix together, then add to fish mixture. Have ready a well-greased plain mould or basin. Put the mixture into the basin, cover with waxed paper and steam gently 1½ hours. Serve with melted butter. *Serves 2.*

Potted Ham

Ham, lean, 2 lbs.	Cayenne, a pinch
Mace, ¼ teaspoon	Fat, ½ lb.
Nutmeg, ¼ teaspoon	Butter, clarified, 4
Pepper, ¼ teaspoon	tablespoons

Pass the ham 2 or 3 times through a grinder with the seasoning and fat or chop extremely fine, pound it well in a mortar, and rub it through a sieve. Put it into a greased pie dish, cover with waxed-paper, and bake in a moderate (350°F.) oven for about ¾ hour. When done, press into small pots and cover with clarified butter. *Serves 6.*

Fillets of Veal

Veal fillet, 1½ lbs.	Rind of 1 lemon, grated
Egg, 1	Lemon juice, 1 teaspoon
Parsley, finely chopped, ½ teaspoon	Bread crumbs, ¾ cup
	Butter, 4 tablespoons
Thyme, ¼ teaspoon	Tomato sauce, 1 cup

Cut the veal into slices about ½ inch thick, and cut each slice into rounds between 2¼-2½ inches in diameter. Beat the egg lightly, add to it the parsley, thyme, lemon rind, and lemon juice and mix together. Dip each meat round into this mixture, coat gently with seasoned bread crumbs, and fry in the hot butter until golden brown on both sides. Remove from the butter and keep hot. Warm the tomato sauce in the pan with a little added butter and flour. Cutlets should be dished into a border of mashed potatoes, and the sauce should be strained over them. *Serves 4.*

Note: An alternative sauce can be made with 1 cup white stock, ½ oz. flour, 2 tablespoons cream, ½ teaspoon lemon juice, a little meat glaze, salt, and pepper. Mix the flour in the butter after cooking the fillets, then pour in the stock and stir until it boils. Add the lemon juice, cream, and glaze, and simmer for a few minutes. Strain this over the fillets before serving, instead of the tomato sauce.

Exeter Stew

Beef, lean, 2 lbs.
Vinegar, 2 tablespoons
Fat, 2 tablespoons
Onions, sliced, 2-3
Flour, 1½ oz.
Water, 3 cups
Salt and pepper, to taste

Flour, 4 oz.
Suet, finely chopped, 1½ oz.
Parsley, finely chopped, 1
    tablespoon
Mixed herbs, ½ teaspoon
Salt, 1 teaspoon
Baking powder, ¼ teaspoon

Pepper, a pinch

Remove all the fat from the meat and cut into 8-10 pieces. Put them into a pan with the vinegar, and place in a cool oven. Heat the fat in a frying pan and fry the onions and flour until brown; add the water, bring it to a boil, and pour over the meat in the pan. Season, cover tightly, and cook gently either in the oven or on the stove for 3 hours. Mix the remaining ingredients together, add water to bind into a stiff mixture, and separate into 12 balls. About 40 minutes before serving, bring the stew to the boiling point, drop in the balls, and simmer for the remaining time. Serve by piling the meat in the center of a hot dish, strain the gravy over the meat, and arrange the balls around the base. *Serves 3-4.*

Artichoke Soup

Artichokes, 1 lb.
Butter, 1½ teaspoons
Onion, chopped, 1

Celery, chopped, ½ stalk
White stock, 3 cups
Milk, 1 cup

Salt and pepper, to taste

Wash the artichokes, and pare down to the hearts, making sure you have at least ¾ pound of heart altogether. Heat the butter in a saucepan and fry the vegetables in it for 10-15 minutes. Pour in the stock and boil until the vegetables are tender. Rub the vegetables through a fine sieve, return to the saucepan, add the milk and seasoning, and bring to the boil. Serve hot. *Makes 4 portions.*

Note: If you want a thicker soup, add ½ teaspoon flour or cornstarch to the milk seasoning mixture, and add to the soup a few minutes before serving.

Fish and Oyster Pie

Cod or haddock, 1 lb.	Grated nutmeg, ½ teaspoon
Oysters, 1 dz.	Parsley, finely chopped, 1
Salt and pepper, to taste	teaspoon
Bread crumbs	Melted butter or white sauce

Clear the fish from the bones and skin. Layer it, flaked, into a pie dish or casserole. Add a few oysters, with nutmeg and chopped parsley. Repeat layers until dish is quite full. Pour in some melted butter or thin white sauce and the oyster liquid. Cover with bread crumbs. (For a fancier pie, cover with puff pastry cut in strips and criss-crossed over top of pie with a layer around edge.) Bake in moderate oven for ½ hour.

Beef Pudding

Flour, 3 oz.	Mixed herbs, ½ teaspoon
Egg, 1	Roast beef, cold, finely
Milk, 1 cup	chopped, ½ lb.
Salt and pepper, to taste	

Make a batter from the flour, egg, and milk, and season with salt and pepper. Add the mixed herbs and beef, and put into a pie dish or casserole with a little melted dripping. Bake until set and nicely browned in a moderate (375°F.) oven.

Stewed Oxtails

Oxtail, 1	Bouquet garni of parsley,
Butter, 2 tablespoons	thyme, and bayleaf
Onion, sliced, 1	Cloves, whole, 2
Flour, 1½ oz.	Mace, 1 blade
Stock, 2 cups	Salt and pepper, to taste
Lemon juice, 1 tablespoon	

Wash the tail, cut into pieces 1½ inches long, dividing the large pieces in half. Heat butter in a saucepan and fry the oxtail until browned. Take the meat out of the saucepan and put in the onion and flour. Fry these until well browned, then add the stock, bouquet garni, cloves, mace, salt, and pepper and stir until it is boiling. Replace the meat and cover; simmer gently 2½-3 hours. Arange the meat in a hot dish, season the sauce to taste, add lemon juice, and strain over the meat. Garnish with croutons of bread, or cooked carrot and turnip.

Mushrooms au Gratin

Mushrooms, fresh, 1 lb.
Salt and pepper, to taste
Shallots, chopped, 2
Parsley, ¼ cup

Parmesan cheese, grated,
 ½ cup
Bread crumbs, ¾ cup
Butter, 2 tablespoons

Wash and peel the mushrooms and place in a casserole dish. Sprinkle lightly with salt, pepper, shallot, parsley, cheese, and bread crumbs. Dot with butter; bake in a moderate (350°F.) oven for 15 minutes and serve. *Serves 3-4.*

Golden Buck

Cheese, Chesire or Ched-
 dar, chopped, ½ lb.
Butter, 1½ teaspoons
Ale, 2-3 tablespoons
Worcestershire sauce, ½
 teaspoon

Lemon juice, ½ teaspoon
Eggs, beaten, 2
Celery salt, ⅛ teaspoon
Toast, 4 slices
White pepper, to taste

Put the cheese into a saucepan with butter and ale and stir vigourously until creamy. Add Worcestershire sauce, lemon juice, and eggs. Season with the celery salt and pepper, and continue to stir until the mixture thickens. Trim the toast, butter well, and cut each piece into four squares. Arrange toast on plates and pour mixture over them. Serve as hot as possible. *Makes 4 portions.*

Asparagus Soup

Asparagus, fresh, about 25
Spinach, ½ lb.
Stock, 3 cups
Butter, 1½ teaspoons

Flour, ½ oz.
Milk or cream, 1 tablespoon
Salt and pepper, to taste
Cream, 1 cup

Cut off the points of the asparagus and put them aside; trim the stalks and cut into small pieces. Wash and pick the spinach. Bring the stock to a boil, add the spinach and asparagus, and cook until tender. Rub the vegetables through a fine sieve. Have ready a small saucepan of boiling salted water, put in the asparagus points, and cook for 10-15 minutes. Melt the butter or fat in a saucepan, sprinkle in flour, add milk, and stir until it boils. Put in the stock, the pureed asparagus and spinach, salt, and pepper, and simmer gently for about 10 minutes. Place the asparagus points in the tureen, add the cream and necessary seasonings, and serve as soon as possible. *Serves 4-6.*

Tongue with Cherries

Tongue, sliced, ½ lb.	Peppercorns, 3-4
Brown gravy, ½ cup	Cherries, canned or fresh,
Carrot, sliced, 1	6 oz.
Onion, small, sliced, 1	

Warm tongue in a brown gravy flavored with carrots, onion, peppercorns, and cloves. When very hot, arrange the slices in a dish with the gravy strained over. Serve with cherries on the side. *Serves 2.*

Stuffed Lettuce Leaves

Variation # 1

Raw beef, ground, ½ lb.	Rice, 3 oz.
Celery salt, ¼ teaspoon	Stock, 1 cup
Paprika, ¼ teaspoon	Egg, 1
Worcestershire sauce, 2	Milk, 1 tablespoon
teaspoons	Lettuce, 1 head
	Butter, 3 tablespoons

Take minced raw beef, season with celery salt, pepper, salt, paprika, and a little Worcestershire sauce. Boil rice in stock, drain, and cool. Mix rice with meat; bind this mixture with an egg beaten with milk. Wrap a tablespoonful of this mixture in a large lettuce leaf, and brown the rolls in butter. Cover with good stock; cover dish with waxed paper, and bake slowly until nearly all the liquid has disappeared, leaving only a small amount of sauce to serve them with. *Serves 4-6.*

Variation # 2

Onion, fried, 1 teaspoon	Bread crumbs, 6 oz.
Veal, cooked, chopped,	Stock, ½ cup
6 oz.	Salt and pepper, to taste

Celery salt, ⅛ teaspoon
Egg, beaten, 1
Lettuce, 1 head
Tomato or white sauce,
   1 cup

Cheese, grated, ¼ cup
Bread crumbs, 2
   tablespoons

Mix onion, veal, and bread crumbs moistened with stock, salt, pepper, and celery salt; bind with beaten egg. Put in lettuce leaves and cook as above. Take from stock, arrange on a hot plate, and pour the tomato sauce or white sauce over them. Sprinkle with grated cheese and bread crumbs, and brown quickly in oven. *Serves 4-6.*

Fish Salad

Lettuce, 1 head
Fish, cooked, 1 lb.
Mayonnaise, ¼ cup

Capers, 1 tablespoon
Tomatoes or potatoes
   (cooked), sliced, 4

Anchovy fillets, 4

Make a nest of lettuce leaves in salad bowl, and arrange on them fish, flaked or divided into fairly large pieces. Coat fish with mayonnaise, sprinkle with chopped capers, and garnish with tomato or potato slices (or both) and anchovy fillets. *Serves 4.*

Raised Veal, Pork, and Egg Pie

Pie dough, yeast, 1 lb.
Veal, stewing, 1 lb.
Pork, stewing, 1 lb.
Flour, 1 oz.
Salt, 1½ teaspoons

Pepper, ¼ teaspoon
Eggs, hard-boiled, 3
Water, 2 tablespoons
Egg, beaten, 1
Veal and pork bones

Grease a seven inch tin with lard; make the pastry dough and when risen, cut one-quarter off. Roll out remaining dough about 2 inches bigger than the tin and line the tin with dough, making sure there is a little edge left. Cut the meat into small pieces, removing any gristle and fat. Mix together the flour, salt, and pepper, and toss the meat in this mixture. Put half the meat mixture into the pie, and add the shelled but uncut eggs. Add the rest of the mixture of meat and water. Roll out the rest of the dough, and dampening the edge of the pie, cover with this dough. Beat an egg and brush onto the pie crust, then cut a hole in the center of the pie. Bake for 15 minutes at 400°F., then reduce heat to 290°F. and cook for another 2½ hours. In the interim cook the bones from the veal and the pork in a little water. Strain the stock and pour into the pie to fill it when it is done baking. This pie should be served cold. *Serves 6.*

Fillets of Beef with Fried Bananas

Beef fillet, 1½ lbs.
Salt and pepper, to taste
Bananas, 3
Egg, beaten, 1

Bread crumbs, ½ cup
Butter, 2 tablespoons
Meat glaze, ¼ cup
Brown sauce, 1 cup

Cut the meat into neat fillets after trimming off fat and bone; wipe dry and season with salt and pepper. Peel and cut the bananas into quarters, coat with egg and bread crumbs, and fry in deep fat until golden brown. Drain and keep hot until ready to use. Fry the fillets of beef in hot butter for about 7 minutes, turning them often. Drain them, glaze, and arrange on a circle in a hot dish. Place the bananas in the center and pour some hot brown sauce over, serving the rest of the sauce separately. *Serves 4.*

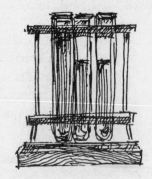

TEA

Tea is the most English of all meals, and naturally, the most civilized. Whether it is served with silver in the drawing room of some noble home, or whether its just a "cuppa" from a street wagon in Whitechapel, the beverage, and the refreshing mid-afternoon meal tradition it has given its name to are symbols of the British Empire and British civilization that are universally respected.

Unfortunately, since many of the cases Dr. Watson recorded take place in the afternoon, those intimate early evening gatherings around the fireplace in that immortal sitting room remain more a matter of imagination than documented fact. But even if the Canon remains silent about these refreshing daily pauses, we know they must have taken place. Imagine Watson, silently involved in the latest *Lancet* (perhaps with a yellow-backed novel hidden inside); and Holmes, filing newspaper clippings according to his rather bizarre system, while watching a toasting scone carefully out of the corner of his eye; the scene is no less real because it was never put on paper.

If Mrs. Hudson's breakfasts were in the good, hearty style of Scotland, then the teas she must have served would have been on occasion substantial affairs, with meat and egg dishes as well as the better known scones, crumpets, and other sweets. On those occasions when her tenants were going to be busy during the dinner hour, they probably ordered up a big meal to tide them over to a late supper. In early summer, tea was a less filling affair, with a few light cakes and probably a mild tea. In winter, when the wind howled and the street outside became a sea of frozen mud, buttered crumpets, eggs, and a strong tea were in order to help fight the chill.

We will probably never know how Holmes and Watson drank their tea, with or without lemon, with a little milk, or sugar and thick cream (though, like most Englishmen, they probably never drank it "black"). But we can create a high tea they would have enjoyed and drink to their continued good health.

HOW TO BREW A GOOD POT OF TEA

The single most important ingredient for a good pot of tea is, of course, the tea. Most connoisseurs prefer China tea although there are several very good India teas. Choose one to your preference.

A good china teapot is the best for brewing tea, though some prefer silver pots. China cups are also the choice for tea drinking, though heavy porcelain ones will do.

Heat the teapot with boiling water and drain just before making the tea. Put in one teaspoon of tea leaves for every cup of tea to be poured, plus 1 teaspoon extra (for the pot). Pour freshly boiling water over the leaves, and allow the tea to steep for 3 to 5 minutes, according to taste. Serve at once. It is better to make a fresh pot of tea for a second cup rather than allowing extra water and tea to sit in the pot, since the tea will just continue to get stronger.

At high teas, the water for tea is heated in a special pot at the table and poured directly into the teapot. Failing one of the special pots, it is better to make the tea in the kitchen than to bring the boiling water to the pot at table, since it will cool. Fresh lemon slices instead of lemon juice, and granulated sugar rather than lumps, are best. If cream is to be served, warm it to room temperature, since cold cream will curdle in the hot tea.

Candied Peel Biscuits

Flour, ½ lb.	Sugar, superfine, 2 oz.
Baking soda, ¼ teaspoon	Lemon peel, candied, 2 oz.
Mixed spices, ¼ teaspoon	Butter, 2 tablespoons
Ginger, ground, ½ oz.	Golden syrup (treacle), 4 oz.

Sift together baking soda, mixed spice, ginger, and flour, and then add sugar and the lemon peel. Cream the butter and syrup together, add the other ingredients and mix into a stiff dough. Leave this for 4 hours, then roll into long, flat biscuits, 3 × 1½ inches, and bake in a quick (450°F.) oven for 8-10 minutes.

Macaroons

Sugar, superfine, 8 oz.	Egg whites, 2
Almonds, ground, 4 oz.	Rice, ground, ½ oz.

Vanilla, ½ teaspoon
Almond extract, 2 drops

Almond halves
Rice paper

Cream together sugar, almonds, and egg whites for 5-10 minutes, and then add ground rice, vanilla, and almond extract. Add a few drops of water if the mixture is too stiff. Put into pastry bag with a ½ inch nozzle, and pipe the mixture onto small circles of edible rice paper; brush each with beaten egg white, press a split almond half onto each, and bake for about 20 minutes in a moderate (375°F.) oven.

Raspberry Buns

Butter, 4 tablespoons
Flour, 8 oz.
Sugar, 2 oz.
Baking powder, 1 teaspoon

Salt, a pinch
Egg, 1
Raspberry jam
Sugar, powdered

Rub butter into flour, sugar, baking powder, and salt. Beat an egg well and mix with flour mixture into a stiff dough. Shape this into balls; make a hole in each and into each hole put a little raspberry jam. Close the hole, brush the ball with a little milk, and sprinkle with a little sugar. Bake in a moderate (375°F.) oven for 20 minutes.

Marmalade Cake

Butter, 1 cup
Sugar, 1 cup
Eggs, separated, 2

Marmalade, 2 tablespoons
Flour, self-rising, 2 cups
Milk, ½ cup

Cream butter with sugar and beat in egg yolks. Add the marmalade and mix in the flour alternately, slowly with the milk. Finally fold in the stiffly whipped egg whites, and bake in a greased shallow cake tin in a moderate (350°F.) oven for about 1 hour.

Orange Cake

Butter, 4 oz.
Orange rind, grated, 1 orange

Sugar, superfine, 4 oz.
Eggs, 2
Flour, sifted, 6½ oz.

Baking powder, ¾ teaspoon   Lemon extract, a few drops
Orange juice, 2-3
   tablespoons

Cream the butter; add rind and sugar; cream again. Slowly add eggs, beating well. Lightly add ⅓ of the flour sifted with baking powder; add the rest of the flour alternately with orange juice mixed with a few drops of lemon extract. Put the mixture into a 6-inch cake pan lined with waxed paper, and bake in a moderately hot (375°F.) oven for 1½ hours. Ice the cooled cake with lemon cream or chocolate icing.

Madeira Cake

Butter, ½ lb.   Milk, 1-3 tablespoons
Sugar, superfine, 6 oz.   Flour, ¾ lb.
Rind of ½ lemon, grated   Lemon peel, candied, 2 thin
Egg, 1 large or 2 small   slices

Put the butter and sugar in a bowl, add the lemon rind, and beat the mixture with a wooden spoon until it becomes a very light cream. Add the egg and a little milk and beat well. When the batter is light and creamy, add the flour; stir it in lightly with the hand, and when well mixed divide the mixture in half. Place in two well-greased cake tins of the same size. Put two thin slices of lemon peel on top, and bake in a moderate (350°F.) oven for 1-1¼ hours.

Queen Cakes

Baking powder, ½ teaspoon   Egg, 1
Flour, ½ lb.   Currants, ¼ lb.
Butter, ¼ lb.   Lemon or almond extract,
Sugar, superfine, ¼ lb.   to taste
Cream, ½ cup

Sift the baking powder and flour onto a piece of paper. Put the butter, sugar, and cream in a mixing bowl and beat to a light cream. Add the egg. When the egg is beaten in, add the flour and the fruit; moisten with milk to the consistency of a cake batter. Stir in almond or lemon extract. Put into small greased baking tins (or cupcake tins). Bake for ¼-½ hour in a moderate (350°F.) oven until springy. Grated lemon rind may be substituted for lemon or almond extract.

Yorkshire Ginger Cake

Egg, 1 large or 2 small   Castor Sugar, ¼ lb.
Cream, ½ cup   Ginger, ground, 1¼ oz.
Butter, ½ lb.   Flour, 1 lb.
                       Salt

Whisk the egg thoroughly, add cream and beat together. Put mixture into a saucepan and stir until warm. Add butter, sugar, and ginger, stirring carefully over a very moderate fire. When butter has melted, stir in flour and very little salt. Make into a paste. Roll out the paste and cut into rounds. Put on a greased baking sheet and bake in a moderate oven.

Lemon Biscuits

Butter, 3 tablespoons   Rind of 1 lemon, grated
Flour, ¾ lb.   Eggs, well-beaten, 2
Sugar, superfine, 6 oz.   Lemon juice, 1 teaspoon

Rub the butter into the flour; stir in the sugar and the lemon peel. When these ingredients are mixed, add the eggs and lemon juice. Beat the mixture well for a few minutes, then drop from a spoon onto a buttered baking sheet, about 2 inches apart. Bake the biscuits from 15-20 minutes in a moderate (350°F.) oven, until they lightly brown.

Ginger Biscuits

Ginger, ground, ½ oz.   Egg, 1
Butter, ¼ lb.   Milk, 1-3 tablespoons
Flour, ½ lb.   Sugar, superfine, 4 oz.

Rub the ginger and butter into the flour and sugar on a board; make a well in the center, break in the egg, and work into a paste, using a little milk if necessary. Roll into thin sheets and cut into rounds with a cutter. Set rounds onto a greased baking sheet and bake in a cool (300°F.) oven, for about 5 minutes.

Rice Biscuits

Butter, ¼ lb.   Rice flour, ½ lb.

Sugar, ¼ lb.   Egg, well-beaten, 1

Beat the butter to a cream, stir in the rice flour and sugar, and moisten the whole with the egg. Roll out the paste, cut into small rounds, put on a greased baking sheet, and bake for 12-15 minutes in a very slow (300°F.) oven.

Genoa Cake

Butter, 6 oz.   Cherries, glacéd, sliced, 2
Sugar, superfine, 6 oz.   oz.
Eggs, well-beaten, 4   Rind of 1 lemon, grated
Milk, 2 tablespoons   Almonds, blanched,
Flour, 12 oz.   chopped, 2 oz.
Sultanas, or currants, 4 oz.

Put the butter in a mixing bowl, cream it thoroughly with a wooden spoon, add the sugar, and beat well. Stir in the eggs, and add milk and flour alternately, continuing to beat the mixture. Add the fruits, lemon rind, and almonds. Mix well and put into a greased cake pan. Bake in a moderately hot (375°F.) oven for 1½ hours, until springy. Cool on a rack and serve.

Sally Lunns

Flour, ½ lb.   Yeast, cake, ¼ oz.
Salt, ¼ teaspoon   Sugar, superfine, ¼
Butter, 1 tablespoon   teaspoon
Milk, warm, ½ cup   Egg, beaten, 1

Mix the flour and salt in a bowl; make a hole in the center. Melt the butter in the warm milk. Cream the yeast and sugar, add egg, and stir in the milk and butter. Add gradually to the flour and beat with the hand until smooth. Warm and grease two round cake pans; put in the dough, cover with paper and cloth, and leave in a warm place until the dough rises to nearly double its original size. Bake in a hot (400°F.) oven for about 25 minutes.

Bath Buns

Salt, ½ teaspoon   Sugar, 3 oz.
Flour, warm, 1 lb.   Yeast, ½ oz.
Butter, 3 tablespoons   Milk, warm, 2 oz.
                                Eggs, 2

Mix the salt with flour and rub in the butter. Mix in most of the sugar. Mix into a light dough, adding yeast mixed with warm milk, the rest of the sugar, and eggs. Put in a warm place until it rises to double its original size; then knead lightly. Divide into two dozen pieces and shape each 3½-4 inches long and 1 inch wide. Place on a greased baking sheet close enough together so that they join up. Prove 15 minutes. Bake in a hot (400°F.) oven for 10-15 minutes.

To make the glaze: boil together water and sugar until slightly syrupy. Brush this mixture on the buns as soon as they come out of the oven so that it hardens on the warm buns. Sprinkle heavily with fine sugar and break apart before serving.

Date and Walnut Cake

Flour, ¾ lb.

Salt, ¼ teaspoon

Butter, 4½ tablespoons

Sugar, 5 oz.

Nutmeg, a pinch

Baking powder, 1½ teaspoons

Cream of tartar, 2 teaspoons

Eggs, 2

Milk, 1 cup

Dates, chopped, 4 oz.

Walnuts, chopped, 1½ oz.

Sift the flour and salt together; rub in the butter. Add the other dry ingredients and mix with the eggs and milk to a dropping consistency. Add fruit and nuts. Put into a well-greased 8-inch cake pan and bake at 375°F. for 15 minutes; reduce heat to 350°F and bake for 1¼-1½ hours in all.

Swiss Rolls

Flour, 3 oz.

Salt, a pinch

Baking powder, 1 teaspoon

Eggs, 3

Sugar, superfine, 3 oz.

Vanilla extract, ¼ teaspoon

Raspberry jam, 2 tablespoons

Grease a baking sheet. Sift flour, salt, and baking powder together. Beat eggs and sugar in a bowl over a pan of hot water until thick and pale in color. Add vanilla. Do not let the bottom of the mixing bowl touch the water. Lightly fold in the flour mixture. Spread evenly on the baking sheet and bake at 425°F. until spongy, but still moist. Sprinkle the sugar onto a piece of waxed paper, and place the baked roll into this. Cut halfway through the roll, about 1 inch from the bottom. Spread the roll with the heated jam, 1 inch from all edges. Turn up the 1 inch at the bottom to make the original roll, and continue to roll up firmly with the aid of the paper. Press gently to keep in place. Remove the paper and sprinkle with the sugar.

Note: If the edges turn crisp during baking, trim them before rolling, or the roll may break.

Sponge Drops

Flour, 4 oz.	Sugar, superfine, 4 oz.
Salt, a pinch	Jam, several tablespoons
Baking powder, 1 teaspoon	Whipped cream,
Eggs, 2	sweetened, ½ cup

Sift together the flour, salt, and baking powder. Whisk eggs and sugar together in a mixing bowl over hot water until they are thick and creamy; fold the flour in lightly. Force out in drops or put in spoonfuls onto a greased baking sheet. Sprinkle heavily with sugar and bake at 350°F. for 10-15 minutes. When cold, spread half with jam, force a rose of whipped cream on the others, and sandwich them together.

Brandy Snaps

Sugar, 2½ oz.	Golden syrup (treacle), 1 oz.
Butter, 1 tablespoon	Flour, 1 oz.
Ginger, ground, 1 teaspoon	

Cream sugar, butter, and syrup together; stir in sifted flour and ginger. Make this into 12-16 small balls and place far apart on a well-greased baking sheet. Bake at 310°F. until nicely browned. Allow these to cool slightly; remove from the sheet with a knife and while soft enough, roll around the handle of a wooden spoon. The snaps may be filled with sweetened and flavored whipped cream.

Parkin Biscuits

Flour, 2 oz.	Cinnamon, ½ teaspoon
Oatmeal, 2 oz.	Mixed spice, ¼ teaspoon
Sugar, 1½ oz.	Shortening, 1 tablespoon
Ginger, ground, ½ teaspoon	Baking soda, 1 teaspoon

Golden syrup (treacle), Almonds, blanched, for
1½ oz. garnish
Egg, ¼

Sift and mix flour, oatmeal, sugar, and spices; rub in the shortening. Add the baking soda, syrup, and egg. Mix well to a fairly stiff consistency. Form into balls and place a little apart on a greased baking sheet. Put one-half a blanched almond on top of each. Bake in a moderate (350°F.) oven for 15-20 minutes and allow to cool slightly before removing from baking sheet.

Rich Oatcakes

Salt, ½ teaspoon Oatmeal, 1 lb.
Baking soda, 2 teaspoons Sugar, 1 oz.
Cream of tartar, 2 Butter, mixed with lard, 4
   teaspoons   tablespoons
Flour, 3 oz. Milk, ½-¾ cup

Sift the salt, soda, cream of tartar, and flour together; add the oatmeal and sugar, and rub in the butter and lard. Add enough milk, mix into a stiff, but not hard, dough. Dust the baking board with a mixture of flour and oatmeal, and roll out thinly. Rub the surface with oatmeal and cut out with a 3½-4-inch circular cutter, or cut into triangles. Place on a baking sheet and bake at 325°F. for 20-30 minutes.

Bakewell Tart

Short crust pastry, 8 oz. Egg, 1
Raspberry jam Almonds, ground, 2 oz.
Butter, 2 oz. Cake or cookie crumbs,
Sugar, 2 oz.   2 oz.
Almond extract, few drops

Line a 7-inch pie plate with the dough. Place a good layer of raspberry jam on the bottom. Cream together the butter and sugar until thick and white. Beat in the egg and add the ground almonds, crumbs, and almond extract. Spread the mixture on top of the jam and bake in a fairly hot oven for about ½ hour. Sprinkle icing sugar on top; serve hot or cold.

Red Currant and Raspberry Tart

Red currants, 1½ lbs.   Raspberries, ½ lb.
Sugar, 2-3 tablespoons   Short crust pastry, 10 oz.

Strip the currants from the stalks, rinse, and place half of them in a 3-cup pie dish. Add the sugar, hulled raspberries, then the remaining red currants. Line the edge of the dish with pastry. Cover the pastry, sprinkle with sugar, and bake at 400°F. for about ¾ hour.

Frangipane Tart

Short crust pastry, 8 oz.   Egg, 1
Butter, 2 tablespoons   Almonds, ground, 2 oz.
Sugar, 2 oz.   Flour, 1 tablespoon

Line a 7-inch pie plate with the pastry. Cream the butter and sugar until thick and white. Add the egg, beating well, and then mix in the almonds and flour. Place the mixture in the pastry shell and bake in a moderate (375°F.) oven for 25-30 minutes. When cool, sprinkle with icing sugar.

Chelsea Buns

Flour, ½ lb.   Milk, warm, ½ cup
Salt, ½ teaspoon   Currants, ½ oz.
Butter, 2 tablespoons   Candied peel, chopped,
Yeast, ½ oz.   ½ oz.
                    Sugar, 1 oz.

Mix the flour and salt; rub in the butter; cream the yeast and add to the flour with milk. Beat well and set in a warm place to rise to double its size. Knead the risen dough slightly and roll out into a square about 10 inches on a side. Sprinkle with the fruit and sugar and roll up like a swissroll. Cut roll into seven pieces and put cut side up. Put the cut buns in a square or round 8-inch cake pan so when they are baked they will join up. Allow them to prove until they rise to the top of the pan. Brush with milk or egg, bake in a hot (400°F.) oven for 20-25 minutes. Make sure they are done to the bottom. When the buns are ready, brush with a sugar and water glaze and dust with sugar.

Gingerbread

Flour, ¾ lb.

Salt, ¼ teaspoon

Ginger, ground, ¼ oz.

Sugar, 3 oz.

Lard, 3 oz.

Blackstrap molasses, ½ lb.

Milk, 4-6 tablespoons

Baking soda, 1 teaspoon

Egg, 1

Sift the flour, salt, and ginger. Add the sugar. Put the fat, molasses, and most of the milk into a pan and warm them. Dissolve the baking soda in the rest of the milk. Pour the warm liquid into the flour, add the beaten egg and dissolved soda, and beat well. The mixture should be soft enough to run easily from a spoon. Pour into a greased 8-inch cake tin and bake in a moderate (350°F.) oven, reducing heat to lower temperature after 20 minutes. Bake for 1½ hours, or a little less, overall.

Potato Scones

Pototoes, cooked, cold,
   ½ lb.

Butter, melted, 1½
   teaspoons

Salt, to taste

Flour, 3 oz.

Sieve or mash the potatoes very fine; mix with the butter and salt. (The scones are very flat tasting without salt.) Work in as much flour as the mixture will take up and roll the mixture out thinly. Cut into 3½-inch rounds or triangles and prick well. Place on a moderately hot (375°F.) griddle and cook for 3 minutes on each side. Cool in a towel. If desired, scones may be served hot and buttered.

DINNER

Dinner for Sherlock Holmes was often an uneasy meal. It often preceded the dangerous business of a cimrinal investigation. Nor was Watson particularly fond of writing about dinner, since he rarely describes the meal and is often more interested in the post-prandial coffee, port, and cigars.

Holmes and Watson often dined out before the opera or a concert. Their tastes (at least the record we have of them) run from Italian restaurants to good English cooking. It is pleasant to speculate that on occasion Holmes and Watson might have even patronized the Café Royale, or a similar expensive restaurant, celebrating the end of a particularly remunerative adventure.

But before well-off clients began to patronize the world's first consulting detective, many, many dinners must have been shared by gaslight (or whale-oil light) in the sitting room of Mrs. Hudson's establishment. These must have usually been rather simple meals, since Holmes remarked on his landlady's rather limited cuisine.

The meal probably began with soup, prepared from the pot of stock kept on the stove continually. It was followed by a meat course, though this would often be a leftover dish, cooked with meat from an earlier meal (quite a few recipes of this sort are listed here under lunch). Almost certainly, boiled, mashed or baked potatoes accompanied the meal, along with vegetables fresh from the coster's barrow. There would be bread freshly baked, with sweet butter, and rolls hot from the oven. If drink was served with the meal, it would have probably been alcoholic (an ugly word to describe a delightful liquid). More than likely, it was beer or ale of one sort or another. Holmes showed a remarkable fondness for

43

beer through the first of his adventures, and Watson had probably lived on the brew in India. And of course, in the beginning neither could afford the good wines they were later to indulge in.

After the main course, a sweet course would have been served, and not necessarily a light sweet either, since in England dessert has always been considered an integral part of the meal's substance, rather than just a pleasant after thought. Mrs. Hudson might have served a sweet pudding, or an apple pie or layer cake. After the sweet, the savoury. "Savouries," or what today are called hors d'oeuvres, were usually served after the final course, and were intended to finish the meal pleasantly. They might have been cheese toasts, or small sandwiches. (See the chapter on Supper for these.)

After the meal was finished, brandy or scotch and soda from the gasogene, and cigars from the coal scuttle would aid digestion. Special occasions, or a lucky horse for Dr. Watson, might bring in the odd ancient and cobwebby bottle of port for the friends' after-dinner conversation.

As Holmes became more affluent, Mrs. Hudson seems to have become a better cook, preparing delightful cold suppers and fancy dinners. These must have improved apace, however. (In fact, I rather doubt Mrs. Hudson's cooking was all that bad to begin with. It is more probable that, as Holmes increased his rent to her, she could afford to buy better and more varied foodstuffs. After all, she was running a business, and couldn't afford to be extravagant on a low rent any more than could her roomers on a low income.)

On holidays, Mrs. Hudson must have outdone herself, though Holmes and Watson certainly would buy the goose and other special provisions that had become traditional. The Christmas pudding Mrs. Hudson prepared from an old family recipe is long since lost. I've included an old recipe for plum pudding, which probably isn't as good as Mrs. Hudson's, but which will stand well in its place.

(It should be noted here that in England, as in just about every other country in the world, the dishes served at each meal are generally interchangeable. Thus, some things listed under Lunch will serve well here for dinner; sweets in the chapter on Tea will often go well with dinner; some dinner recipes can be served at supper; and in general everything can be changed around. Rather than try and find a system to let you know which can go where, I leave it to your judgment and good cooking sense. Chacun a' son gout!)

I begin this section with a few recipes for the only foods actually mentioned as dinners in the Canon: grouse, oysters, green peas, roast Christmas goose, and woodcock. The goose, of course is the one that hid the Blue Carbuncle in its crop (I hope the one you choose to roast is a bit fresher than it would be after eighty-odd years). The oysters are not the world-dominating kind found in "The Dying Detective"; rather they are the accompaniment to a brace of grouse served in "The Sign of the Four." The green peas are the ones babbled about by the landlady in "The Three Students." The woodcock figures in a 7 o'clock dinner in "The Blue Carbuncle" (the only story in the Canon to definitely mention two different dinners in some detail).

Roast Grouse

Grouse, 1 brace
Toast, 2 slices
Butter or drippings
Flour

Brown gravy, good
Bread sauce
Bread crumbs, fried
Bacon

Let the birds hang in a cool, dry place for 3-4 days. When they are ready to use, pluck, draw, and truss them as you would a chicken for roasting. Tie over each breast a thin slice of bacon and roast in a moderate oven for ½ hour, basting frequently with hot fat. When nearly done, remove the bacon, cover with flour and baste well to give the birds a nice brown color. Toast the bread lightly, when the birds are about ¾ done, put the toast into the dripping pan to catch the fat that drops from them. Dish the birds onto the toast, and serve the gravy, bread sauce, and bread crumbs on the side. *Serves 2-4*

OYSTERS

The oysters Sherlock Holmes mentions might well have been steamed in their own shells and served with lemon wedges and butter. I have included here two slightly more ornate recipes for them.

Fried Oysters

Oysters, 6
Frying batter
Parsley, finely chopped, ¼
   teaspoon

Lemon rind, grated, a pinch
Fat for frying

Blanch the oysters in their own liquor, strain them just before they boil, and dry. Add the parsley and lemon rind to prepared frying batter. Dip each oyster separately in the batter; fry in the hot fat until crisp and lightly browned. Drain well and serve hot. *Serves 2.*

Oyster Fritters

Oysters, large, 6	Salad oil, ½ tablespoon
Flour, 1½ oz.	Egg white, stiffly-beaten, 1
Water, lukewarm, 3 oz.	Salt, to taste
	Frying fat

Make a batter by stirring the water and the salad oil into the flour. When the batter is very smooth, add the salt and the egg white. Beard the oysters, dip in the batter, and fry a golden color. *Serves 2.*

Green Peas with Mint

Add a couple of sprigs of mint to boiling peas. This is a favorite English way of cooking peas.

Roast Woodcock

Woodcock, 1	Toast, 2-3 slices
Bacon, 2 strips	

Dress the woodcock without drawing it. Truss as for roast chicken, but leave on the head and skin. Brush with warm fat, tie a thin slice of fat bacon over each breast, and put toast underneath the fowl to catch the drippings. Baste frequently while roasting for 15 minutes in a moderate (375°F.) oven (or less time if you prefer them underdone). Serve on toast, garnish with the watercress, and serve gravy separately. *Serves 2.*

Roast Goose

Clean and truss the goose, stuff with the dressing (see below) and baste with hot fat. Roast or bake for 2-2½ hours, depending on size and age. Baste frequently and if not well browned, sprinkle well with flour when the bird is three-quarters done. Remove the trussing string and serve on a hot dish with apple sauce and gravy. *Serves 4.*

Stuffing

Onions, chopped, 2 lbs.	Sage, fresh, 1 tablespoon
Butter, 2 tablespoons	(or dried, 1 teaspoon)
Bread crumbs, 1 cup	Salt and pepper, to taste

Put the onions in cold water and bring to a boil, then boil for 5 minutes. Remove the onions from water, drain, and fry in butter for nearly 10 minutes, but not until browned. Add bread crumbs and sage, and season with salt and pepper. Mix well. Stuffing is then ready to use. *Makes 3 cups.*

Pigeon Pie

Pigeons, 2
Rump steak, ¾ lb.
Ham or lean bacon, 3 oz.
Egg, hard-boiled, 1

Puff pastry, ½ recipe
Salt and pepper, to taste
Stock, strong, 1 cup
Egg yolk, beaten, 1

Cut each pigeon into 4 pieces. Cut the beef into thin, small slices, the ham into julienne strips, and the egg into slices. Put these ingredients into a pie dish in alternating layers, season with salt and pepper, and pour in enough stock to ¾ cover. Top with rolled puff pastry dough, brush with the egg yolk, and cut a small hole in the center. Bake the pie in a hot (400°F.) oven until the pastry sets; then cook at a cooler temperature for an hour or so. Have ready a few of the pigeon's feet, scalded, with the toes cut off. Also have ready the rest of the stock. Before serving the pie, pour the rest of the stock into the pie through the hole on top, and decorate the pie top with the pigeon feet. The pie may be served hot or cold, though the stock must jell if it is to be served cold. *Serves 4.*

Spanish Sauce

Butter, 2 tablespoons
Ham, lean, raw, or bacon,
  1½ oz.
Carrot, sliced, ½
Onion, sliced, 1 small
Clove, whole, 1

Peppercorns, 2
Bouquet garni, 1
Flour, 1 oz.
Sherry, ¼ cup
Tomato pulp, ¼ cup
Stock, 3 cups

Salt and pepper, to taste

Melt the butter in a saucepan and add the ham or bacon, cut into small pieces. Simmer a few minutes. Then add the vegetables, herbs and spices. Stir these ingredients over a slow fire for a few minutes, then add the flour and brown it carefully. Add the sherry, tomato pulp, and stock, stir until boiling; then reduce the temperature and let boil for about 1 hour. Skim off the fat, pass the mixture through a fine sieve or a cloth, season, and serve warm. *Makes about 3½ cups.*

Faggots (also called Savoury Ducks or Poor Man's Goose)

Pig's liver, ¾ lb.	Thyme, to taste
Onion, ½	Egg, beaten, 1
Fat pork, ¼ lb.	Nugmeg, to taste
Salt and pepper, to taste	Bread crumbs, ¼-½ cup
Basil, to taste	Pig's caul, 1
Sage, to taste	Gravy, ¾ cup

Chop the liver and onion rather finely and dice the pork. Put all three into a saucepan, add salt, pepper, basil, sage, and thyme; cover tightly and cook for about ½ hour without browning. Drain off the fat and cool the meat mixture a little. Add the egg, nutmeg to taste, and enough bread crumbs to make a fairly stiff dough. Mix this thoroughly, then form into squares, surround with pig's caul, and place into a baking pan. Add a little good gravy and bake until nicely browned. Serve with gravy. *Serves 3-4.*

Baked Spanish Onions

Spanish onions	Water
Salt	Butter

Put the onions, still in their skins, in a pan of salted, boiling water and boil for about 1 hour. Remove each one, wipe dry and wrap in buttered paper. Bake in a moderate (350°F.) oven for 2 hours or more depending on their size. Serve in their skins, with butter and salt and pepper, or peeled, with gravy.

Eel Pie

Eels, 1½ lbs.	Worcestershire sauce, 1
Salt and pepper, to taste	tablespoon
Lemon juice, 1 teaspoon	Stock, beef, 1 cup
Puff pastry, ½ recipe	

Clean and skin the eels and cut into pieces about 2 inches long. Put the heads, tails, and fins into a saucepan with the stock; simmer for about ½ hour, then strain and skim the stock. Place the eels in a pie dish, salt and peppered well. Add the lemon juice and Worcestershire sauce a little at a time between layers of eel. Pour about half the stock into the pie dish, and cover with rolled puff-pastry, leaving a hole in the center. Bake in a fairly hot (400°F.) oven for about 1 hour. Warm the rest of the stock and pour in through the hole into the pie as soon as the pie is removed from the oven. *Serves 4.*

Braised Duck with Chestnuts

Chestnuts, 1 lb.
Onion, Spanish, 1
Salt and pepper, to taste
Egg, 1
Duck, 4-5 lbs., 1
Bacon, several strips
Butter, 2 tablespoons
Onions, sliced, 2
Carrots, sliced, 2
Turnip, small, sliced, 1

Celery, diced, 2 stalks
Stock, 2 cups
Spanish sauce, 1½ cups
 (see above recipe)
Port, ¼ cup
Red currant jelly, 1
 teaspoon
Bouquet garni, 1
Allspice, whole, 6
Cloves, whole, 2

Boil the chestnuts and remove the skins. Cook the Spanish onion in stock or water until tender. Chop both finely, season with salt and pepper, add the egg, and use these for stuffing the duck. Truss the duck and lard it well with the bacon. Put the butter in a large roasting pan, add the sliced vegetables, put the duck on top, cover and fry for about 20 minutes. Add as much stock as will ¾ cover the vegetables, add the spices and the rest of the stock as that in the pan boils away. Cover the duck with greased paper, put on the lid, and cook gently for about 2 hours, or until the duck is perfectly tender. Heat the Spanish sauce, add to it the port, add the jelly, and season to taste. Remove the trussing strings, and put the duck in a hot (400°F.) oven for a few minutes to crisp the bacon. Serve with a little sauce poured over the duck and the rest served separately. *Serves 4.*

Stewed Carp

Carp, large, 1
Onions, sliced, 2-3,
 small
Butter, 2 tablespoons
Stock, 2 cups

Mushrooms, button, 12
Bouquet garni, 1
Nutmeg, a pinch
Salt and pepper, to taste
Flour, 1 tablespoon

Wash the fish in vinegar and water, and cut it into thick slices. Fry the onions until brown in half the butter. Add the stock, mushrooms, herbs, a pinch of nutmeg and seasonings. When this mixture is warm, add the fish. Simmer gently for 30-40 minutes. Take the fish out and keep it hot. Have ready the flour and the rest of the butter, kneaded together into a smooth paste. Add to the contents of the saucepan and simmer until smooth and slightly thickened. Place the fish on a hot dish, strain the sauce over it, and garnish with the mushrooms, fried roe, and snippets of toast. *Serves 3-4.*

Stuffed Breast of Lamb

Breast of lamb, 4-5 lbs.	Butter, 2 tablespoons
Salt and pepper, to taste	Bouquet garni, 1
Ground veal, cooked, 1 cup	Peppercorns, 6
Onions, 2	Stock or brown sauce,
Carrots, 2	¾ cup
Turnip, small, 2	French beans, 1 lb.

Remove the bones from the breast of lamb and flatten with a rolling pin or a meat mallet. Season well with salt and pepper. Spread on the breast the ground cooked veal; roll up tightly and tie with strings. Slice the vegetables, put them into a large saucepan or roasting pan, add half the butter, season, and place the meat on top. Cover and cook gently for about 20 minutes. Add the herbs, peppercorns, and enough stock to nearly cover the vegetables. Cover the meat with a greased paper or foil, cover the pan, and cook for 2 more hours. Cook the beans in slightly salted water and drain well. Melt the remaining butter in another pan, add the drained beans and shake up. Serve the meat garnished with the beans on a hot plate. Serve the strained sauce separately. *Serves 4.*

Coburg Pudding

Butter, 1½ tablespoons	Currants, 1½ oz.
Sugar, superfine, 1½ oz.	Brandy, 1 teaspoon
Egg, 1	Baking powder, ¼ teaspoon
Milk, ½ cup	Nutmeg, a pinch
	Salt, a pinch

Cream the butter and sugar together; add the egg gradually and beat in well. Mix in the rest of the ingredients, pour into well-greased pans, and bake for ½ hour in a moderate (350°F.) oven. Serve with a sherry wine sauce. *Serves 4.*

Boiled Pork and Pease Pudding

Split peas, dried, 1 quart	Celery, diced, 1 stalk
Pork, salt or pickled, 1 leg or	Peppercorns, 12
other joint	Parsnips, cut, 6
Onion, quatered, 1	Cabbage, quartered, 1 head
Turnip, sliced, ½	Egg yolks, 2
Carrot, sliced, ½	Butter, 1 tablespoon

Salt and pepper, to taste

Soak the peas for about 12 hours. Place the pork in a large pot, and cover with warm water (cover with cold water if it is very salty). Bring to the boil, boil for about 10 minutes, and skim. Add the onion, turnip, carrot, and celery. Add the peppercorns and simmer gently until the meat is well cooked. Boil the parsnips and cabbage separately. Drain and cut into small squares. Serve the pork in a large dish, garnished with the cabbage and parsnips.

There are two ways to make the pease pudding. In the first, the peas are drained, tied in a cloth, cooked with the boiling pork for 1½ hours, then removed and rubbed through a fine sieve. They are then mixed with the egg yolks and butter, seasoned with salt and pepper, and returned to the cloth and boiled again for 40 minutes in the pork pot. In the second method, the peas are drained and cooked in boiling water in a saucepan for about 2 hours. Drain them and rub through a fine sieve. Then combine the peas with the egg yolks and butter, season with salt and pepper, and put into a well-greased pudding tin. Steam or bake the pudding for about 40 minutes, until done. *Serves 8 or more.*

Grilled Mackerel with Gooseberry Sauce

Mackerels, large, 2	Butter, 1 tablespoon
Flour, seasoned, 1	Tomatoes
tablespoon	

Trim and clean the mackerel, and divide into fillets. Dip each piece into flour, and fry in melted butter for 8-10 minutes. Cut the tomatoes in half and fry with the fish. Serve the fillets and tomatoes on a hot dish, with the gooseberry sauce served separately. *Serves 4.*

Gooseberry Sauce

Green gooseberries, ½ lb.   Nutmeg, a pinch
Water, ½ cup   Chives, chopped, ½
Butter, 1½ teaspoons   teaspoon
Sugar, 1 oz.   Sorrell, a few leaves
Lemon juice, 2 teaspoons   Salt and pepper, to taste

Stir the gooseberries very gently with the water and butter until they are pulpy. Beat them until they are very smooth, or rub through a very fine sieve. Reheat the sauce, stir in the sugar, add the lemon juice and spices. *Makes about 1½ cups.*

Hunter's Soup

Partridges, Carcass and   Parsnip, sliced, ½
  Trimmings, 2 (or equal   Celery, diced, 1 stalk
  amount of any game   Flour, 1 oz.
  meat)   Stock, 4 cups
Bacon, lean, 1 oz.   Bouquet garni, 1
Butter, 1 tablespoon   Clove, 1
Onion, sliced, 1   Partridge or game breast
Carrot, sliced, 1   meat, 2 cups
            Salt and pepper, to taste

Put the carcasses, the trimmings, and bacon in a saucepan with butter; fry them until browned. Remove the game, add the vegetables, and brown. Add the flour and fry until golden brown. Add the stock to this and bring to the boil. Add the herbs, clove, and game, and simmer for 1½-2 hours. In the meantime, cut the pieces of breast or meat into small cubes. Strain the soup, add to it the diced meat, reheat carefully, and serve. *Makes about 6 cups.*

Mushrooms Stewed with Wine

Mushrooms, button, 1 lb.   Chives, chopped, 1
Bacon, 6 slices   teaspoon
Parsley, finely chopped, 1   White wine or cider, ¼ cup
  teaspoon   Flour, ¼ cup
            Salt and pepper, to taste

Wash the mushrooms. Cut the bacon into small pieces and cook in a saucepan for 15 minutes. Add the mushrooms, parsley, chives, and a little salt. Moisten with white wine or cider, sprinkle heavily with flour, and stew gently until the sauce thickens. Season with salt and pepper. *Serves 3-4.*

Apricot Fritters

Yeast, ¼ oz.

Sugar, superfine, ¼ teaspoon

Milk, warm, about 1 cup

Flour, 6 oz.

Salt, a pinch

Butter, melted, 1 tablespoon

Cinnamon, ¼ teaspoon

Apricot halves, fresh or canned, 12

Frying fat, ¼ cup

Make the batter by creaming the yeast and sugar and adding a little milk. Sift together 2 oz. of the flour and the salt into a warm bowl. Mix into a batter with the yeast mixture, adding more yeast, if necessary. Leave this to rise until it doubles in size. When the dough has risen, add the rest of the flour and the milk to make a batter, and work in the melted butter and cinnamon. Leave the mixture to rise again. Drain the apricots. Coat them with the batter, and put them on a piece of waxed paper. Leave them for 30 minutes, then fry in hot fat until browned. Drain and sprinkle with superfine sugar before serving. *Makes 12 fritters.*

Hotch Potch

Mutton, neck, 2 lbs.

Water, cold, 2 quarts

Salt, 2 teaspoons

Pepper, to taste

Bouquet garni, 1

Carrot, diced, 1

Turnip, small, diced, 1

Scallions, sliced, 6

Cauliflower, 1 small head

Lettuce, 1 small head

Broad beans, cut, 1 cup

Peas, shelled, 1 cup

Parsley, chopped, 1 tablespoon

Wash the mutton, remove all fat, and cut the meat into small pieces. Put the bone and meat into a pan, add cold water and bring very slowly to a simmer. Add salt and herbs, and simmer for ½ hour. Add the carrot, scallion, and turnip to the water and simmer for an additional 1½ hours. Break the cauliflower into small pieces, and shred the lettuce. Add these with beans and peas to the mixture and simmer for ½ hour. Season the broth, skim off the fat, and remove the bones and the bouquet garni. Add parsley just before serving. *Makes about 6 cups.*

Cornish Pasties

Beef, chopped, 6 oz.	Flour, 8 oz.
Potatoes, raw, diced, 4 oz.	Baking powder, 1 teaspoon
Onion, small, chopped, 1	Butter, 6 tablespoons
Salt and pepper, to taste	Water, to moisten

Salt, a pinch

Mix the beef, potatoes, onion, and a little salt and pepper together and set aside. Make a dough from the flour, baking powder, sufficient water, and salt. Roll the dough out to about ¼ inch thickness, and cut it into large squares. Fill half each square with the meat and potatoes mixture; dampen the edges and fold up to seal. Bake at first in a hot (400°F.) oven, so the dough rises slightly, then cool the oven. Bake for 30-45 minutes overall. To improve the appearance, brush these with a little beaten egg yolk after about 20 minutes of baking. (Uncooked calves liver may be added to the chopped beef, if you like.) *Makes about 12.*

Colcannon

Parsnips	Butter
Potatoes	Salt and pepper, to taste
Milk	Milk, enough to make
Cabbage	smooth

Boil the potatoes, cabbage, and parsnips. Mash the potatoes and parsnips together, chop the cabbage, and mix all together. Add butter and salt and pepper to taste, and heat over a moderate fire with a little milk to smooth the mixture.

(Also try this with carrots and boiled small onions added. Try as I may, I can't get people to believe this is any good. It really is a delightful and wonderful way to vary the traditional meat and potatoes fare.)

Pea Soup

Split peas, diced, 2 cups	Celery, sliced, 2-3 stalks
Stock, 2 quarts	Turnip, sliced, small, 1
Onions, sliced, 2	Salt and pepper, to taste
Carrots, sliced, 2	Cayenne, a dash

Soak the dried peas in cold water for 12 hours. Drain and put them into a large pot with the cold stock, and bring to a boil. Cook the vegetables in butter until onions begin to turn clear; then add to boiling stock. Season with pepper and salt. Simmer gently for 2½-3 hours, until peas are very tender. Strain vegetables, sieve, and return to the stock. Stir well and season with a little cayenne pepper. Serve with croutons or with celery cooked in stock until tender. *Makes about 6 cups.*

Jugged Hare

Hare, 1	Stock, strong, 3 cups
Butter, 2 tablespoons	Flour, 4 tablespoons
Salt and pepper, to taste	Butter, 4 tablespoons
Onion, sliced, 1	Parsley
Cloves, 3-4	Thyme
Lemon juice, 1 tablespoon	Bay leaf, 1
Port, 1 cup	Red currant jelly

Salt and pepper

Joint the hare and brown in a frying pan with a little butter. Season with salt and pepper. Put the pieces of hare into a saucepan and add the onion, herbs, and lemon juice. Pour in ¼ cup wine and warm stock, and season again with salt and pepper. Cover the saucepan tightly and cook in a moderate (350°F.) oven for 3 hours. Just ½ hour before it is done, thicken the sauce with a roux of flour and butter, and add the rest of the wine. *Serves 4.*

Veal Forcemeat Balls

Veal, lean, ½ lb.	Lemon juice, 2 teaspoons
Bacon, ¼ lb.	(or lemon rind, ½
Bread crumbs, 1½	teaspoon)
tablespoons	Nutmeg, a dash
Mixed herbs, 1 teaspoon	Salt and pepper, to taste

Eggs, 1-2

Chop the veal and bacon very fine; mix with the bread crumbs, season with mixed herbs, add lemon juice or grated lemon rind, nutmeg, and salt and pepper. Bind with one or two beaten eggs. Shape into small meatballs and fry in butter. *Makes about 12-15 balls.*

Serve the jugged hare with the veal forcemeat balls and red currant jam served separately.

Beefsteak Pudding

Beafsteak, 2 lbs.   Salt, 1 teaspoon
Flour, 1 tablespoon   Pepper, ½ teaspoon
            Paste of suet and flour, 1 lb.

Cut meat into thin slices, about three inches long and the same width, though not necessarily uniform in shape. Mix the flour, salt and pepper on a plate, and dip each slice of meat into the mixture. Cutt off about a quarter of the flour-suet paste, and set aside for a lid. Roll the rest out and line a pudding basin (a deep round tin) with it, after greasing the tin. Put the meat in layers, leaving room for some water between the meat, to keep the pudding from drying out. Salt and pepper each layer. Cover the meat to a level three quarters deep with boiling water. (Boiling water will extract less of the meat juice than cold water.) Moisten the top edges, cover with the rest of the paste, rolled out, and tie the whole in a pudding cloth. Put the pudding into a pot of boiling water for 3½ hours. (If you prefer, the pudding may be steamed above boiling water for about 4 hours, instead.)

Tipsy Cake

Sponge cakes, small, 4   Sherry, ½ glass
Raspberry jam   Cherries
Custard, boiled, 1 cup   Angelica
            Almonds

Split the cakes, spread them with a layer of jam, replace the tops and arrange them close together on a dish. Pour the sherry over them and let soak for about an hour. Make the custard and when cooled, pour over the cakes. Garnish the cake with cherries, angelica and almonds.

Syllabub

Macaroons, 10   Lemon rind, grated, ½
Cream, 1 cup   lemon
Castor sugar, 4 oz.   Madiera or Sherry, 1 glass
Lemon juice, 1 lemon   Cinnamon, ground, pinch
            Ratafia, essence of

Mix the sugar, lemon juice, and lemon rind; cinnamon and wine together in a large bowl. Add a few drops of essence of ratafia and mix until sugar is fully dissolved. Add cream and whip to a froth. Arrange the macaroons on bottom of a deep dish, and as liquid froths, skim the froth off and put on top of cookies. When whole mixture has frothed and been put on top of macaroons, cool the dish and let stand 12 hours, then serve.

Fried Dover Sole

Dover soles

Butter

Flour

Egg, beaten

Bread crumbs

Dip the fish into the flour, brush with the beaten egg, and coat with bread crumbs. Fry in butter until golden brown. Serve with lemon and parsley.

Fried Whiting

Whiting

Butter

Flour

Egg, beaten

Bread crumbs

Prepare as in Dover sole, but before frying, fasten the fish's tail in its mouth with a skewer. This is the typical English manner of preparing this fish. Serve with lemon and parsley.

Mixed Grill

Per Person:

Lamb chop, or cutlet

Sausage

Kidney

Bacon, 2 slices

Mushrooms, several

Tomato

Flour

Slice the tomato in half, dip in flour. Slice the kidney in half, remove the core, and wash well. Fry the kidney, tomato, lamb chop or cutlet, mushrooms, and sausage. Serve hot, with bottled sauce.

Oxtail Soup

Oxtail, 1	Stock, 2 quarts
Ham, lean, 2 oz.	Thyme, ½ teaspoon
Flour, 2 tablespoons	Bay leaf, 1
Butter, 1 tablespoon	Mace, 1 blade
Onion, sliced, 1	Cloves, whole, 2-3
Carrots, sliced, 2	Salt, to taste
Turnip, sliced, 1	Peppercorns, 2-3
Parsley, chopped, 1	Egg, 1
tablespoon	Sherry, ¼ cup

Clean the oxtail thoroughly and cut into 1½ inch lengths. Put these lengths into a saucepan, cover with water, and bring to a boil. Strain, dry the oxtail, and roll in flour. Put these into a saucepan with melted butter and fry until they begin to brown; then add all the vegetables, and fry until brown. Add the slightly warm stock, bring it to a boil, and skim. Add the herbs and seasonings and simmer gently for 4 hours. Strain this mixture and clarify the soup with a little egg white and egg shell. Strain again through a cloth, put in a saucepan, and boil. Garnish with a few pieces of oxtail, add the sherry, and serve.

Sometimes fancy cut vegetables are added as a garnish. Thick oxtail soup is made in the same way, but a little cornmeal is added to thicken the mixture. *Makes 6-8 cups.*

White Soup

Flour, ½ cup	Lemon rind, grated, a pinch
Milk or water, ½ cup	Rice, cooked, 2½
Milk, 4 cups	tablespoons
Onion, finely chopped, 1	Salt and pepper, to taste
teaspoon	

Mix the flour into a smooth paste with a little milk or cold water. Bring to a boil, and add the flour to it, stirring until it begins to thicken. Add the onion, lemon rind, and cooked rice, and season with salt and pepper. Simmer for about 20 minutes, stirring occasionally. *Makes 3-4 cups.*

Rice Pudding

Rice, raw, 3 tablespoons Salt, a pinch
Milk, 2 cups Eggs, 2-3
Sugar, 2 tablespoons Vanilla, 1 teaspoon
Bay leaf, 1 (optional)

Put the rice, well washed, in a buttered dish; add the milk, sugar, and salt. Beat the eggs into this mixture. Add the vanilla, and a bay leaf, if you like. Bake in a slow (300°F.) oven for 1½-2 hours, until the top is lightly browned. Serve with milk and sugar. *Makes about 2 cups.*

Halibut Bristol

Halibut, center cut, 1 lb. Butter, 1½ teaspoons
Salt and pepper, to taste Cheese, grated, 1½ oz.
Milk, ½ cup Mussels, 12
Flour, ½ oz.

Put the halibut in a greased baking dish; sprinkle with salt and pepper, and cover with milk. Cover with waxed paper and bake in a hot (425°F.) oven for 20 minutes. Remove the dish from the oven, drain off the liquid, and remove the bones from the fish. Use the liquid to make a sauce with the butter, flour, and 1 oz. of the cheese, adding seasonings. Arrange freshly-cooked mussels around the halibut, cover with the sauce, and sprinkle with the remaining cheese. Return the dish to a very hot (425°F.) oven for 10 minutes to brown. *Serves 2-3.*

Steak Pudding

Steak, round, ½ lb. Drippings, 4-5 tablespoons
Ox kidney, cleaned, ½ lb. Flour, ¼ cup
Salt and pepper, to taste Eggs, 2
Milk, 1½ cups

Cut the steak into finger-shaped pieces. Cut the kidney into thin slices and season well. Fry the steak for a few minutes in the drippings to seal the surface. Mix the flour, eggs, and milk into a smooth batter and season. Melt about 2 tablespoons dripping in a casserole or pie dish and add half the batter. Bake in a moderate (350°F.) oven until it sets. Place the steak and kidney on top of the batter, fill the dish with the rest of the batter, and bake in a hot (400°F.) oven for 10 minutes; reduce the heat to a moderate (350°F.) temperature and bake for about 1 hour. Serve with a good brown gravy. This pudding is equally good served hot or cold, accompanied by the gravy and mustard on the side. *Serves 4-6.*

Liver and Sausage Pâté

Liver, 1 lb.	Mixed herbs, 1 teaspoon
Salt and pepper, to taste	Bay leaf, 1
Celery salt, a pinch	Garlic, 1 clove
Worcestershire sauce, a dash	

Take the liver in one piece and put it in a large bowl. Pour over it enough boiling water to cover, and let it stand for 5 minutes. Drain and chop it up into small pieces, then run it through a grinder twice. Season with salt and pepper, celery salt, Worcestershire sauce, and mixed herbs, and mix with the sausage meat, using first a fork and then a wooden spoon, until it is well mixed. Put this mixture through the grinder once again and then press into a greased ovenproof dish which has a bay leaf on the bottom. Add a little minced garlic to this mixture if you like garlic, otherwise just rub a clove of garlic around the dish before greasing it. Cover with a lid or with waxed paper and bake for about 40 minutes in a moderate (350°F.) oven. *Makes 8 servings.*

The pâté can be eaten hot, served with a thick gravy or tomato sauce. Served cold, it is a perfect dish for picnics. Try it with pickled walnuts.

Note: *The texture of this dish depends on the number of times it is passed through the grinder. Three times produces a rather smooth consistency, but if you prefer a very smooth texture, merely run it through a grinder several more times.*

Stuffed Lambchops

Lambchops, 4	Bread crumbs, 1 cup
Veal forcemeat, ½ cup	Eggs, beaten, 2
	Butter, 2 tablespoons

Make sure the lamb chops are cut thick. Cut them through the middle to the bone, making a pocket for the stuffing. Fill with veal forcemeat (or sage and onion dressing, if you prefer). Close the cut by pressing, then cover with bread crumbs, pressing them well into the meat. Dip in egg, then dip in bread crumbs again. Bake in a moderate (350°F.) oven, basting with melted butter, turning at least once. Bake about ½ hour or longer, depending on the thickness of the chops.

White Fish with Asparagus and Cheese

Asparagus, ½ lb.
Cream, ½ cup
Butter, 1 tablespoon
Salt and pepper, to taste
White fish fillets, 4
Lemon juice, 1 tablespoon

Stock, fish, 4 tablespoons
Wine, white, ¼ cup
Flour, 1 tablespoon
Butter, 1 tablespoon
Cheese, grated, 2
  tablespoons

Boil the asparagus until soft, then drain and chop in into medium-sized pieces. Add the asparagus to a saucepan filled with enough cream to cover, add butter and salt and pepper, and simmer gently for a few minutes. Put the fish fillets into a greased baking dish and sprinkle them with lemon juice. Add the stock to the fish, then add the wine, cover and bake in a moderate (350°F.) oven for ½ hour. When done, drain, and put the fish into a shallow ovenproof dish. Thicken the asparagus mixture with a little flour and butter mixed together, and mix in the liquid from the baked fish. Pour the sauce over the fillets, sprinkle with grated cheese, and brown lightly in the oven, melting the cheese. Garnish with asparagus tips. *Serves 4.*

Friar's Omelet

Apples, baking, sour, 4
Sugar, 2 oz.
Butter, 1 tablespoon
Rind of ½ lemon, grated

Juice of ½ lemon
Egg, well-beaten, 1
Bread crumbs, 2 oz.
Butter, 1 tablespoon

Pare, core, and slice the apples. Stew them with the sugar, butter, lemon rind, and lemon juice until tender. Stir in the egg. Put half the bread crumbs at the bottom of a well-greased pie dish, pour in the apple mixture and cover with the rest of the bread crumbs. Add a few bits of butter and bake in a moderate (350°F.) oven for about ¼ hour. *Serves 4.*

Hasty Pudding

Milk, 2 cups
Flour or tapioca, 1-2 tablespoons

Salt, to taste
Sugar, to taste

Boil the milk and sprinkle in enough flour or tapioca to thicken the milk, stirring briskly. Add a little salt, and sugar to taste, stir and cook for about 10 minutes. Serve with cream and sugar, jam, or treacle syrup. *Serves 3.*

Chestnut Pudding

Chestnuts, shelled, 3 oz.	Flour, 1 tablespoon
Chocolate, semi-sweet, ½ oz.	Cake or cookie crumbs, 1 oz.
Milk, ½ cup	Egg, separated, 1
Butter, 2 tablespoons	Vanilla extract, ¼ teaspoon

Bake for roast the chestnuts and remove the shells and skins. Put into a saucepan with a very little water; cook until tender, then rub them through a fine sieve. Break the chocolate into small pieces and put these with the milk into a small saucepan. Simmer until the chocolate melts. In another saucepan melt the butter and stir in the flour. Cook for a few minutes, then add the milk and cook until it boils. Add the cake crumbs, and stir and cook the mixture until it does not stick to the sides of the saucepan. Allow the mixture to cool slightly, then beat into it the egg yolk. Add the chestnut pureé and the vanilla. Whisk the egg white until it is very stiff, and fold it into the mixture. Pour the mixture into a well-greased pudding tin, cover with waxed or greased paper, and boil for 1½ hours, or bake in a moderately hot (375°F.) oven for 1 hour. Serve with vanilla sauce. *Serves 4.*

Roast Beef

Beef	Drippings

Roast Beef is the most famous English dish and the one the English most enjoy. Served with a horseradish sauce, and Yorkshire pudding, it is a simple and elegant meal.

Usually the sirloin, ribs or aitchbone are roasted, basted in their own drippings. Sometimes, shortly before serving, the roast is covered with flour, to brown and crust the meat.

Yorkshire Pudding

Flour, 4 heaping tablespoons	Milk, 2 cups
Salt, a pinch	Beef drippings, 2 tablespoons
Eggs, 2	

Put the flour and a good pinch of salt into a large mixing bowl, and make a well in the center. Break the eggs into the well, mix in the flour slowly from the sides, and add the milk gradually until a thick, smooth batter is formed. Beat well for 10 minutes, then add what's left of the milk, beat a little more, and let the bowl and mixture stand, covered for at least 1 hour. When ready to use, cover the bottom layer of a baking pan with beef drippings, and heat the pan and drippings in the oven. While they heat, beat the batter again. Bake the pudding in a hot (400°F.) oven for about 10 minutes, until the bottom sets, in the pan with the drippings. (Actually, this pudding was usually cooked in front of the fire in Yorkshire homes; one cooked in an oven was called a "batter pudding.")

Hot Horseradish Sauce

Horseradish, finely-grated, 2
    tablespoons
White sauce, 1 cup

Vinegar, 1 teaspoon
Sugar, to taste
Salt, to taste
Cayenne, to taste

Add the horseradish to the white sauce, add the vinegar, and season to taste with sugar, salt, and cayenne pepper. *Makes about 1½ cups.*

Horseradish Sauce

Eggs, hard-boiled, 2
Vinegar, 3 tablespoons
Horseradish, finely-grated, 2
    tablespoons

Cream, 1 tablespoon
Salt, to taste
Sugar, to taste

Work the egg yolks into a paste. Add vinegar gradually, and work into a cream. Add the horseradish, cream, and salt and sugar to taste. *Makes about ½ cup.*

Queen's Pudding

Suet, finely-chopped, 4 oz.
Sugar, superfine, 2 oz.
Bananas, sliced, 6

Flour, whole wheat, 2 cups
Milk, 1 cup
Eggs, 2

Mix the suet, sugar, bananas, and flour together; add the milk and cover tightly. Let the mixture stand for at least 1 hour before adding the eggs. Add a little more milk if the mixture is at all stiff, and beat well. Turn into a greased pudding tin and steam gently for 1 hour. Serve with a white sauce or wine sauce. *Serves 6.*

Rolled Loin of Lamb

Loin of lamb, about 6 lbs.	Carrots, 2
Salt and pepper, to taste	Turnip, small, ½
Onions, 2	Butter, 1 tablespoon
Meat glaze, ¼ cup	

Remove the bones from the meat. Season the inner surface with salt and pepper, roll the flap under, and tie tightly with string. Chop onions, slice the carrots and turnip, and brown in a baking pan with butter. Put meat on top, cover, and bake for 2 hours in a moderate (350°F.) oven. Brush with glaze and serve on a bed of cooked peas or spinach. Serve with mint sauce. *Serves 4.*

Mint Sauce for Lamb

Mint leaves, fresh, chopped, 4 tablespoons	Vinegar, ½ cup
	Sugar, 2 tablespoons

Mix mint leaves with vinegar in a bowl with sugar. Be sure to make this sauce an hour or so before it is to be served, to give the mint time to mix well with vinegar and sugar.

Baked Trout

Trout, 2	Capers, 1 teaspoon
Forcemeat, veal, 1½ cups	Lemon juice, 1 teaspoon
Butter, 3 tablespoons	Anchovy extract, ½
Flour, 1 oz.	teaspoon
Stock, fish, about 1 cup	Salt and pepper, to taste

Clean, scale, and dry the fish. Put forcemeat inside the fish and sew up the openings. Place fish in a baking pan with 2 tablespoons of butter, and bake for about ½ hour in a moderate (350°F.) oven, basting frequently. Fry the flour and the rest of the butter together. When the fish is ready, remove it to a hot dish. Strain the liquor from the baking dish into the flour and butter mixture. Add stock and stir the mixture until it boils and smooths out. Add the capers, lemon juice, and anchovy extract, and season to taste with salt and pepper. Simmmer the sauce about 10 minutes, then pour it over the fish and serve garnished with parsley and lemon wedges. *Serves 2-4.*

Paradise Pudding

Apples, chopped coarsely, 3 oz.
Sugar, 3 oz.
Currants, 3 oz.
Bread crumbs, 4 oz.

Eggs, 2
Rind of ½ lemon, grated
Brandy, 1 tablespoon
Salt, to taste
Nutmeg, a pinch

Mix all the ingredients together well, turn them into a well-greased pudding tin or basin, and steam for about 2 hours. Serve with a suitable sauce. *Serves 4.*

Empress Pudding

Rice, 2 oz.
Milk, 2 cups
Butter, 1 tablespoon
Sugar 1½ teaspoons

Salt, ⅛ teaspoon
Flour, ½ cup
Water, ½ cup
Jam or stewed fruit, 1 cup

Simmer the rice in the milk until tender and fairly dry. Add the butter, sugar, and salt. Line the edge of a pie dish with a paste of flour and water; then spread a thin layer of rice on the bottom of the dish, and cover thickly with jam or stewed fruit. Repeat until the dish is full, the top layer should be rice. Bake in a moderate (350°F.) oven for ½ hour and serve with a boiled custard sauce. *Serves 4-6.*

Chicken Soufflé

Chicken, raw, ¼ lb.
Butter, 2 teaspoons
Egg, separated, 1

Salt and pepper, to taste
Cream, heavy, 1 tablespoon
Béchamel sauce, ½ cup

Shred the chicken meat finely, or grind it, and then mix it in a mortar with the butter and egg yolk. Season with salt and pepper, and rub through a sieve. Whip the cream slightly, whip the egg white thoroughly, and add both to the chicken pureé. Add a little milk if the mixture is too thick. Place in a well-greased soufflé pan, cover with waxed paper, and steam gently for about 1 hour. Serve with béchamel sauce poured over, and decorate the souffle, if you like, with a little chopped truffle. *Serves 2-3.*

Bachelor's Pudding

Apple, pared, cored, and
   coarsely chopped, 3 oz.
Bread crumbs, 3 oz.
Currants, 3 oz.
Sugar, 1½ oz.

Rind of ½ lemon, grated
Salt, ⅛ teaspoon
Eggs, well-beaten, 2
Baking powder, 1 teaspoon
Nutmeg, a pinch

Add the apples to the bread crumbs, currants, sugar, lemon rind, and salt, and mix well together. Then stir in the eggs. Let the mixture stand for about ½ hour. Stir in the baking powder and nutmeg, add milk if the mixture is stiff, and turn the mixture into a greased pudding tin. Steam for 3 hours, or boil for 2½ hours. Serve with a sweet melted butter sauce. Serves 3.

Sole au Gratin

Sole, large, 1
Salt and pepper, to taste
Wine, white, ¼ cup
Lemon juice, a few drops
Mushroom liquor, 1
   tablespoon
Parsley, chopped, 1
   tablespoon

Mushrooms, canned, sliced,
   12
Italian sauce, 1 cup
Bread crumbs, toasted, ¼
   cup
Butter, 1 tablespoon

Skin both sides of the sole, cut off its head, remove the fins, and make several slices on one side of the body. Place, cut side up, on a well-buttered baking dish. Season with salt and pepper, add wine, lemon juice, mushroom liquor, and chopped parsley. Place a row of mushrooms down the center of the fish, and cover with Italian sauce (see below). Sprinkle with brown bread crumbs, put a few bits of butter on top, and bake in a moderate (350°F.) oven for 20-30 minutes according to the size of the sole. *Serves 2.*

Italian Sauce

Shallots, chopped, 4
Oil, 1 tablespoon

Thyme, 1 sprig
Bay leaf, 1

Wine, chablis, ¼ cup	Stock, ¼ cup
	Spanish sauce, 1 cup

Put the shallots in a small piece of muslin, and squeeze them in cold water to extract some of the flavor. Place them in a saucepan with the oil and fry, but do not brown them. Add the wine, mushrooms, herbs, and stock. Reduce the mixture well and add the Spanish sauce. Boil for about 10 minutes, remove the herbs, and skim off the oil before using. *Makes about 1½ cups.*

Roast Pheasant

Pheasant, 1	Bacon, sliced thin, 4 strips
Beefsteak, ¼ lb.	(or fat bacon)
	Flour, ¼ cup

Pluck and draw the bird, truss like a roast chicken, leaving the head on. Put the beefsteak inside the pheasant. (The beefsteak is to improve the flavor of the bird and to keep it moist and tender; it is not intended to be eaten with the bird, though it may be kept to use as cold meat in some other dish.) Cover the bird's breast with bacon, or lard it with fat bacon, and roast for 40-50 minutes in a moderate (350°F.) oven. Baste frequently with hot fat. When about ¾ done, remove the bacon and sprinkle the breast with flour, basting well to give the bird a nice brown appearance. Serve on a hot dish, untrussed, on watercress seasoned with oil, salt, and pepper. Serve bread crumbs, sauce, and gravy separately. *Serves 2.*

Baked Plaice

Bread crumbs, 2 tablespoons	Nutmeg, a pinch
	Salt and pepper, to taste
Suet, finely-chopped, 1 tablespoon	Egg, 1
	Milk, to moisten
Parsley, finely-chopped, 1 teaspoon	Bread crumbs, toasted, 2 tablespoons
Mixed herbs, ¼ teaspoon	Drippings, a few pieces

Mix the bread crumbs, suet, parsley, herbs, and nutmeg together; season well with salt and pepper, add half the egg and enough milk to thoroughly moisten the mixture. Make an incision down the center of the fish as for filleting, and pull each side of the fish up as far as possible. Fill with the mixture. Instead of bringing the sides together, fill the gap with the stuffing and level with a knife to the edge of the fish. Brush with the remaining half of the egg, cover lightly with the browned bread crumbs, place a few small pieces of drippings on top, and bake in a moderate (350°F.) oven for 20-30 minutes. *Serves 2.*

Baked Mackerel

Mackerel, medium, 2	Drippings, 1 oz.
Veal forcemeat, 1 cup	Flour, ¼ cup
	Salt and pepper, to taste

Clean the fish, take out the roe, fill with forcemeat, and sew up the opening. Put the fish with the roe into a baking dish. Add the dripping, sprinkle heavily with flour, season with salt and pepper, and bake for 30-40 minutes in a moderate (350°F.) oven, basting occasionally. Serve with melted butter mixed with lemon juice and chopped parsley. *Serves 4.*

Baked Pork

Pork, loin or leg, about 6 lbs.	Salt and pepper, to taste
Onions, sliced, 2	Mixed herbs, 1 teaspoon
Carrots, sliced, 2	Drippings, 3 oz.
Turnip, small, sliced, 1	Onions, button, 24
Celery, diced, 2 stalks	Gravy, 1 cup

Score the pork in narrow lines. Slice all vegetables except the button onions and place in a baking dish, sprinkle with salt and pepper, and add the herbs and drippings. Lay the meat on the top and cook in a moderate (350°F.) oven, about 20 minutes for each lb. basting often. About ½ hour before serving, peel the small onions and fry them in fat. Serve the meat on a hot dish, garnish with the onions, and serve the gravy separately. Serve with applesauce. *Serves 4.*

Roast Loin of Veal

Veal loin, 4-5 lbs.	Meat glaze, ¼ cup
Forcemeat, veal, 1½ cups	Brown sauce, 1½ cups
Salt and pepper, to taste	Bacon, 4-6 slices
	Lemon, quartered, 1

Bone the veal and fill the inside with forcemeat after seasoning with salt and pepper. Skewer or tie the meat in the form of a roll. Baste well with hot drippings, cover with greased or waxed paper, and either bake or roast from 2½-3 hours, basting frequently. Boil the bones for stock for the brown sauce. About ½ hour before serving the meat, remove the paper and brush with glaze. Drain all the fat from the baking pan but leave the brown sediment. Pour the brown sauce into the pan, return to the oven to finish cooking, and baste the meat frequently. Roll the bacon, put on a skewer, and fry or bake until crisp. Remove the meat to a hot dish, garnish with bacon and lemon quarters. Strain the sauce and serve it separately. *Serves 8-10.*

Baked Carp

Carp, 1	Salt, to taste
Salad oil, 3 tablespoons	Cayenne, to taste
Worcestershire sauce, 1 tablespoon	Butter, clarified, 1½ tablespoons
Lemon juice, 1 tablespoon	Flour, 1½ oz.
Parsley, finely-chopped, 1 tablespoon	Milk, 1½ cups
Onion, finely-chopped, 1 teaspoon	Gherkins, coarsely chopped, 2 tablespoons

Wash, scale, and clean the fish; place it in an earthenware baking dish. Mix together the salad oil, the Worcestershire sauce, lemon juice, parsley, and onion, season well with salt and cayenne pepper, and pour this mixture over the fish. Let it remain in the mixture for at least 2 hours, basting occasionally. Cover with a greased paper, bake for about 1 hour in a moderate (350°F.) oven, basting well. When nearly done, melt the butter in a saucepan, stir in the flour, add the milk, bring to a boil, and simmer for 5-6 minutes. Place the fish on a hot dish, strain the gravy in the baking dish into the sauce, add the gherkins, season to taste, and pour over the fish. *Serves 2-4.*

Stewed Veal

Veal, neck or breast, 2 lbs.	Milk, 2 cups
Salt and pepper, to taste	Butter, 1 tablespoon
Onion, small, quartered, 1	Cornstarch, 1 tablespoon
Mace, 1 blade	Cream, 2 tablespoons

Cut the meat into pieces convenient for serving. Place them in an ovenproof stew pot, season with salt and pepper, and add the onion and mace. Pour in the milk, cover tightly, and cook in the oven or over a fire for about 2½-3 hours. A few minutes before serving, knead the butter and cornstarch together; divide into very small pieces, and mix them into the cream. Put the meat onto a hot dish, add the cream to the sauce, season to taste, and pour over the meat. *Serves 4.*

Gooseberry Pudding

Gooseberries, 3 cups   Butter, 1½ tablespoons
Bread crumbs, 1 cup   Sugar, 2 oz.
Eggs, 2   Short crust pastry, ½ recipe

Cut the tops and tails off the berries, cook them until tender in a jar placed in a saucepan full of boiling water. Then rub the gooseberries through a fine sieve. Add the pureé to bread crumbs which have been beaten with eggs, butter, and sugar. Have a pie dish ready, lined with pastry, the bottom well greased. Pour in the preparation, and bake for about 40 minutes, or until the fruit sets, in a moderate (350°F.) oven. Sprinkle heavily with sugar and serve. *Serves 4-6.*

Blanquette of Lamb

Lamb, loin, neck, or breast,   Butter, 1½ tablespoons
   2 lbs.   Flour, 1 oz.
Onion, sliced, 1   Egg yolk, 1
Bouquet garni, 1   Cream or milk, 2
Peppercorns, white, 6   tablespoons
Salt, to taste

Cut the meat into pieces about 2 inches square and put them into a saucepan with the sliced onion, peppercorns, and salt. Cover with cold water, and cook gently for about 2 hours. Melt the butter, add the flour to it, and fry for a few minutes without browning the flour. When the meat is ready, strain from it 1 cup of the liquor it was cooked in. Add the liquor to the flour and butter mixture. Stir this until it boils. Simmer the mixture for a few minutes, then add the egg yolk and cream, previously beaten together. Stir and cook gently for a few minutes, taking care the sauce does not boil. (Boiling may cause the mixture to curdle.) Arrange the meat nicely on a hot dish, strain over it the sauce, and serve. Garnish with boiled new potatoes or with flower-sliced tomatoes. *Serves 4.*

To finish this section, here are two typical and traditional English Christmas dishes: the world famous Christmas pudding, and mince pie—both very British.

Christmas Pudding

Beef Suet, ½ lb.

Raisins, ½ lb.

Mixed fruit peel, finely
shredded, ¼ lb.

Sultanas, ¼ lb.

Currants, ¼ lb.

Rind of ½ lemon, chopped

Bread crumbs, ½ lb.

Coconut dried, 2 oz.

Flour, 2 oz.

Nutmeg, grated, ½

Cinnamon, ½ oz.

Mixed spice, ½ oz.

Milk, ½ cup

Eggs, 4

Rum or brandy, ¼ cup

Juice of 1 lemon

Skin the suet and chop it finely. Put all the fruit and dry ingredients into a mixing bowl and mix well together. Add the milk, stir in the eggs one at a time, add the rum or brandy, and the strained juice of the lemon. Work the whole thoroughly for some minutes, so that the ingredients are well blended. Put the mixture into a well-greased basin or pudding cloth. Boil for 4 hours or steam for at least 5 hours.Garnish with holly springs, pour brandy over the top, light, and serve flaming. *Serves 6-8.*

Mince Pie

Lemon, 1

Suet, 1 lb.

Raisins, chopped, 1 lb.

Sultanas, ½ lb.

Currants, 1 lb.

Apples, peeled, cored,
and chopped, 1 lb.

Sugar, powdered, ¼ cup

Mixed candied peel,
shredded, ¼ lb.

Cinnamon, ¼ teaspoon

Mace, a dash

Nutmeg, ⅛ teaspoon

Lemon juice, 1 tablespoon

Brandy, ½ cup

Pie crust, 1 receipe

Pare the lemon and boil the rind until it is tender. Rub the rind through a fine sieve. Skin and finely chop the suet. Mix the raisins, sultanas, currants, apples, sugar, candied peel, sieved lemon peel, spices, lemon juice, and brandy together. Put the mixture into an airtight jar and let it stand at least a month before using for pie. Make a shortening pie crust and save ¼ of the dough. Line a pie tin with the rest, and fill it to the top with the aged mincemeat mixture. Spread the mixture out evenly and even with the top of the crust. Roll the remaining crust out about ¼ inch thick; cut into long strips of the same width. Arrange these in a lattice over the top of the pie. Bake the pie in a moderate (350°F.) oven until the crust is light and flaky. Sprinkle the crust with sugar before baking, if you like. *Serves 6-8.*

SUPPER

*" . . . if we are too late for dinner, I think we are both ready for our
supper."*
— *Sherlock Holmes*

Supper is the least understood of Victorian meals. Seventy or more years of
changing customs have served to obliterate the word's original meaning, and except for some old-fashioned homes in Britain and Ireland, supper has passed into
history.

I thought supper was merely a forgotten tradition until a stay on an Irish
farm in Longford, ancestral home of my family, convinced me otherwise. There
the five meal-a-day tradition lingers on. I had my supper served before a crackling
fire in the family's 200-year-old Georgian farm house. Tea, fresh tomato
sandwiches, berry tarts, fresh bread and butter made up the simple fare. It was an
excellent finish to a very restful, old-fashioned day.

Supper is or was the last meal of the day, what we might now call a "mid-
night snack." But it was more than just a snack, as the Canon clearly indicates.
Often it was just toast and tea, or a favorite savoury and coffee or whiskey and
soda. But it was also an important meal, substantial and formal, when the occasion called for it. If dinner was missed, or eaten in haste, when an important
client was waiting, supper would fill the empty void. And if a full-length
Wagnerian Opera caused an early curtain, an after-theatre supper was called for,
either through Mrs. Hudson's good offices or at one of the restaurants that
specialized in that sort of fare.

Sherlock Holmes probably did not often call on his landlady for supper. He once told Watson "you have never appreciated my merits as a housekeeper," and proceeded to produce what the hungry doctor called "a quite epicurean little cold supper." Instead of keeping Mrs. Hudson up to all hours of the night, Holmes preferred to practice his talents as a chef. (Is it possible that during his prolonged stay in the south of France, Holmes did more research into French provincial cuisine rather than into coal-tar derivatives, a rather boring subject at best when compared with the delights of cooking? Perhaps the Legion d'Honneur Holmes accepted was to accompany his cordon blu from the French academy.) It shows the affection Mrs. Hudson held for her lodger that she would allow him to work in her kitchen, at night and presumably alone. Despite the incident of the bullet-scarred wall, Holmes must have been a more reasonable boarder than is usually thought.

Scholarly debate has centered around that supper in "The Noble Bachelor." Watson describes the tables set for five, but some contend that Holmes had only prepared food for four, knowing that Lord Robert St. Simon would not stay for the meal. While it is possible that the almost omniscient Holmes deduced Lord St. Simon's intentions beforehand, I suspect that Holmes' elaborate preparations were intended to impress the nobleman. Despite objections that the phrase "a couple of brace of cold woodcock" meant two birds, with one-half a bird being a serving, I suggest that the "couple" might well have been three. The group of "ancient and cobwebby bottle" seem more than enough for four, and the pheasant added to the meal with the pâté de fois gras pie would certainly serve five.

Supper was, as I said earlier, a changeable feast. What was served depended on dinner, and might include just about anything. Here I have included mostly recipes for "savouries," dishes that might as easily be served after a heavy dinner in the English manner as for supper. Tea cakes, lunch, and even breakfast dishes often found there way onto supper menus. Cold suppers were both served, according to tasfe, throughout the year.

I have of course included receipes for the supper served by Holmes in "The Noble Bachelor," but I have refrained from recreating the supper in "Silver Blaze." That meal consisted of a dish of curried mutton, you will remember. But the ingredients included a small dose of a powerful drug, and the groom Hunter was still under its influence some hours after the murder was discovered. I have included a curried mutton elsewhere (see Lunch). If you are interested in drugging a stable boy, though, look elsewhere. That is not within my purview.

ANCIENT AND COBWEBBY BOTTLES

I have neither the money nor the age to have become an expert on wines, though I do appreciate them. Nor am I widely acquainted with the wines of France. With that caveat, I'll attempt a few suggestions.

Watson describes the bottles on the sideboard in "The Noble Bachelor" as a group of "ancient and cobwebby bottles." We may be sure that these were suited to the meal Holmes had prepared. One was most probably an ancient, crusted port, intended for consideration after the meal. Holmes and Watson had a liking for port.

It is possible a Côté de Beaune, a brother of the one Watson nodded over at lunch one day, might have been featured, along with, perhaps, a fine burgundy or claret. Beyond that I will not venture my limited knowledge.

I will, however, in deference to my native state, offer a few suggestions about California wines that would serve well. A fine Cabernet Sauvignon, or Pinot Noir would go well with the meal Holmes planned. A Gamay, or Gamay Noir might also be included.

Pâté de Fois Gras Pie

Butter, ½ cup   Flour, 4 cups
Salt, 1 teaspoon   Pâté de fois gras, 3½ lbs.

Mix the butter, salt, and flour together into a dough, adding a little cold water. Let the dough stand in a cool spot for 6-8 hours. Line a croute pan or pie pan with dough rolled ¼ inch thick, leaving a little dough over for the top. Fill with pâté, cover with pastry, and bake in a moderate (350°F.) oven for 1-1½ hours. Cool before serving. *Serves 6-8.*

Though Sherlock Holmes never goes shooting for game in any recorded case, he shows a marked fondness for it. Woodcock is one of the few foods to be mentioned on two different occasions in the Canon. It figures in a dinner in "The Blue Carbuncle" and reappears in "The Noble Bachelor" as a cold supper dish.

(It should be noted here that there is some confusion about the term "brace of woodcock." The *Oxford English Dictionary* suggests it may be used either for one bird, or for a pair of birds.)

Cold Woodcock

To prepare the birds, roast them as directed in Dinner; then cool. Serve on a bed of aspic jelly, or with toast and lettuce.

Devils on Horseback

Livers, chicken, 2 (or calve's   Salt and pepper, to taste
   liver)   Cayenne, to taste
Butter, 1 tablespoon   Prunes, stewed, drained, 8
                    Bacon, 8 slices

Cook the liver gently in butter, then cut into 8 pieces. Season well with salt and pepper, and dust lightly with cayenne pepper. Stone the prunes and stuff with the liver. Stretch the bacon to double its size with a knife. Roll each prune in a piece of bacon and fasten with skewers or toothpicks. Grill or fry in a little butter until bacon is crisp. Serve on toast squares, garnished with the olives. *Serves 4.*

Dutch Flummery

Lemon, 1
Water, 2 cups
Gelatin, unflavored, 1 oz.

Maderia or sherry, ¼ cup
Eggs, beaten, 2
Sugar, to taste

Cut thin strips of lemon rind after washing the fruit. Put the rind in water and infuse it by heating. Simmer gently and add the gelatin, stirring until it dissolves. Add the wine to the eggs, then add juice from the lemon and the gelatin-water. Pour through a strainer into a saucepan, and stir gently over a low fire until the mixture thickens. Sweeten the mixture to taste, and pour into a wetted 1-quart mold. Chill until set, then remove from the mold. *Serves 4.*

Russian Salad

Cauliflower, small, 1
Peas, ½ cup
Carrot, cut, ½ cup
Turnip, cut, mixed with
  French beans, ½ cup
Potatoes, 3
Beetroot, small, 1
Tomatoes, 2
Aspic jelly, 1-1½ cups

Ham, diced, 2 oz.
Fish, shrimp, prawns, or
  lobster, 2 oz.
Salmon, smoked, 2 oz.
Gherkins, cut, 3
Lettuce, ½ small head
Mayonnaise, ¼ cup
Egg, hard-boiled, 1
Olives, for garnish

Anchovy fillets, for garnish

Prepare and cook the vegetables, or use canned vegetables. Drain them well. Divide the cauliflower into small pieces and dice all the other vegetables except the peas. Skin and slice the tomatoes. Line a ring mold with aspic jelly and decorate with a little diced vegetables. Set layers of jelly, cooked meat, cooked fish, vegetables, and gherkins alternately in the mold, but do not use all the vegetables. Let the mixture set, and turn out from the mold. Chop the lettuce, and toss it with the mayonnaise, then mix in the remaining vegetables and pile the mixture in the center of the mold. Decorate the mold with sliced egg white, olives, and anchovy fillets. If you prefer, make the salad without the aspic jelly. Arrange the vegetables, meat, and fish in layers in a large bowl, alternating with layers of mayonnaise. Arrange the whole in the shape of a pyramid, and cover the outside with a layer of mayonnaise. Decorate with egg whites, anchovies, and olives; chill and serve. *Serves 6.*

Cheese and Onion Pie

Onions, small, 3
Short crust pastry, 10 oz.
Salt and pepper, to taste

Flour, ½ oz.
Cheese, 4 oz.
Milk, 2 tablespoons

Parboil the onions. Roll the pastry ¼ inch thick and use half of it to line an 8-inch ovenproof plate or shallow pie dish. Mix the salt and pepper with the flour. Dip the onions, sliced thickly, into the seasoned flour and cover the bottom of the dish with them. Grate the cheese over the onions, then add the milk. Wet the edges of the pastry and put on the top. Decorate as you like, and then brush the top with a little milk or beaten egg. Bake for about 40 minutes in 425°F. degree oven. (Make this as an open tart, if you prefer, using half as much pastry dough.) *Serves 4-6.*

Anchovy Eclairs

Puff pastry, 6 oz.
Anchovy fillets, 12-15
Milk, 2-3 tablespoons

Cheese, Parmesan, grated,
3 tablespoons

Roll out the pastry to about ¼ inch thickness, and cut into oblong pieces about twice as wide as the anchovies, and a little longer. Enclose an anchovy fillet in each piece, and fold the edges over and seal them with a little milk or water. Sprinkle with cheese, and bake in a hot (425°F.) oven for about 15 minutes. *Makes about 12 eclairs.*

Hot Potato Salad

Potatoes, large, 6
Parsley, chopped, 1 heap-
   ing tablespoon
Chives or Scallion,
   chopped, 1 tablespoon

Lemon juice, 1 tablespoon
Salt and pepper, to taste
Vinegar and oil, seasoned, 4
   tablespoons

Boil the potatoes in their jackets until they are just soft, then peel them and cut into thick slices. Arrange a layer in an ovenproof dish, and sprinkle with a little parsley, chives, lemon juice, salt, and pepper. Continue layers until potatoes are used up. Bring the vinegar and oil to a boil and pour over the potatoes. Cover the dish and put into a moderate (350°F) oven until they are very hot. *Serves 4-6.*

Chili Savouries

Cream cheese, 4 oz.   Vinegar, from chili peppers
                         Rounds of toast, 4

Mix the cheese and vinegar together to form a smooth paste, and spread on toast rounds. *Serves 4.*

Deviled Shrimp Toasts

Shrimp, cleaned, cooked,   Curry powder, ½ teaspoon
  4 oz.   Toast, 4-6 slices
Cream, 4 oz.   Parsley, 1 teaspoon
                      Paprika, to garnish

Mix the cooked shrimps with cream flavored with curry powder and a few drops of liquid from chutney. Spread them on toast rounds, and sprinkle with parsley and paprika. *Serves 4-6.*

Maids of Honor

Puff pastry, 6 oz.   Flour, ½ oz.
Almonds, ground, 4 oz.   Cream, 2 tablespoons
Egg, 1   Orange-flower water, 1
Sugar, superfine, 2 oz.   tablespoon

Roll the dough out to less than ¼ inch thick, and line twelve cupcake tins with it. Mix the almonds, egg and sugar together, and mix in the flour, cream, and orange-flower water. Put a little of the mixture into each shell and bake in a fairly hot (400°F.) oven until the pastry is brown and the mixture is set. *Makes 6-8 tarts.*

Ham Mousse

Ham, cooked, ½ lb.   Aspic jelly, ¾ cup
Salt and pepper, to taste   Stock, white, 2 tablespoons

Nutmeg, to taste

Spanish sauce, 1 cup

Tomato, 1

Gelatin, unflavored, ½ oz.

Red food coloring, 1 drop

Cream, heavy, 1 cup

Truffles, chopped, 1

   tablespoon

Tie a piece of stiff paper around a china or earthenware souffle dish so that it is overall about 7 inches deep. Grind the ham twice and then pass it through a sieve. Season with salt, pepper, and nutmeg. Add the Spanish sauce, well colored with tomato. Dissolve the gelatin and ½ cup of the aspic jelly in the stock. Color the mixture with red food coloring and add to the ham. Whip the cream very lightly and fold into the mixture. When it begins to set, pour it into the souffle dish and let it set th' roughly. When the mixture is set, pour over it the remaining aspic jelly mixed with the truffes. Cool, and when the jelly sets, serve. *Serves 4-6.*

Stuffed Onions in Batter

Onions, large, 8

Pork, roasted, cold ½ lb.

Apple, small, 1

Drippings, 1 oz.

Sage, dried, 1 teaspoon

Salt an pepper, to taste

Flour self-rising, 1 oz.

Milk, 6 tablespoons

Eggs, 3-4

Milk, 1 cup

Flour, ¼ cup

Salt, ½ teaspoon

In salted water boil the onions for 15-20 minutes. Scoop the center out of each onion. Chop the onion from the center and mix with the chopped pork and chopped apple. Fry the mixture in the drippings for a few minutes. Add the sage, salt, pepper, flour, and milk, and cook a few minutes longer. Fill the onions with the mixture. piling it up on top. Grease a shallow baking dish and place the onions in it. Cover and bake for 2 hours in a 335°F. oven. While the onions cook, mix the eggs, milk, flour, and salt and let it set. Remove the onions from the oven, stir the batter, and pour it into the dish. Bake another 30 minutes in a hot (425°F.) oven, until the batter browns. *Serves 8.*

St. Honore Trifle

Sponge cake, round, 1

   inch thick, 6 inches

   diameter, 1

Egg whites, 2-3

Sugar, 4 oz.

Macaroons, ½ lb.

Sherry, ½ cup

Cream, heavy, 1 cup

Cherries or angelica, for

   garnish

Place the sponge cake on a baking sheet. Make a meringue with the beaten egg whites and sugar. Pipe a border of meringue around the top of the cake, and dry in a very (225°F.) cool oven. Don't let the meringue color. Place a thick layer of macaroons on top of the cake and soak with sherry for at least 1 hour. Don't touch the meringue with the sherry, since it may crumble. Pile whipped, sweetened cream on top and decorate with cherries and angelica. *Serves 6.*

Swedish Salad

Roast beef, cold, 4 oz.
Herring, pickled, 1
Potaotes, cooked, 4 oz.
Apples, cooking, 4 oz.
Beetroot, boiled or
pickled, 4 oz.
Gherkins, chopped, 1
tablespoon
Capers, chopped, 1
tablespoon

Chervil, chopped, ½
teaspoon
Salt and pepper, to taste
Oil, 1 tablespoon
Vinegar, 1 tablespoon
Oil, 1 tablespoon
Egg, hard-boiled, 1
Anchovy fillets, 3
Oysters, 6

Dice the beef, herring, potatoes, apples, and beetroot. Mix with gherkins, capers, and chervil, and moisten with oil and vinegar. Pile in a dish and garnish with hard-boiled eggs, anchovy fillets, and bearded oysters. This salad is often served with a stiffly-beaten sour cream colored with beet juice. *Serves 4.*

Pear and Chocolate Trifle

Sponge cakes, small, 6
Pear halves, canned, 6
Butter, 1 tablespoon
Cocoa, ¾ oz.
Flour, 1 oz.

Milk, 2 cups
Gelatin, unflavored, ¼ oz.
Water, 1 tablespoon
Sugar, to taste
Whipped cream, 1 cup

Place sponge cakes into individual dishes or arrange them neatly in a large glass dish. Place one drained pear half rounded side up on each cake. Melt the butter in a saucepan, add the cocoa, and stir it until it is well mixed in. Add the flour and mix well, then slowly mix in the milk. Soak the gelatin in the water and heat it to dissolve. Bring the milk and cocoa mixture to the boil, stirring continuously to keep it from becoming lumpy. Sweeten the mixture to taste. Add the dissolved gelatin and remove the mixture from the fire. Stand the saucepan in a bowl of cold water so that the mixture cools to a coating consistency. Pour the mixture over the pear halves to cover them, and allow it to run smoothly in the dish. Chill, and when cold decorate with whipped cream and angelica. *Serves 6.*

Apple Amber

Short crust pastry, 6 oz.	Brown sugar, 3 oz.
Apples, cooking, 1½ lbs.	Eggs, separated, 2
Water, 2 tablespoons	Sugar, superfine, 2-3 oz.
Rind of 1 lemon	Cherries, glacé, to decorate
Butter, 2 tablespoons	Angelica, to decorate

Lightly grease a 3-cup pie dish, and line it with the rolled pastry dough. Core the apples and peel and slice them. Put them in a saucepan and stew them with the water and the lemon rind. When they are soft, pass through a fine sieve. Return the apple pulp to the pan, and reheat slightly. Add the butter, brown sugar, and egg yolks to the apple. Put the mixture into the pie dish and bake gently in a moderate (350°F.) oven for about 30 minutes, until the apple is set. Stiffly whisk the egg whites and fold in the sugar. Pile this on top of the apple mixture, sprinkle lightly with sugar, and decorate with glacé cherries and angelica. Bake in a very cool (225°F.) oven until the meringue is done. Serve hot or cold. (Ground cinnamon and nutmeg added to the apples before mixing with the eggs is a pleasant way to vary the dish.) *Serves 4-6.*

Cheese Pudding

Eggs, 2	Salt and pepper, to taste
Cheese, grated, 4 oz.	Milk, 1 cup
Mustard, prepared, 1 teaspoon	Bread crumbs, 1 oz.

Beat the eggs slightly and add them to the cheese, mustard, salt, and pepper. Boil the milk and pour it over the eggs, then add the bread crumbs. Pour into a pie dish or soufflé dish and bake for 25-30 minutes in a fairly hot (400°F.) oven. Serve at once. *Serves 4.*

Apricot Bouchees

Puff pastry, 10 oz.	Whipped cream, 1 cup
Apricots, canned, medium sized	

Roll out the pastry to less than ½ inch in thickness; cut into 2½-inch rounds. Make an incision halfway through the rounds with a smaller round cutter, and bake them in a hot (425°F.) oven for about 12 minutes, until browned. When they cool, remove the tops and scoop out the insides. Drain the apricots, and place one half an apricot, rounded side down, in each case. Pipe a rosette of whipped cream into each apricot. *Makes about 12 bouchees.*

SCOTLAND AND INDIA

English cooking, like the English race, is a healthy sampling of several cultures. The good old-fashioned English cooking dates back to the middle ages. But another part of British cuisine was adopted along with colonial power. The Scots, whom the act of union made one with the English in Great Britain, contributed much to English eating. And when India joined the empire, the provincial tastes of English cooks took on a new and exotic flavor. Sharp, hot spices and tropical fruits joined time-tested staples to produce a blend that now remains a last testament to the empire on which the sun never set.

Mrs. Hudson, Sherlock Holmes, and Dr. Watson, often thought of as the epitome of the English, reflect the blend of cultures. Watson may have been a Scot, though the evidence is inconclusive. Holmes as much as says Mrs. Hudson is Scots, remarking that she has as good an idea of a breakfast as a Scotswoman.

Watson served in India and was wounded there during the fatal battle of Maiwand. Like many others of his generation, Watson sacrificed himself for the empire, and like all the others, he came back with an impression of faraway places that left a gap in his life—a gap filled on occasion by a curry that could refresh the memory of lithe young women and strange sights.

SCOTLAND

Scottish food is simple and straightforward, like the Scots. Unlike their reputation, it is not frugal but generous, rich, hearty, and well prepared, making use of the high quality of Scottish meat, Scottish grain, and Scottish fish. It is suited to the climate of Scotland, with its cold winters and none-too-hot summers, and is often descended from food prepared over peat fires glowing in the hearths of highland huts.

It reflects the Scottish love of tradition, as in haggis, the Scottish national dish. And so it reflects the Scottish love of home in foods meant to be enjoyed in the privacy of a Scottish home (for example, in scones and shortbread). It features recipes for the game plentiful in the highlands, and recipes of fishermen and sailors; and it features recipes derived from those thrifty Scottish housewives who found ways to make their meager budgets stretch.

It is a cuisine designed for hungry men, men tired from hard work or hard fighting or hard drinking, all Scottish qualities and all likely to produce a large appetite. It is also a cuisine for those who enjoy good food and aren't afraid of a dish that is simple and straightforward, a dish that satisfies hunger without apology for its simplicity.

The national dish of Scotland, the haggis, seems a little unappetizing to some. Yet, like Scotch whiskey, it is an acquired taste and many admire it.

Haggis

Sheep's stomach, 1	Suet, mutton, ½ lb.
Sheep's heart, 1	Oatmeal, pinhead, 1 lb.
Sheep's lights (lungs), 1	Onions, chopped, 3
Sheep's liver, 1	Salt and pepper, to taste

Wash the stomach bag in cold water until it is perfectly clean. Turn it inside out, scald it, then scrape it with a sharp knife. Steep the stomach in salt water until needed. Parboil the heart, lights (lungs), grinding the suet in also. Toast the oatmeal and mix with the meat, mixing in the chopped parboiled onions as well. Season to taste with salt and pepper. Add a little of the water the onions were cooked in, and put the mixture into the stomach, sewing it up tight. Make sure there is a room for the oatmeal to swell.

Prick the bag with a needle to prevent bursting. Put the haggis on an enamel plate in a large saucepan with enough water to cover it. Boil for 4-5 hours, making sure the haggis is covered with water at all times. Place on hot, flat dish, and cut strings. Serve with a spoon, and accompany it with Scotch whiskey and mashed potatoes. *Serves 4-6.*

Angus Potatoes

Potatoes, baking, 6	Butter, 4 tablespoons
Milk, ½ cup	Smoked haddock, diced, 2
Salt and pepper, to taste	cups

Cut a slice from the top of each potato and remove the insides. Add to the potatoes milk, salt, pepper, and butter to make potatoes to the consistency of mashed potatoes. Beat until light. Mix in the flaked fish. Refill the potatoes with the mixture, place a dab of butter on top of each, and sprinkle with pepper. Bake in a moderate (350°F.) oven until browned, then top with a pat of butter and serve.

Vinegar Curry

Drippings, 1 oz.
Meat, any kind, 1 lb.
Onions, large, peeled, 3
Coconut, dried, 3 teaspoons
Allspice, ½ teaspoon

Curry powder, 1 large
   teaspoon
Stock, 1 cup
Malt vinegar, 1 tablespoon
Wine vinegar, 1 tablespoon

Melt the fat slowly in a shallow saucepan. Cut the meat into small pieces and fry slowly until brown all over; then add all the ingredients in the order given, except the vinegars. Cover and simmer gently for 2 hours, stirring occasionally. Stir in the vinegars and cook for a minute or two longer. Pile in the center of a ring of boiled rice. Serve with chutney. *Makes 1½ cups.*

Brandon Bannocks

Oatmeal, 1 large cup
Baking soda, a dash

Drippings, 2 tablespoons
Water, tepid, to moisten

Place the oatmeal in a large bowl. Stir in soda, drippings, and enough water to make a dough. Strew the pastry board with oatmeal. Place the dough on the board. Sprinkle the dough with oatmeal. Spread out into a cake from about ¼-½ inch thick. Cut into quarters. Lift one quarter at a time and toast on a spatula over an open fire. Place in a toaster to finish toasting. *Serves 4.*

Cullen Skink

Finnan haddock, 1
Onion, chopped, 1
Milk, 2 cups

Mashed potatoes, ½-1 cup
Butter, 1 tablespoon
Salt and pepper, to taste

Skin the haddock and place it in a shallow saucepan. Add just enough water to cover it. Bring the water slowly to a boil and add the onion. When the haddock turns creamy, remove it from the pan and gently removed the flesh from the bones. Flake the fish. Add the bones to the water in the pan and gently simmer, covered, for 1 hour. Strain the stock and return it to the pan. Boil the stock, and in a separate pan, boil the milk. Add the stock to the milk; add the fish and simmer gently for about 5 minutes, then add enough mashed potatoes to make a creamy soup. Add butter, bit by bit, and salt and pepper to taste. If you like, stir in a couple of tablespoons of cream and a teaspoon of minced parsley. *Serves 2-3.*

Poloni

Steak, minced, ½ lb.	Ketchup, 1 teaspoon
Ham, lean, minced, ½ lb.	Egg, beaten, 1
Bread crumbs, stale, 1 cup	Salt and pepper, to taste

Mix all the ingredients together in the order listed. Pack into a straight-sided, well-greased jam jar. Steam for 2 hours, then cool slightly and carefully turn the mixture out of the jar. Brush with the melted glaze and let cool. *Makes about 3 cups.*

Glaze

Gelatin, unflavored, ¼ oz.	Salt and pepper, to taste
Water, hot, 1 cup	Ketchup, 1 tablespoon
Fat, melted, 1 teaspoon	

Dissolve gelatin in hot water. Add salt and pepper to taste, ketchup, and melted fat. Leave until almost cold before using. *Makes about 1 cup.*

Cabbie Claw

Haddock, medium-sized, 1	Horseradish, grated, 1
Salt	tablespoon
Water	Egg sauce, 1 cup
Parsley, 3 sprigs	Cayenne or paprika, for garnish

Clean, skin, and dry a fresh haddock. Leave the head on but remove the eyes. Rub inside and out with salt, and leave for 12 hours. Hang it up in the open air for at least 24 hours. Place in a saucepan of boiling water to cover. Add the parsley and horseradish. Simmer very gently until cooked. Remove the fish to a platter. Lift all the flesh from the bones, dividing it into small pieces. Arrange on a flat, hot dish. Cover with an egg sauce. Sprinkle lightly with cayenne pepper or paprika, and spoon mashed potatoes around the edge. *Serves 2.*

Egg Sauce

Milk, ½ cup

Stock, fish, ½ cup

Egg, beaten, 1

Salt and pepper, to taste

Mix all ingredients thoroughly and heat gently to a boil. Simmer until slightly thick and serve. Makes 1 cup.

Dundee Scotch Broth

Water, cold, 2 quarts

Mutton, neck, 1 lb.

Salt, 1 teaspoon

Pearl barley, 2 tablespoons

Carrots, sliced, 2

Leeks, chopped, 2

Onion, sliced, 1 medium

Cabbage, chopped, ½

Celery, chopped, 1 stalk

Peas, dried, soaked for 12 hours, 1 cup

Parsley, 1 sprig

Parsley, minced, 1 teaspoon

Pour water into a large saucepan. Prepare the meat and place in the saucepan. Bring very slowly to a boil and add salt. Skim thoroughly. Add barley and prepared vegetables. Bring slowly to the boil again. Simmer gently for about 2 hours, adding the parsley a scant 2 minutes before serving. *Makes about 7 cups.*

Garrion Barley Bannocks

Barley meal, 1 lb.

Flour, ¼ lb.

Salt, ½ teaspoon

Buttermilk, 2 cups

Baking soda, 2 teaspoons

Mix the barley meal with the flour and salt. Pour the buttermilk into a jug. Add the baking soda. As the mixture fizzes up, pour it into the meal and flour. Work into a soft dough, then dredge with flour and roll out to about ½-inch thickness. Cut into large rounds. Bake on a hot griddle, turning the scones when brown on one side. *Makes about 15 bannocks.*

Scotch Flippers

Flour, 1 oz.

Salt, to taste

Cayenne, to taste

Butter, 1½ teaspoon

Cheese, grated, 1 oz.

Egg yolk, ½

Lemon juice, a few drops

Savoury cream, 2 tablespoons

Sift the flour with the salt and cayenne pepper into a small mixing bowl. Rub the butter into the mixture well. Stir in the cheese, egg yolk, lemon juice, and cream. Roll the dough out into a round or oval. Prick well all over with a fork. Cut into small rounds or ovals. Bake on a well-greased baking sheet, set a little apart, in a moderately hot (375°F.) oven, for about 10 minutes, until pale gold. Cool. Serve as below:

Savoury Cream

Tomato, 1
Gelatin, ¼ oz.
Water, 1 cup
Shrimp, jellied, minced, 1
  tablespoon
Aspic jelly, liquified, 3 oz.
Mayonnaise, 1½ teaspoon

Salt and pepper, to taste
Lemon juice, a few drops
Red food coloring, 1-3
  drops
Cream, heavy, 3 oz.
Cayenne or paprika, for
  garnish

Peel a scalded tomato, then rub through a sieve. Heat slightly in a saucepan. Add gelatin and stir over hot water to dissolve. Place jellied shrimps in a bowl; strain in tomato pureé, then add aspic jelly. Add to that tablespoon mayonnaise, salt and pepper to taste, a squeeze of lemon juice, and a few drops of red food coloring. Half whip the cream and gradually stir in the shrimp mixture. Pour in a flat, wet dish about ¼-inch deep and leave until set. Cut into rounds or ovals to fit biscuits and with a spatula, place one round on top of each biscuit. Whip a little cream stiffly. Season to taste with salt and paprika, or with cayenne pepper, and add a little red food coloring. Pipe this mixture in rosettes onto each biscuit. *Makes 1-2 cups.*

Butterscotch Scones

Flour, 7 oz.
Cornstarch, 1 oz.
Salt, a pinch
Baking powder, 1 teaspoon
Butter, 2 tablespoons

Milk, to moisten
Butter, 3-4 tablespoons
Brown sugar, 2-3
  tablespoons

Sift the flour, cornstarch, salt, and baking powder into a mixing bowl. Rub the butter in thoroughly. Mix to an elastic dough with milk. Turn onto a floured board and knead lightly. Roll out into an oblong ¼-inch thick. Spread this with butter and sprinkle liberally with brown sugar. Roll up. Cut into slices and bake in a hot (400°F.) oven for 8-10 minutes. *Makes about 24 scones.*

INDIA

The English reign in India lasted until 1946, and in the century that preceded Indian independence, the cuisine of that strange and ancient land had a marked effect on British cooking. Exotic spices, tropical fruits, and strange, mellifluous names like Mulligatawny all reflect the eastern heritage of English cuisine.

But an Englishman's home-grown version of curry has as little relationship to the original, fiery Indian dish as "The Mazarin Stone" has to "Silver Blaze." Traveling over the thousands of miles between Bombay and London, the cooking of India suffered a sea change, a change that washed the spice and color from the food, leaving only the name and a vague, quiet similarity to the original.

There were, and still are, restaurants in London that cater to the British love for the exotic and to the former Indian soldiers' nostalgic taste for the past. Dr. Watson, who served in India, if only for a brief spell, must have had a few opportunities to eat in the Indian manner, if he didn't stick to the officer's club. Watson's unfortunate accident at the battle of Maiwand cut short his stay, but back in England, he must have enjoyed reminiscing over a Madras curry, or a real kedgeree.

Like Indian civilization itself, cookery in India is ancient and has been an art form for countless centuries. Food is an important aspect of the Hindu religion, and its preparation is regarded as an art form granted to man by the gods. Holy cookbooks provide prayers to be said before cooking, as well as recipes that are subtle and ingenious. Rice forms an important part of the cook's repertoire, but in India, it is the blend and not the main ingredient that matters. The use of spices are one of the Indian secrets. A land of spice, India's cuisine is noted for its subtle use of condiments.

Crisp Kedgeree (Bhoonee Khichree)

Butter, 4 tablespoons	Peppercorns, 2-4
Onion, sliced, 1-2	Cloves, 2
Rice, 1 cup	Bay leaf, 1
Lentils, 1 cup	Cinnamon, 1 stick
Ginger, fresh, a few slices	Salt, to taste

Melt the butter and fry the onion to a golden color. Remove the onion from the pan and put the rice and lentils into the butter. Cook them until all the butter has been absorbed. Add the ginger and other ingredients and cover with hot water. Cover the saucepan and simmer very slowly until the water has been completely absorbed. Stir occasionally with a wooden spoon and shake the pan so the kedgeree will not burn. Serve hot, with the fried onions strewn over the dish. *Serves 10-12.*

Sour Pork Curry (Soowar Ka Gosht Vindallo)

Pork, lean, cut into ¾-inch
    cubes, 2 lbs.
Vinegar, ½ cup
Onions, medium,
    chopped, 4
Garlic, minced, 1 teaspoon
Ginger, fresh, minced, 1
    tablespoon

Mustard seed, 1 tablespoon
Tumeric, 1 teaspoon
Cayenne, ½ teaspoon
Oil, ¼ cup
Bouillon, chicken, 1 cup
Potatoes, medium, peeled
    and sliced, 6

Marinate the pork in the vinegar, onion, garlic, and seasonings for 2 hours or more. Place in a stove-top casserole with oil and bouillon. Cook over medium heat for 20 minutes. Add potatoes and cook slowly, covered, for about 40 minutes, or until they are tender. Add more bouillon if necessary. *Serves 6.*

Chopped Meat with Peas (Keema Matar)

Lamb, ground, 1½ lbs.
Garlic, minced, 1
    tablespoon
Curry powder, 2
    tablespoons
Cinnamon stick, 1

Ginger, fresh, minced, 1
    teaspoon
Salt, 1 teaspoon
Peas, frozen, one 10-oz.
    package

Sauté the meat in a skillet, chopping and turning it to break it up. As soon as the pan becomes moist, add all the other ingredients except the peas. Stir and cook until the meat is done, keeping it crumbly. Add the peas and cook until just thawed and heated through. *Serves 4.*

Madras Curry

Onions, small, 2-3
Garlic, 2 cloves
Curry powder, 1 tablespoon

Salt, to taste
Stock, 2 cups
Mutton or veal, 1 lb.

Juice of ½ lemon

Slice the onions and fry with the garlic until browned. Add the curry powder and season with salt. Mix well, add the stock, and simmer for 20 minutes. Add the meat, cut into inch-long strips, and simmer for 1 hour, until the meat is quite tender. Add the juice of one-half lemon just before serving. *Serves 3.*

Channa Kari

Curry powder, 1 tablespoon
Garlic, minced, 1
 tablespoon
Green pepper, chopped, ½
 cup

Chick peas, canned, 3 lbs.
Salt, 1 teaspoon
Coriander or parsley, for
 garnish

Sauté curry powder, garlic, and green pepper in oil. Add chick peas and salt and heat through. Simmer for 5 minutes and serve sprinkled with coriander or parsley. *Serves 8.*

Potato Chakee

Mustard oil, ⅓ cup
Onions, ground, 4
 teaspoons
Chili peppers, ground, 1
 teaspoon

Tumeric, ½ teaspoon
Garlic, ground, ¼ teaspoon
Salt, 1½ teaspoon
Potatoes, 1 lb.
Water, hot, 1 cup

Brown all the condiments in the mustard oil, then add peeled and quartered potatoes. Stir the potatoes, mix thoroughly with the condiments, and cook for 10-15 minutes. Add the hot water and simmer until the potatoes are quite tender. *Serves 4.*

Kekda Bengali

Onions, medium,
 chopped, 2
Oil, 6 tablespoons
Ginger, fresh, minced, 1
 tablespoon
Yogurt, plain, 1 cup

Coriander, 1 teaspoon
Tumeric, 1 teaspoon
Cumin, 1 teaspoon
Chili pepper, green, hot,
 minced, 1 teaspoon
Crabmeat, 12 oz.

Salt, 1 teaspoon

Cook onions in oil until brown; add all other ingredients except the crabmeat, and simmer for 5 minutes. Add the crabmeat and simmer another 20 minutes, or until the meat is tender. *Serves 3.*

Sarson Bhara Kekda

Mustard seed, ground, 2
   tablespoons
Tumeric, 1 teaspoon
Water, to moisten
Oil, ¼ cup

Onion, large, chopped, 1
Shrimps, cleaned, 1½ lbs.
Chili pepper, green, hot,
   minced. 1 tablespoon
Salt, 1 teaspoon

Make a paste of the mustard seed and tumeric with a little water. Add all the other ingredients, cover and cook at a gentle simmer until the shrimps are fully pink, for 5-10 minutes. *Serves 4.*

The following recipes are English versions of Indian dishes and thus, are not quite as spicy as their original countrparts. However, they are tasty and surely Mr. Holmes had his share of the tempered British renditions, either as a breakfast meal, supper dish, or as part of a full-fledged luncheon or dinner.

Curried Eggs

Rice, cooked, 4 oz.
Eggs, hard-boiled, 4
Onion, chopped, 1 small
Butter, 1 tablespoon

Flour, 1 teaspoon
Curry powder, 1 teaspoon
Stock, ¾ cup
Lemon juice, to taste

Cook rice until tender and rinse with cold water. Shell eggs and cut into quarters. Fry the onion slightly in butter; sprinkle in flour and curry powder. Cook slowly for about 5-6 minutes. Add stock and lemon juice and simmer for 15 minutes. Put in eggs and heat thoroughly. Serve with rice as a border. *Makes 2 portions.*

Indian Style Buttered Eggs

Eggs, hard-boiled, 3
Curry powder, ½ teaspoon
Cayenne, a dash
Eggs, raw, 2

Salt and pepper, to taste
Bread crumbs, 2
   tablespoons

Cut the eggs into thick slices. Place in a well-buttered baking dish and sprinkle with curry powder and a few grains of cayenne pepper. Beat raw eggs slightly, season with salt and pepper, and pour over hard-boiled eggs. Sprinkle dried bread crumbs and butter on top; bake at 350°F. for 10 minutes. *Serves 2.*

Curried Cod

Cod, 2 lbs.
Butter, 2 tablespoons
Onion, sliced, 1 medium
Flour, 1 tablespoon

Curry powder, 1 teaspoon
Stock, white, 2 cups
Lemon juice, 1 tablespoon
Salt and pepper, to taste

Wash and dry the fish and cut into pieces about 1½ inches square. Melt the butter in a saucepan, fry the cod slightly, then take out and set it aside. Add the onion, flour, and curry powder to the butter and fry for about 15 minutes, stirring constantly to prevent the onion from becoming too brown. Pour in the stock and stir until the mixture boils, then simmer gently for 20 minutes. Strain the mixture and return to the saucepan. Add the lemon juice and season to taste, bring nearly to the boil, and add the fish. Lower the temperature and let simmer for about ½ hour, until the fish absorbs the flavor of the stock. Stir occasionally to prevent the fish from sticking to the bottom of the pan. Dish up and serve on boiled, drained rice. Serves 6.

Fancy Mulligatawny Soup

Chicken, cut up, 1
White stock, 7 cups
Onions, chopped, 2
Carrot, small, sliced, 1
Mushrooms, chopped, 1
   tablespoon

Celery, chopped, 1 stalk
Parsley, 2 sprigs
Salt, to taste
Butter, 1½ tablespoons
Flour, 1½ tablespoons
Curry powder, 1 teaspoon

Cream, ½ cup

Place 8-10 chicken pieces in a saucepan with stock, one chopped onion, carrot, mushroom, celery, parsley, and a little salt. Bring to a boil and carefully skim. Simmer gently for 1½-2 hours. Brown the other onion in a little butter; sprinkle with flour and curry powder. Gradually add a few spoons of the chicken broth and stir until smooth. Strain through a coarse seive, put back in saucepan, and stir in cream. To serve, put pieces of chicken, carefully skinned, in soup tureen. Strain the stock over chicken, and stir in the cream and curry mixture. Rice is generally served with this soup. *Serves 6-8.*

Lobster Curry

Butter, 2 tablespoons
Onion, coarsely chopped,
  1 large
Flour, 1 teaspoon
Curry powder, 1 teaspoon
Stock, fish, mixed with milk,
  1½ cups

Curry paste, 1 teaspoon
Coconut, grated, 1
  tablespoon
Apple, sliced 1 (or green
  gooseberries or rhubarb)
Salt, to taste
Lobster, boiled, 1

Lemon juice, to taste

Melt the butter in a saucepan, put in the onion, flour, and curry powder, and fry gently for about 10 minutes. Add the stock and milk, curry paste, coconut, apple, and salt, and stir the mixture until it boils. Cover and simmer gently for about 1 hour, occasionally stirring. Remove the flesh from the lobster and cut it into 1-inch square pieces. When the sauce is ready, pour it through a fine strainer, return it to the saucepan, season to taste and reheat. Just before the sauce boils, put in the lobster, cover and lower the temperature, almost simmering for 15-20 minutes, allowing the lobster to heat and soak up the flavors in the sauce. Add lemon juice and serve with boiled rice, chutney, coconut, chopped nuts, and chopped chives as garnishes. *Serves 2-3.*

Curried Rice

Variation #1

Rice, cooked, drained, 3
  cups
Curry powder, 1 teaspoon

Anchovy paste, 3 teaspoons
Egg yolks, beaten, 2
Cayenne, to taste

Mix together all ingredients and heat through well to cook the eggs. Serve very hot. *Serves 6.*

Variation #2

Rice, raw, 4 oz.
Onions, minced, 2
Butter, 1½ teaspoons

Curry powder, 1 teaspoon
Stock, 1½ cups
Salt and pepper, to taste

Brown rice and onions in butter; add curry powder, and cook for 4-5 minutes. Mix well together and then add boiling stock; season to taste and boil for

10 minutes. Cover and simmer gently for 40 minutes. Serve with tomatoes and crisply fried onions. *Serves 4.*

Curry of Prawns

Prawns, 24
Butter, 4½ teaspoons
Onion, small, sliced, 1
Curry powder, 1 teaspoon
Flour, 1 teaspoon
Stock, white, 1 cup

Apple, sour, coarsely
  chopped, 1
Coconut, grated, 1
  tablespoon
Salt and pepper, to taste
Lemon juice, 1 teaspoon

Shell the prawns and set them aside. Melt the butter in a saucepan and fry the onion without browning it. Add the curry powder and the flour, and fry slowly for at least 20 minutes. Add the stock, apple, coconut, and a little salt. Simmer gently for about ½ hour, then strain and return to the saucepan. Season to taste, add the lemon juice, put in the prawns, and when they are cooked, serve on boiled rice. *Serves 6.*

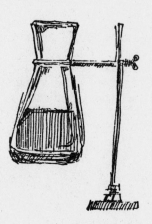

SHERLOCK HOLMES ON THE MOVE

Travel and good food were two of Sherlock Holmes' great pleasures. They were so closely associated with his life that he rarely thought to mention them. And Dr. Watson, world traveler before he met Holmes, found the pleasures of the grand tour and the table much to his liking. Both thought nothing of a half-day train trip through the English countryside. Travel to the continent, though more rigorous, was almost as much a matter of course.

Holmes travelled a good deal on business, as evidenced in his recorded cases, and more importantly in his unrecorded cases. In only two Canonical stories do Watson and Holmes leave England for foreign climes, and on both occasions they find Switzerland figuring large in their operations. In "The Final Problem," fleeing Professor Moriarty, they travel through France, Luxembourg, and Germany on their way to the fatal rendevous at the Reichenbach Falls. Searching for the disappeared Lady Frances Carfax, Switzerland, France, and Germany hear the tread of the detective and doctor. Except for Holmes' American experiences, which figure in his final victory over the German agent Von Bork, no other recorded case leads Holmes out of Great Britain.

But many of the tantalizing unrecorded cases mentioned by both Holmes and Watson take place outside the confines of the empire ruled by Queen Victoria. "The Affair of the Vatican Cameos" must have involved Holmes in travel to Italy, and his other undertakings for the Papacy may have involved further journeys south. Holmes' investigation of Cardinal Tosca's death involved travel to that unfortunate's see; though where the cardinal presided is as yet (to my knowledge) undetermined. An "Intricate Matter in Marseilles" may have helped earn Holmes his French reputation that eventually was represented in the Legion

D'Honneur he was awarded. Travel to Odessa, Warsaw, and one of the Scandinavian countries was also necessary to Holmes' investigations.

Watson confessed to knowledge of women on three continents. The Indian subcontinent and Europe make up two of the three, but the third remains a matter of speculation. Sir Arthur Conan Doyle, the doctor's literary agent, wrote a play, still extant in manuscript, based on the doctor's early life, placing him in California, but that must be regarded as only partially conclusive. It was never published, perhaps because it was not entirely factual. Some scholars have suggested Australia as the third continent and the place of Dr. Watson's birth, but again the evidence is scant. In any case, it is certain that travel was more a pleasure than a burden to Watson.

Holmes was bitten by the same urge as may of his contemporaries—the urge to explore. If his account of his three-year hiatus from practice after Moriarty's death is to be believed (and many eminent Sherlockians, including Edgar W. Smith, doubt it), Holmes spent much of his time traveling in the Mid East and Far East, distinguishing himself as the first white man to reach the Tibetan holy-of-holies, Lhassa, first "historically" visited by an expedition led by Colonel Francis Young-Husband in 1903. Holmes also traveled through Persia and visited Mecca (obviously in disguise). The detective claims to have met the Khalifa at Khartoum*, and told Watson he worked in Montpelier in the south of France doing chemical research.

Holmes spent at least two years in the United States and probably much more time since he is familiar both with American police officers and obscure criminal cases from the states. It is possible that his acquaintance with the American criminal scene was purely second hand, but it is hard to believe a man with Holmes' internationalist leanings and affection for Britain's former colonies could avoid the U.S. for an entire lifetime. New York and Chicago would have been on Holmes' itinerary in his disguise as the Irish incendiary Altamont. He may also have managed a journey farther west, perhaps to Salt Lake City, the place where his first "public" adventure began.

*Much controversy surrounds this point. When Holmes was away from London on his wanderjahre, the Khalifa Abdullah was residing not in Khartoum but in nearby Omdurman, since the historic city of Khartoum had been levelled shortly after it fell to the Mahdi's forces some years earlier. Obviously Holmes could not have visited Khartoum, the scholars say. Some even go so far as to postulate the fictitious nature of Holmes' whole trip on this evidence. Personally, I accept the Canonical account. Watson, an admirer of the late General Gordon, who died in the final defense of Khartoum, would have been well acquainted with the subject. Holmes would not have attempted to fool Watson with such a patent falsehood. Even if the city had been levelled, Khartoum continued to exist as a geographical location. To preserve his rather uncertain rule, the Khalifa might well have been willing to talk *to an English governmental official, but to admit such a person to his court might have weakened the Khalifa's power. A meeting, arranged in the ruins of Khartoum, would have been both secret and plausible, and when we remember Mycroft Holmes' position in the government, it becomes evident that his brother was serving the crown on this mission.*

The far-flung travels of Watson and Holmes were equalled by their far-flung experiences with international cuisine. A gourmet like Holmes or a man of the world like Watson would not hesitate to try local specialities, and with their varied opportunities, they must have eaten some of the best (and some of the worst) food the world then had to offer.

Imagine, if you will, Holmes and Watson strolling along the Via del Corso in Rome: two gentlemen definitely English and well-to-do, yet more than just tourists, sure of themselves, talking quietly of the ancient and new buildings of the peculiar and pitiful sights of this mother of all civilization and cradle of all that was uncivilized. Holmes probably spoke enough Italian to easily handle most situations, if he wasn't actually fluent. His mastery of Latin would have made the unavoidable pontifical paeans to humility and service easily decipherable, and Watson, fortified by perhaps two glasses of the pungent Italian liquer Grappa, would have been in the mood to marvel at his friends ability. Even in the Rome of the late nineteenth century, in the enlightened world of modern science and thought, the Pope still wielded silent authority, and Holmes' service to His Holiness opened the doors of the Italian nobility to him. Elegant dinner parties in his honor, and quiet lunches in a pine-scented garden antiqued by Roman weather and darkened by Roman soot must have delighted Watson, ever impressed by the upper strata of society. Holmes, I fear, must have been tolerant, but a little bored. His marked interest in the ancient must have been piqued by the decaying ruins of the Imperial City, and he begrudged the time spent dining, time that he might better have spent digging in the forum or in the stacks of the Vatican Library.

Holmes' investigations were not always criminal, or even literary, though, and he certainly spent some time sampling the excellent Roman cuisine, in cafes along the Tiber as well as in the dining rooms of elegant palaces. These investigations, featuring both wonderful food, wine, and beautiful women, were more to Watson's liking. A few glasses of sparkling Asti Spumante, and his war wound would start to pain him again, much to the concern of his beautiful companions. And if the story of the double-barreled tiger cub which Watson fired at a musket came up, the ladies probably attributed the confusion to their imperfect understanding of the English language, and not to the wine Watson had drunk or the comapny he was keeping.

Italian cooking is heavily influenced by regional tastes and regional products. Italy was not united as a single country until 1861, and even now it retains its provincial attitude. The cuisine varies greatly, as evident in the difference between sun-soaked Sicily and the alpine terrain of the Piedmont. The cooking methods differ also, right down to the basics of frying fats. Southern Italians use olive oil, but the northerners stick to butter, simply because the olive does not flourish in the north of Italy. The tomato and garlic, both thought of as absolutes of Italian cooking, often are not used at all in local cuisine, and even pasta, noodles, and spaghetti sometimes vanish in regional dishes.

While it would be hard to find a series of dishes that are "typically" Italian, because Holmes and Watson spent some of their time in and around Rome eating in local restaurants, we can get some idea of what they tasted by preparing a meal in the Roman manner.

Italian meals can be divided into three main portions, much like English and American meals. The antipasto, or hors d'ouevre course, generally comes before the main meal. Soup, pasta, or rice comes as the first part of the main meal, followed by entreés of fish and meat, with fresh and cooked vegetables. Finally a "dolci" or sweet is served for dessert, along with coffee and apertifs.

Spaghetti Carbonara

Pork sausage, Italian, ½ lb.
Prosciutto, thinly-sliced, ¼
  lb. (or cooked ham)
Butter, 4 tablespoons
Spaghetti, ½ lb.

Parsley, chopped, ½ cup
Eggs, beaten, 3
Cheese, Parmesan, grated,
  1 cup
Pepper, to taste

Remove the sausage meat from the skins and chop it or crumble it up. Add half the prosciutto (or cooked ham), well-chopped, to the sausage meat. Put the meat mixture into a frying pan with half the butter, and cook over a low flame until the sausage is lightly browned; add the rest of the chopped ham. Cook the spaghetti in boiling salted water without breaking it until it is al dente, that is, still slightly chewy. Remove from the water and drain thoroughly. Mix into the hot spaghetti the meat, butter, and chopped parsley. Add the eggs and mix well with the spaghetti, until the egg coats all of it. Add one-half of the cheese, season with pepper, and mix again. Serve hot with the rest of the cheese. *Serves 4.*

Easter Soup (Brodetto Pasquale)

Beef, lean, 1 lb.
Onion, large, stuck with
  cloves, 1
Carrots, 2
Celery, 1 stalk

Tomatoes, 2
Parsley, 2 sprigs
Water, cold, 12 cups
Lamb, shoulder or breast,
  1 lb.

Egg yolks, well-beaten, 6
Cheese, Parmesan, grated,
 ¾ cup

Marjoram, 1 sprig
Pepper, a pinch
Juice of 1 lemon

Put the beef and vegetables, with a little salt, into a large pot with the water. Bring the water to a boil and simmer for at least 1 hour. Add the lamb and continue cooking for another hour with the pot tightly covered. Remove the skum every so often after water boils. Take the meat out of the stock, strain, and return to the pot. Reheat the stock, but do not boil. Pour the egg yolks into a soup tureen, add the Parmesan cheese, marjoram, pepper, and the lemon juice and mix together well. Add the hot stock, which should not be boiling or the egg will curdle. Stir constantly while slowly pouring the stock into the bowl. Put a slice of well toasted bread into each soup bowl and add soup slowly. Serve with more grated Parmesan cheese. *Serves 10.*

Zucchine Ripiene

Zucchini, medium, 8
Ground beef, ½ lb.
Egg, 1
Cheese, Parmesan, grated,
 3 tablespoons
Roll, white part, soaked in
 milk and squeezed dry, ½

Garlic, minced, 1 clove
Nutmeg, a dash
Salt and pepper, to taste
Olive oil, 1 tablespoon
Onion, chopped, 1
Wine, white, dry, 2-3
 tablespoons

Tomato sauce, 2 cups

Wash the zucchini in cold water and remove the smaller end. Scoop out enough of the insides to leave room for stuffing, but not so much as to soften the outside. Mix the next 7 ingredients and fill zucchini. Put some oil and the onion into a casserole dish. Cook the onion over a low flame until it begins to brown. Add the wine, tomato sauce, and salt and pepper. Cook the sauce for a very few minutes, then add the zucchini, laying them side by side in the dish. Cook for about 20 minutes in a moderate (350°F.) oven, then turn them over and cook them until tender. Do not serve these hot; allow them to cool before serving, since the flavor is lost in the heat. If you like, serve as cold appetizers. *Serves 4-8.*

Saltimbocca

Veal steaks, about ½ inch
 thick

Proscuitto, thinly sliced, 24
 slices (about 6 oz.)

Cheese, Swiss, cut into 12   Basil, ¼ teaspoon
   sticks, ¼ lb.   Mustard, prepared, Dijon, ½
Butter, 4 tablespoons   teaspoon
Sage, ¼ teaspoon   Wine, white, dry, 3 oz.

Remove bone from meat, trim fat, and pound until quite thin; then divide into 12 pieces of approximately equal size. Top each piece of veal with several
slices of prosciutto and a piece of cheese. Roll meat to enclose filling completely,
and turn in the sides. Secure the sides with skewers. Melt the butter in a large frying pan, and blend in sage, basil, and mustard. Add the meat rolls and brown
quickly on all sides, turning them frequently. Remove the meat and add the wine
to the fat, scraping loose all brownings. Simmer. Pour the sauce over the veal and
serve with noodles on the side. *Serves 6.*

Zabaglione

Egg yolks, 8   Wine, sauterne, Marsala, or
Sugar, 3-4 tablespoons   Madiera, ½ cup

Beat the egg yolks, sugar, and wine together on top of a heated double
boiler. Beat thoroughly until the mixture is stiff enough to retain a peak. Serve in
stemmed glasses. Try this with a little of your favorite liqueur added to a dry white
wine.

SWITZERLAND

Sherlock Holmes chose Switzerland as the place for his final appointment
with Professor James Moriarty, and it was more than the practical advantages of
the Reichenbach Falls that attracted him. Holmes was familiar with Switzerland,
and both he and Watson were enjoying their walk through the countryside
before the Napoleon of crime brought things to a halt.

   Searching for the kidnapped Lady Frances Carfax, Watson visits Lausanne,
but leaves sooner than he might have wished, on the lady's "trail." Switzerland
thus became the only foreign country visited twice by Holmes or Watson in the
recorded cases.

   Surely the occasional vacations Holmes allowed himself must have included
a more leisurely and less sinister visit to the ancient cantons. A few weeks amidst
the alpine splendor of Meiringen, or enjoying the more civilized pleasures of
Zurich, and Holmes would be ready to return to London. Watson, of course,
could always find someone to take his practice.

   Physical conditioning is a sine qua non of the detective's profession, and
both men managed to remain in excellent shape despite the temptations London

had to offer. When Dr. Doyle introduced skiing to Switzerland, perhaps he invited Holmes and Watson along to try the novelty of rushing downhill at high speed. I rather doubt Watson really would enjoy the sport, but Holmes might well have taken a liking to its challenge. For Watson, if the ole wound was acting up from the cold, there were always pleasant hours to spend in the comfort of a hotel bar with a hot, strong drink and pleasant company.

Swiss cooking is a cosmopolitan combination of three cuisines, with a heavy mixture of local specialities. German, French, and Italian influences mix in the tiny country of high mountains and rich valleys. In the south, the Italian influence favors strong spices. French cooking is dominant in the north and west, while German tastes are reflected in the east. Add to these tendencies the fine cheese and beef of the Swiss, and the result is varied and imaginative.

Stufato

Salt, 1 teaspoon
Rosemary, crumbled, 1
    teaspoon
Wine, red, dry, 2 cups
Onion stuck with 2 cloves, 1
Celery, chopped, 1 stalk
Parsley, 1 sprig
Bay leaf, 1

Bottom round or chuck
    roast, rolled and tied,
    3-4 lbs.
Marrowbone, 1
Bacon, chopped, 2-3 strips
Onion, 1 small
Flour, ½ cup
Stock or wine, 2 cups

Mix together salt, rosemary, red wine, onion stuck with cloves, celery, parsley, and bay leaf. Marinate the meat and marrow bone overnight in this mixture, the longer the better. Fry the bacon until all the fat is melted, and remove and reserve the crisp bacon bits. Chop the small onion and brown in the bacon fat. Remove meat and bone from wine marinade and wipe them dry. Dust the meat heavily with flour and brown it in the onion-flavored bacon fat. Remove the meat when browned and pour off the fat. In a large baking pan, place the meat on a rack. Add the strained marinade, bacon bits, and enough stock to cover the meat. Simmer this in a slow (275°F.) oven for about 30 minutes per pound of meat. Turn the meat at least twice while cooking it, and when it is tender remove it from the broth. Take the marrow from the marrowbone, and when the remaining stock is reduce to about half, add the marrow, and thicken the sauce with a roux of flour and butter. Stir in the sour cream and heat. Serve the sauce separately, and garnish meat with sautéed mushrooms. Serve with boiled potatoes.

Fondue is the classic Swiss dish, made from the cheese for which Switzerland is so famous. Delicious and simple, it is perfect for intimate meals.

Fondue

Garlic, 1 clove
Wine, white, dry, 2 cups
Cheese, Swiss, finely
  chopped, 1 lb.

Cornstarch, 1 teaspoon
Kirschwasser or brandy or
  vodka, 3 tablespoons
French bread

Rub garlic around the inside of a casserole dish or fondue pot, enamel if possible. Pour the wine into dish, and heat until it just begins to form bubbles. Add the chopped cheese by handfuls, stirring constantly with a wooden spoon. Continue stirring until the cheese is melted. Dissolve the cornstarch in liquor and mix into the cheese mixture. Stir a few minutes more, then add nutmeg and stir a little longer. Place the pot over a hot plate or other warmer that keeps the cheese just bubbling. Serve with bite-sized chunks of French bread. *Enough for 4.*

Rehruecken

Butter, ⅓ cup
Bread crumbs, dry, fine, 2
  tablespoons
Eggs, separated, 5
Eggs, whole, 2
Sugar, ½ cup
Cinnamon, ½ teaspoon
Citron, finely chopped, 2½
  tablespoons
Almonds, blanched, grated,
  ¼ lb.

Chocolate, unsweetened,
  grated, ⅓ cup
Salt, ⅛ teaspoon
Butter, ¼ cup
Chocolate, unsweetened,
  4 oz.
Water, boiling, ¼ cup
Vanilla extract, ½ teaspoon
Sugar, confectioner's,
  sifted, 2 cups

Butter two 9-inch layer cake pans well and dust thoroughly with bread crumbs, shaking the excess crumbs off. Combine the egg yolks, whole eggs, and sugar and beat until light and lemon colored. Add to this mixture the cinnamon, citron, almonds, and chocolate and mix together well. Beat the egg whites until they are quite stiff but not dry. Fold the egg whites into the chocolate mixture until they are no longer visible. Pour this mixture into the two cake pans and bake in a preheated moderate (350°F.) oven for about 35 minutes, when cakes test done. Remove the pans and cool on a rack. Melt together butter and chocolate for the glaze. Beat in boiling water, salt, vanilla extract and confectioner's sugar. Frost cakes with this mixture, allow it to harden slightly, and stud with rows of slivered almonds. *Makes one 9-inch cake.*

Like many northern Europeans, Sherlock Holmes had a special fondness for the warm sun of the south of France. In "The Adventure of the Empty House," he tells Watson he spent some time in Montpelier doing research into coal tar derivatives. Whether that was merely a ruse to cover up some months of soaking up the sun, we shall never know. I suggested elsewhere that he may have been studying French cooking instead of coal tars, but that is of course mere speculation on my part.

I am sure whatever Holmes was doing in the south of France, at least some of his time was spent sampling French provincial cuisine in local inns and taverns and even at a few more exclusive places. In the several months he spent studying, Holmes must have had ample opportunity to become well acquainted with local delicacies.

French cooking is considered by many to be the apex of the chef's art. It is impossible to hope to convey even a part of that art here. Instead, I've chosen several typical dishes, which at least hint at the totality of French food.

Onion Soup

Broth, beef, clear, 8 cups	Butter, 4 tablespoons
Onions, large, red, 18	Salt and pepper, to taste
Bread, 6 slices	Sugar, at least 2
Cheese, Parmesan, grated	tablespoons
1½ cups	

Heat beef stock to nearly boiling. Thinly slice the onions without producing rings. In a large frying pan, put in enough good olive oil to fry the onions, and cook the slices until they are soft and begin to clear. Be sure they are not browned. Divide the broth evenly between 6 earthenware bowls. When the onions are done, add butter, salt, pepper, and sugar. Put an equal portion of onions into each bowl, and float a round of toasted bread on top. Cover each piece of toast with Parmesan cheese, and cover each dish, either with lids or inverted saucers. Bake the dishes in a 375° oven for 15 minutes, and serve sizzling hot. *Serves 6.*

Chicken Marengo

Olive oil, 3 tablespoons
Chicken, jointed, 1
Tomatoes, 3
Tomato pureé, 3
  tablespoons
Flour, 1 tablespoon

Onions, small, 12
Butter, 2 tablespoons
Wine, white, 6 tablespoons
Stock, veal, 6 tablespoons
Mushrooms, 12
Garlic, 1 clove

Salt and pepper, to taste

Heat the oil in a large saucepan, and when very hot, add the chicken pieces. Cook to a golden brown on all sides. Add the tomatoes and tomatoe pureé. Sprinkle a little flour onto the chicken, and cook, stirring, until the flour browns. Brown the onions in a little butter, and add them along with the wine, stock, mushrooms, and a clove of garlic. Season with pepper and salt and simmer for about 1½ hours. Put the pieces of chicken into a dish, garnish with the onions and mushrooms, and pour the sauce over them. Sprinkle with chopp d fresh parsley and serve. *Serves 4.*

GERMANY

Holmes and Watson passed through Germany on at least two occasions. From Luxembourg, the great detective and his companion passed through Germany on their way to Switzerland fleeing the Napoleon of crime. Watson visited Baden-Baden, the famour spa, on the trail of Lady Frances Carfax. On both occasions, Watson and Holmes certainly found time to sample the substantial Teutonic fare.

Whether it was beer and bratwürst or a delicate Rhine-Hesse or Mosel vintage and schnitzel, the English tastes of the duo must have been pleasantly sated by the abundance and nourishing qualities found at table in Germany. The Germans appreciate haute cuisine, of course, and did then; but the fare offered at German restaurants always tended toward the peasant's or farmer's tastes for a substantial and filling, rather than a fancy meal. Within that framework, the Germans have created a wide variety of foods for varying tastes, from the strong flavors of sauerbraten and sauerkraut to the delicate flavor of Mumich's favorite weiswürst. While Watson and Holmes may not have had time for leisurely samplings (on both occasions they were in a little haste), they did have time for a few not-too-hurried meals. Holmes, who liked his beer as much as his more expensive tastes, probably insisted on a mid-afternoon stop at an open air bierhall, and Watson, resisting the sumptuous temptations of some of the best European hotels in Baden-Baden, might have settled on a brace of würst and a liter of beer.

If time and train schedules permitted, an evening meal at a rather more expensive restaurant in Frankfurt (on the direct line from Luxembourg to Basel), might have been in order. The meals offered at Frankfurt's Hautbahnhof were probably not as authentic as those to be had elsewhere, and Holmes, as a chemist familiar with German, would have had no fear ordering in a local restaurant.

The recipes I've included here are typically German and together constitute a wholesome German meal, much like what Holmes and Watson might have tried.

Beer Soup with Milk (Bier Suppe mit Milch)

Beer, German, sweet, 1 quart	Egg yolks, 2
	Salt, to taste
Milk, hot, 2 cups	Sugar, to taste
	Croutons

Heat the beer in a saucepan, and when warmed, add the hot milk mixed with the egg yolks. Flavor with salt and sugar, and serve with croutons. *Makes 6 cups.*

Sauerbraten

Beef, lean, boneless, 4 lbs.	Wine vinegar, 1 pint
Water, boiling, 5 pints	Bay leaves, 2
	Peppercorns, 6

Wash the meat and place it in a large bowl. Cover with the other ingredients, and let marinate for at least 12 hours. Wash the meat just before roasting, and baste with butter and suet. Roast in a moderate (350°F) oven for about 15 minutes a pound. *Serves 4.*

Sauerkraut with Wine (Sauerkraut mit Wein)

Sauerkraut, 2½ lbs.	Water, 3-4 tablespoons
Butter, 6 tablespoons	Wine, white, ½ bottle

Put sauerkraut in an earthenware casserole, cover with butter and water, and cook for 30-40 minutes, until tender. Add the white wine and continue cooking until the liquid is reduced by half. *Serves 12.*

Apfelsinenbiscuittorte Ungefüllt

Eggs, separated, 3	Orange liqueur, 2
Sugar, 6 tablespoons	tablespoons
Egg, whole, 1	Flour, ¾ cup
Juice of 1 orange	Butter, creamed, 4
Sugar, 2 teaspoons	tablespoons
Rind of 1 orange	Punch frosting

Beat 3 egg yolks and the sugar together until very smooth. Add the whole egg, orange juice, and a little sugar rubbed with the orange peel. Mix in the orange liqueur and beat thoroughly again. Add the flour, butter, egg whites very stiffly beaten. Pour into a buttered cake pan and bake in a slow (300°F) oven for 30-40 minutes. Let cool and frost with a punch icing. *Serves 4-6.*

THE ADRIATIC

After his supposed death at the Reichenbach Falls, Sherlock Holmes found it healthier to leave Europe for a time, if we are to believe the account Dr. Watson gives of the affair. Holmes spent some three years traveling about the lesser known corners of the world, and doing research in France. If William S. Baring-gould's research is correct, Holmes began his hiatus in Montenegro with Irene Adler. From there, according to Holmes' account, he traveled through Persia, explored Tibet in the guise of the Norwegian explorer Sigerson, and visited the Khalifa at Khartoum in the Sedan before settling down to a more prosaic life in Montpelier.

Dining with The Women, Holmes probably ordered a goulash, which, though Hungarian in origin, had spread over the Balkans. Or he may have sampled the exotic Turkish-influenced dishes that had become native to Montenegro.

Segedínsky Guláš

Onion, medium, chopped, 1	Caraway seeds, ½ teaspoon
Shortening, 2 tablespoons	Water, 1 cup
Pork shoulder, cubed,	Sauerkraut, ½ lb.
1½ lbs.	Flour, 3 tablespoons
Paprika, ½ teaspoon	Lard, 2 tablespoons
Salt, to taste	Sour cream, 1 cup

Fry the onion in shortening. Add meat, paprika, salt, and caraway seeds. Brown well. Add ½ cup water, cover, and simmer for 45 minutes. Add ⅔ of the sauerkraut and simmer another 30 minutes. Brown the flour in lard, stirring well, and add to the meat with the rest of the water. Simmer for another 5 minutes. Add the sour cream and the rest of the sauerkraut. Bring to a boil and serve. *Serves 4.*

Taraba

Spinach leaves, 1 lb.

Mutton, ground, 1½ lbs.

Onion, chopped, 1

Shallots, chopped, 2

Salt, to taste

Cayenne, to taste

Butter, melted, 2
  tablespoons

Lemon juice, 2 teaspoons

Tomato sauce, 1 cup

Blanch the washed spinach leaves for 1 or 2 minutes. Mix together the mutton, onion, and shallots, to taste, and season the mixture with salt and cayenne. Make the meat mixture into little balls, and wrap each in 2 spinach leaves. Mix together melted butter, lemon juice, tomato sauce, and a little salt in a saucepan. Arrange the meat balls close together in the pan, and cover with a plate to keep in place. Simmer gently for 1½-2 hours before serving. *Serves 6.*

PERSIA

In Persia, and later in the Sudan, Holmes must have often traveled in disguise, and lived on the simple fare of the nomads he traveled with. On occasion, he may have supped elegantly in the tent of some sharif, if he dared venture telling true identity. It is pleasant to think that even in the hinterlands of Asia, the name of Sherlock Holmes might have been known.

Persian Shish Kebab

Lamb, trimmed, to cut in
  large cubes, 3 lbs.

Yogurt, 1 cup

Onion, medium, chopped
  fine, 1

Pepper, to taste

Salt, to taste

Sumac, powdered, to taste

Place the lamb in yogurt with onion and pepper to taste, and allow to marinate overnight. Thread the lamb onto skewers and cook over charcoal for 15 minutes, turning frequently. Season to taste with salt, and dust with powdered sumac. If you like, cook a separate skewer full of tomatoes to accompany the dish. *Serves 6.*

Bareh Pello

Lamb, diced or cut into
    small cubes, ½ lb.
Onions, chopped, 2
Butter, 2 tablespoons
Raisins, ¼ cup
Pine nuts, ¼ cup

Garlic, minced, 2 cloves
Tomatoes, peeled and
    chopped, 2
Cinnamon, 1 stick
Cloves, 6
Rice, uncooked, 1 cup

Bouillon, 3 cups

Sauté the meat and onions in butter for 5 minutes. Add all other ingredients except rice and bouillon, and sauté until well mixed. Add rice and bouillon and cook over high heat for 5 minutes after the mixture boils, then cook over a medium heat until the rice is done. *Serves 4.*

Stuffed Roast Chicken

Chicken, roasting, 3½-4 lbs.
Rice, cooked, 1 cup
Chicken liver, chopped, 1
Butter or oil, 2 tablespoons

Raisins, ¼ cup
Pine nuts, ½ cup
Salt and pepper, to taste
Lemons, large, 2

Stuff the chicken with mixture of all ingredients except the lemons. Rub the chicken with lemon juice and roast uncovered in a preheated slow (300°F) oven for 2 hours. Baste every ½ hour with pan juices and lemon juice. *Serves 3-4.*

Maamoul

Farina, cooked, 2½ cups
Butter, soft, ½ cup
Milk, 1 cup
Flour, ½-¾ cup
Almonds or pistachios,
    chopped, 2 cups

Sugar, 1 cup
Rose water, 2 tablespoons
Sugar, confectioner's, to
    decorate

Mix the farina with ¼ cup softened butter. Cover the mixture with milk and refrigerate overnight. Stir several times. When ready to bake, add remaining butter and enough flour to make the dough hold its shape. Mix the nuts, sugar, and rose water. Make small cones out of the dough, and fill with the nut mixture. Bake in a preheated moderate (350°F.) oven for about 15 minutes, until golden brown. Sprinkle with confectioner's sugar while hot. *Makes just over one dozen.*

TIBET

With his enterance into Lhassa, holy capitol of Tibet, Sherlock Holmes guaranteed himself a place in history. He was the first westerner to visit the city and explore the country, and according to his own report spent more than a little time there. There can be no question but that he experienced the local cuisine since no western-style food could possibly have been available.

Holmes must have become familiar, even fond of, the Tibetan version of tea, brewed strong, often for fifteen minutes or more, and mixed with butter and salt in a churn-like device. The Tibetans drink it almost continually, to ward off the cold of the Himalayan heights. Holmes, not innured since birth to the rigors of the high mountains, must have found the hot liquid an essential to survival.*

His arrival and departure must have been celebrated with the popular open-air Tibetan feasts, with meals that by tradition feature fifteen courses served at once, something like an Indonesian rice table. In the brightly colored tents, Holmes must have taken the traditional three cups of warm rice-wine, even if he managed only a sip from each of them.

Momos, the favorite food of Tibetans, much have figured in these feasts, as well in the day-to-day meals Holmes ate. Momos are much like the chinese meat dumplings. Served in several ways and in different sauces, they are quite ubiquitous.

Momos

Top sirloin, ground, 1 lb.	Soy sauce, 1 tablespoon
Scallions, chopped, 8	Ajinomoto, a dash
Fat or suet, cut up, 2	Red pepper, 1 teaspoon
tablespoons	Flour, 3 cups
Salt, ½ teaspoon	Water, 1 cup

Mix together the chopped meat, onions, fat, and spices, and make the mixture into a dough-like consistency. Put it aside to stand for at least 1 hour. Make a dough of the flour and water, but one that is not sticky. Roll out into a 1-inch thick layer, and cut 2½ inch in diameter rounds. Roll these into balls, and then flatten again, making a depression in the center of each. Put a tablespoon of the mixture onto each round, and fold the edges up over the top, sealing by pinching in three places. Put the balls into a cloth, and steam until done. These are served with a sauce of vinegar and soy sauce at the side, and can be made quite ornate by decoration.

I owe this information and the recipes to Ms. Kesang Dolma Ngo Khang, the beautiful Tibetan adopted daughter of Baker Street Irregular John Ball (The Oxford Flyer). Kesang gave me the benefit of her experience and several hours of her time in discussing Tibetan cuisine. I only regret there is not more room for consideration of this subject, which I find fascinating. Despite the efforts of Sherlock Holmes and Col. Young-Husbands, Tibet still remains a land of mystery.

Rhuchuazi

I include this dish not because it is unique, but because the Tibetan spelling took some 10 minutes to anglicize. Rhuchuazi is merely *Momos*, cooked in soup or broth for some 20 minutes. They may be served in the soup, or removed and fried in butter.

Tibetans generally finish their meals with more tea, eschewing sweets except for ceremonials. More rice or millet wine will generally be served after the meal. This wine, called Chang and tasting a little like a margarita, will sometimes be served all night long.

NORWAY

With Holmes' return from his three-year journey, his travels did not cease. Ignoring the thorny problems of dates in the Canon, Sherlock Holmes may have traveled on to Norway, perhaps twice. One of Watson's tantalizing references to unrecorded cases mentions a Scandanavian Royal House. And at the end of "The Adventure of Black Peter," Holmes tells Inspector Stanley Hopkins " . . . my address and that of Watson will be somewhere in Norway." If I choose to believe the royal household was that of Norway, it is merely the blood of my Norwegian great-grandfather influencing me.

Norway is a sea-faring nation, and fish is the prime food. Some Norwegians eat meat so rarely it is a special occasion. Norwegian food is rather plain, not unlike English cooking, with a marked trend toward smoked and salted fish and meats.

Sour Herring (Sur Sild)

Salt herrings, large, 3   Vinegar, 1½ cups
Onion, sliced, 1   Water, 6 oz.

Soak the salt herrings in cold water for at least 12 hours then remove from the water, dry, skin, and bone the fish. Cut the herrings into 1-inch strips, and arrange a layer of fish in a large flat dish. Cover with a layer of sliced onions, and alternate layers until all fish is used. Cover with vinegar and water mixed together, and leave in a cool place for another 12 hours. Remove from vinegar and serve with more sliced onion. *Serves 6.*

Beerbread (Ollebrod)

Beer, light, 1 bottle	Cream, 1 cup
Water, 1 cup	Egg yolks, 2
	Sugar, to taste

Mix the beer and other ingredients in a saucepan. Set on a low fire and whip well, removing the dish from the fire just as it boils. Serve with croutons. *Serves 6.*

Lamb Shanks with Sour Cream Sauce (Lammejjott I Sursaus)

Lamb shanks, 6	Bouillon, beef, ½ cup
Salt and pepper, to taste	Flour, 2 tablespoons
Butter, 3 tablespoons	Water, 3 tablespoons
Onion, chopped, 1 large	Dill, fresh, chopped, 3
Wine, white, dry, 1½ cups	tablespoons
	Sour cream, 1 cup

Trim excess fat from lamb shanks. Wash and pat dry. Rub meat with salt and pepper. Heat the butter in a frying pan and brown lamb shanks on all sides. Transfer shanks to a deep kettle and add wine and bouillon. Add onion to pan drippings and fry until tender. Pour onion and drippings over shanks. Simmer covered for about 1½ hours, or until tender. Remove shanks to a hot platter. Strain stock and return it to the kettle. Mix flour and water into a smooth paste and stir it into the stock. Cook until smooth and thickened, stirring constantly. Stir in dill and sour cream. Return lamb shanks to sauce and heat but do not boil. Serve with steamed potatoes sprinkled with chopped fresh dill. *Serves 6.*

RUSSIA

While he may not have been serving royalty, it is certain Holmes visited Imperial Russia at least twice on cases, once going to the capital of St. Petersburg, the other time solving the Trepoff murder case in Odessa.

Borsch

Beets, large, 5
Stock, beef, 5 cups
Salt and pepper, to taste

Sour cream, 3-4
tablespoons
Butter, 4 tablespoons

Wash and clean the beets and shred them finely. Melt the butter in a saucepan and when hot, add the beets and cook for about 20 minutes. Stir in a little stock, and when it is absorbed, stir in some more. Continue until the beets are tender. Pour the mixture into another saucepan full of stock, simmer for ½ hour, then strain and season. Stir in sour cream just before serving. *Serves 6-8.*

Gouriewskaia Kascha

Walnuts, 1 lb.
Butter almonds, 12
Milk, 6 cups
Semolina, 1 cup
Sugar, 1 cup

Pie crust, 4 oz.
Jam, apricot, ½ cup
Crystallized fruit, several
pieces
Bread crumbs, ¼ cup

Shell the nuts and blanch and skin the almonds. Pound both together. Put the milk in a flat dish and place in a moderate oven until a brown scum is formed. Skim this off carefully and set it aside. Repeat this operation until 5 or 6 skins have formed. Now, add the semolina to the milk and stir it until quite thick. Then add the nuts and the sugar. Make a rim of crust around a pie dish. Put a layer of the nut mixture into this crust, then a skin from the milk. A layer of jam and crystalized fruit is next, followed by a milk skin, until all the ingredients are used up. Make sure the top does not extend beyond the top of the pastry. Sprinkle with bread crumbs and brown the dish in a moderate (350°F.) oven. Remove from the oven when browned and allow the dish to cool thoroughly. When cool, sprinkle with confectioner's sugar, which can be browned with an iron held close to the surface. Let the dish cool slightly, and then refrigerate it until ready to use. Cob nuts may be substituted for the walnuts, and raspberry or any other tart jam, instead of apricot jam. Serve with strong tea. *Serves 6.*

THE NETHERLANDS

Another royal family, this time Holland's House of Orange, was served by Sherlock Holmes. While Holmes may have handled the case from London, it is a fair bet that he traveled to Den Haag to consult with his clients.

Blinde Vinken

Veal slices, round cut, 6
Veal, ground, ¼ lb.
Bread, white, soaked in
   milk, 1 slice
Egg, 1

Salt and pepper, to taste
Nutmeg, a dash
Butter, ¼ cup
Water, 1 tablespoon
Lemon, 2 slices

Pound veal slices until very thin. Combine ground veal, bread, egg, and spices. Cut this mixture into 6 pieces and place 1 piece on each of the 6 slices of veal. Roll up meat to enclose filling and tie with string. Melt butter and brown the meat in it. Add water and lemon slices. Cover and simmer until tender. Remove string and serve. The veal may be filled with fried chopped onions or with slices of hard-boiled eggs if you prefer. *Serves 6.*

Boterhamkoek

Flour, 1 lb.
Brown sugar, 7 tablespoons
Anise seeds, 2 teaspoons
Cinnamon, 1 teaspoon
Nutmeg, ½ teaspoon

Baking powder, 3
   teaspoons
Ginger, 1 teaspoon
Golden syrup (treacle), ½ lb.
Milk, 1 cup

Mix all the dry ingredients in a bowl. Mix the syrup and the milk and work into the dry ingredients gradually, producing a firm dough. Put the mixture into a well-greased sandwich-cake pan, and bake for 1-1½ hours in a moderate (350°F.) oven. Let stand until quite cool. *Serves 8.*

VIENNA

The final foreign recipes I've chosen to include may be arguable in a Sherlockian cookbook, but I can defend their inclusion, if not too strongly. In any case, as Viennese cooking is my favorite cuisine, I can hardly allow any doubt to interfere with my intentions.

Certainly nowhere in the Canon is it said that either Holmes or Watson visited Vienna or Austria (though Nicholas Meyer claims to have evidence of such a journey). But Holmes, after besting Von Bork, shows some acquaintance with the Imperial Tokay from Emperor Franz Josef's cellar, and it is likely he gained an acquaintance with the bouquet of this fine wine while serving the Austrian Emperor on some occasion or other.

Further, I find it hard to believe a music lover like Holmes could manage during his lifetime to avoid the city where much of what is great in music was premiered. Holmes, with his taste for the rather heavier tones of Germanic music, could hardly have avoided Mahler, who was during Holmes' later career conducting the Vienna Opera.

Vienna was, until after the turn of the century, as much a center of culture and art as any European capital. The cuisine of Vienna recalled anything to be found in Europe, and the combination of French techniques and the influences of the far-flung Austro-Hungarian Empire produced dishes which still bow to none in their artistry.

Esterhazy Rostbraten

Carrots, coarsely-chopped, 4

Onions, coarsely-chopped, 2

Parsnips, coarsely-chopped, 2

Celery, coarsely chopped, 2 stalks

Fat, 3-4 tablespoons

Flour, 1½ tablespoons

Sour cream, ¼ cup

Stock, beef, 1 cup

Brown sauce, thick, 2 tablespoons

Paprika, 1 teaspoon

Capers, 2 teaspoons

Steak, round, thickly cut, 3 lbs.

Salt and pepper, to taste

Maderia, ¼ cup

Prepare the sauce by frying the vegetables lightly in the fat. When soft, sprinkle with flour and blend in the sour cream, meat stock, brown sauce, paprika, and capers. Sear the meat quickly on both sides in hot fat. Season with salt and pepper. Place in a large casserole with a tight fitting cover and add the sauce. Cover and bake in a moderate (350°F.) oven for about 25 minutes. Add the madiera and bake another 5 minutes. Serve in the casserole. *Serves 4-6.*

Dobosch Torte

Cake

Eggs, medium, separated, 8

Sugar, ⅔ cup

Flour, cake, sifted 3 or 4 times, 1 cup

Salt, a pinch

Filling

Eggs, medium, 6   Chocolate, baking, 5 oz.
Sugar, 1 cup   Water, 4 tablespoons
                    Butter, 1 cup

Glaze

Sugar, 7 tablespoons   Brown sugar, ⅔ cup
Water, ½ cup   (or white sugar)

Cake: Beat egg yolks and sugar together until lemon colored and smooth. Add stiffly beaten egg white, and gradually and gently sift in flour, stirring carefully after each addition. Divide batter between eight 9-inch well-greased baking pans and bake at 350°F. for 10-15 minutes, or until the layers are a light brown. Let cool and spread with filling, reserving one for the top.

Filling: Beat eggs and sugar together. Place in the upper half of a double boiler and cook over hot water until mixture thickens, beating steadily. Remove from the heat and let the mixture cool. Melt the chocolate, stir in the water, and add to the egg mixture. Cream the butter and combine with the chocolate and egg mixture. Spread the mixture on each cake save one, piling the mixture high in the middle. Place each layer on top of the next, leaving the top layer without filling for the glaze.

Glaze: Caramelize the 7 tablespoons of sugar until it is light brown, then stir in the water and the rest of the sugar. Cook until the mixture begins to thicken. Spread the glaze over the top layer of the cake, and place that layer on top of the others. Mark the glaze in sections with a knife or the cake will be hard to cut.

Serve with espresso or strong coffee.

Spanische Windtorte

Egg whites, medium, 8   Vinegar, 1 teaspoon
Sugar, powdered, 1¾ cups   Cream, heavy, 1 pint
Vanilla extract, 1½   Sugar, ½ cup
    teaspoons   Vanilla extract, ½ teaspoon

Draw four 9-inch circles on a piece of waxed paper. Beat the egg whites with a wire whisk until foamy. Add the sugar, 2 tablespoons at a time, and keep beating. When the mixture begins to form peaks, add the vanilla, vinegar, and the rest of the sugar, if there is any left over. Put the mixture in a pastry bag. Pipe 2 complete circles of meringue on the first 2 circles, 1 for the top and 1 for the bottom of the cake. On the other 2 circles, pipe around the inside edges to form 2 circles about 1 inch deep.

Bake all 4 rings in a slow (300°F.) oven for about 1½ hours, until quite firm. Let cool overnight, and remove from the paper. Put the 2 rings, one on top of the other, on top of the bottom ring, and seal together with meringue mixture, adding another ring to the top for added depth, if necessary. Bake as before, and allow to dry overnight. Finally, pipe fancy design roses and borders on top and sides of cake, and bake again. Whip the cream with sugar and vanilla until stiff. Add fresh fruit if you like, and crumbled dried cookies, and even rum. Fill cake with cream, smooth the top, and cover with a meringue circle. Decorate top with marischino cherries. Chill before serving. *Serves 4-6.*

BAKER STREET MEALS AND MENUS

by
Sean M. Wright

PREFACE

Now that you've read the preceding section, I'm sure you feel well educated in the art of Victorian cookery. (Bully for you!) In today's world, however, you can't always cook in the Victorian manner, probably because there are so few coal stoves around these days.

Most, although not all, of the following recipes are written for informal occasions: lunches, breakfasts, picnics, etc., and there are even a few ideas for parties incorporated into the text.

For each of the sixty recorded cases of Sherlock Holmes, I have listed a few recipes and menu plans, a few of which you may recognize, and all of which are titled after characters and incidents found in their respective adventures. You will find out how to prepare such diversely satisfying dishes as *Cyril Pop-Overtons* (from "The Adventure of the Missing Three-Quarter") and *Mazarin Stones* (from "The Adventure of Mazarin Stone") or *Coronested Eggs* (from "The Adventure of the Beryl Coronet"). These are only a sampling among others whose names are just as badly punned. The auther has done this without apologies; he has taken a rather perverse glee in it, knowing that some ultraserious Sherlockian scholar is gnashing his teeth at this less-than-worshipful attitude. But the furrowed brow and frustrated frown are not to be fretted over, for this type of scholar is not the usual punning, carefree student of the Canon, but is just one of those unfortunates who cannot understand a bit of ribbing. No doubt some nasty notes are already taking shape in the minds of some of these people, but ultimately I shall read them without concern.

I *do* however, hope these meal plans are found somewhat clever and the food is found enjoyable by the greater part of my readers, who are in the end, the salt of the earth.

Sean M. Wright,
18 June 1975

THE ADVENTURE OF CHARLES AUGUSTUS MILVERTON
Thursday, 5 January-Saturday, 14 January
1899

"I can see that you have a strong natural turn for this sort of thing."
—Sherlock Holmes

This party is planned for an out-of-doors escapade, a concert under the stars, a ride through the country, anywhere in fact, it is possible to eat a light meal or snack without difficulty. Actually, this sort of outing may be more suited to a warm spring or a balmy summer evening than the mid-winter case to which I've ascribed it. I hope you won't feel like "the worst man in London" after its consumption.

Holmes and Watson were in a hurry to burgle Appledore Towers and pinch what they could of Milverton's incriminating documents and letters. As you also may be in a rush, this can be eaten hastily and if necessary, it can be taken with you.

Nickel-Plated Jenny Sandwich

Beef tongue, chopped,
1 cup
Cheese, American, grated,
1 cup (or 1 cup Old
English cheese melted

with 2 tablespoons pre-
pared horseradish
mustard)
Mayonnaise, ¼ cup
Bread, rye or sourdough

Combine the chopped beef tongue, the grated American cheese (or the Old English cheese mixture), and mayonnaise. Mix well and spread on rye or sourdough bread. Wrap the sandwiches in foil and place them in the pocket of your ulster, inverness, macfarland, pea-jacket, or greatcoat. *Makes 2 sandwiches.*

After returning from Appledore Towers (or perhaps from somewhere a little less picturesque), or if you've had a light supper, finish up the evening with the following.

Baked Appledore Towers

Apples, medium-sized,
peeled and cored
Raisins, enough to
fill apples

Brown sugar, to taste
Lemon juice
Butter

Peel the applies, cut the tops off, and remove the cores. Place the apple-cup in a shallow baking pan. Fill the cups with a mixture of raisins and brown sugar, sprinkle with lemon juice and dot with butter. Barely cover the pan bottom with boiling water. Bake in moderate oven (375°F.) 25-30 minutes, or until tender.

Serve the sandwiches with beer or ale, light wine, or champagne, in true Milvertonian oppulence. Should the surroundings preclude the use of alcoholic refreshment, tea or coffee, hot or iced, may (unfortunately) be substituted. Coffee or tea would seem to be indicated for use with the dessert.

THE VALLEY OF FEAR
Saturday, 7 January-Sunday, 8 January
1888

"There Watson! What do you think of pure reason and its fruits?"
—Sherlock Holmes

For the celebration of this case, my plan is a dish simple to prepare for those not too infrequent times when friends drop in unexpectedly and stay for dinner, or have been invited for a pot-luck dinner. To prevent the affair from becoming more than just lucky, try these dishes!

Birlstone Beans and Bacon

Kidney beans, two 1-lb. cans   Onions, raw, sliced, 2
Beefsteak tomatoes,   Bacon, ½ lb. (the leaner the
  sliced, 3   better)

In a casserole dish, alternate layers of beans, tomatoes, and onions until you run out. Bake in a slow oven (300°F.) for 2 hours, uncovered. Now cut bacon in half, and lay the strips on top. Place the casserole back in the oven, uncovered, for another 2 hours, by which time the bacon should be browned. Push the bacon into the beans, topping the dish with the rest of the bacon. Bake it uncovered for (you guessed it) another 2 hours. *Serves 5-6.*

With the beans and bacon, serve:

The Scowrer Sandwich

Bread, slices
Butter, enough to spread on
  bread
Eggs, well beaten, 2
Milk, 1½ cups
Salt, ¼ teaspoon

Bacon drippings, 1-2
  tablespoons
Onion, a few slices
Bacon, 3-4 rashers (strips)
  per sandwich, cut in half
  or diced

Spread the bread with softened butter and set aside. Sauté the sliced onions in the bacon fat in the pan until lightly browned. Cook the bacon strips (or dice it) in a heavy skillet until crisp and brown. Remove from pan and pat dry. Spread half the slices of bread with the fried onion. Lay the bacon strips or the dices on the onions and top with remaining slices of bread. Combine the eggs, milk, and salt, mixing slightly. Dip the sandwich in the egg mixture, carefully placing it back in the heated skillet. Add more bacon drippings if necessary and fry quickly on each side.

These sandwiches may also be prepared in a waffle iron, using a richer egg mixture (3 well-beaten eggs, ¼ cup milk, ½ teaspoon salt, and 1 tablespoon melted butter). There are many variations of this sandwich, the fillings including crabmeat, cheese, ham, liver, chicken, fish, and so on. Serve with any tossed salad. For dessert, or perhaps as a salad, serve the following.

The Bodymaster's Brandied Apricots

Apricot halves, 3 or 4
Apricot juice, 1 tablespoon

Apricot brandy, 1
  tablespoon
Grenadine syrup, optional

Place apricot halves in a sherbet glass. Pour over apricot juice and apricot brandy and chill thoroughly. Add a little grenadine syrup if desired to give a rosy color. *Serves 1.*

Just between us, I'm rather sure that Bodymaster McGinty was not the kind of person who nibbled on brandied apricots. But I'm also rather sure that you're not the kind of person he was.

Should the Scowrer Sandwich not appeal to you, here's an alternate.

Birdy Edwards' Re-Veal Surprise

Veal cutlet, ½-1 inch thick,   Salt, ½ teaspoon
  1½-2 lbs.   Pepper, ½ teaspoon
Bread crumbs, 1 cup   Flour, ¼ cup
Parsley, chopped, ¾ cup   Salad oil, 3 tablespoons
Butter, melted, 2   Water, 1 cup
  tablespoons

Cut veal into 6 squares, and pound it very thin with a meat hammer. Combine bread crumbs, parsley, butter, salt, and pepper. Place a spoonful of this mixture in the center of each cutlet square. Roll up meat and fasten each roll with a toothpick or boiled string. Roll each veal square in flour; heat oil and brown on all sides. Add water; cover tightly and simmer slowly 40-50 minutes, or until tender. Remove to hot platter and make gravy, if desired. *Serves one or two depending on their appetite.*

THE ADVENTURE OF THE BLANCHED SOLDIER
Wednesday, 7 January-Monday, 12 January
1903

> *"It is my business to know things. That is my trade."*
> —Sherlock Holmes

This story marked the first time Sherlock Holmes wrote one of his cases in place of Watson. Should this be the first time you've tried the dish described below, I hope you experience it without the difficulties that Holmes encountered, trying to write his adventure in the dry style of a textbook exercise. He decided not to attempt altering its form with a hint of romance, realizing that the reader's attention must be held by the narrative. I hope that your guests find your dinner enough to hold *their* attention!

Ghostly Face Cheese Soufflé (to glimmer on your table)

This recipe is in two parts; prepare the thick white sauce first.

Thick White Sauce

Butter, 3 tablespoons   Salt, ½ teaspoon
Flour, 4 tablespoons   Pepper, ⅛ teaspoon
    Milk, 1 cup

Melt butter over low heat; add flour, salt, and pepper. Stir until well blended and remove from heat. Stir in milk constantly until smooth; return to heat. (To shorten cooking time, heat milk separately.) *Makes 2 cups.* Only half this recipe is needed for the soufflé.

Soufflé

Thick white sauce, 1 cup

Cheese, grated, ¼ lb. (about 1½ cups)

Cayenne, a dash

Eggs, separated, 4

To the hot white sauce, add the cheese and cayenne. Stir over very low flame until cheese is melted and remove from heat. Stir a little of the sauce into slightly beaten egg yolks; combine with rest of sauce. Beat the egg whites until stiff but not dry. Fold into cheese mixture. Pour into greased casserole, about 1½ quart capacity. Bake in slow oven (300°F.) about 1¼ hours. Serve immediately. *Serves 4-6.*

If more people are expected, make a second souffle, and if cooking both together, allow an extra 5-10 minutes cooking time. Serve with a white wine of your choice, and a salad of your own devising.

For dessert try this:

Mr. Kent's Caramel Custard

Caramelized sugar, 3 tablespoons

Milk, 1 quart (4 cups)

Eggs, slightly beaten, 6

Salt, ¼ teaspoon

Sugar, ½ cup

Vanilla, 1 teaspoon

Nutmeg, a dash

Berries or fruit, for garnish

To caramelize the sugar, heat it in a heavy skillet stirring constantly until melted. When it becomes syrupy, add it to the milk. Then combine the eggs, salt, and ½ cup sugar. Add the milk and sugar mixture slowly, stirring constantly; add vanilla. Pour into a large casserole or mold. Sprinkle with nutmeg. Place the casserole in a pan of hot water, 1-2 inches deep and bake in moderate oven (350°F.) for 45-50 minutes, or until a knife inserted in the center of the custard comes out clean. After, and only after, chilling thoroughly, run a knife along the edges and turn the mold onto a serving plate or platter. Garnish with berries, sliced peaches, or other fruit. *Serves 4-6.*

THE ADVENTURE OF THE ABBEY GRANGE
Saturday, 23 January
1897

" . . . I must admit, Watson, that you have some power of selection. . . . "
—Sherlock Holmes

This case, with Holmes waking up the good doctor with, "Come Watson, come! The game is afoot!" seemed right for a good, rollicking breakfast. This breakfast meal, far and above my favorite, consists of pancakes and sausages. My mother has the same ideas as Mrs. Hudson's Scotch notions concerning a filling breakfast. She always reserved this for Sunday mornings, and it was looked forward to ardently by the whole family. It's the perfect meal also for a crowd that might drop in to see you on an early weekend morn.

Hopkins' Inspector-Wrap or
Scotland Yard Pigs-in-Blankets ā la Valentina

Eggs, slightly beaten, 2
Buttermilk, 1 quart (4 cups)
Flour, 2 cups
Salt, 1 teaspoon
Baking powder, 2
    teaspoons
Baking soda, ¾-1 level
    teaspoon
Water ¼-⅓ cup
Sausages, link, enough to
    provide
Sausage drippings, ⅓ cup

Cook the sausages on a hot griddle, reserving ⅓ cup of drippings. Keep the sausages warm. Combine eggs and 2 cups of the buttermilk into a large mixing bowl. Sift the dry ingredients into the milk and eggs. Beat with a wire whisk or egg-beater until smooth. Add the remaining 2 cups milk and stir. Rinse out the empty milk carton with water (a miserly move, but an important one—the water gives a nice crispness to the cakes). Add ¼ to ⅓ cup of the water to the batter and beat until thin. Add another 2-3 tablespoons of this water if necessary to thin out the batter. Blend drippings with the batter and mix well. Drop batter by the spoonful on a heavy griddle, turning once. *Makes 50-60 silver-dollar or 35-40 standard-sized cakes.* Roll the link sausage into the cakes. Spread with melted butter and serve immediately. Use syrup only if you must. A fruit juice or coffee or tea are the recommended beverages.

A STUDY IN SCARLET
Friday, 4 March-Monday, 7 March
1881

"They would be likely to agree on some meeting place beforehand."
—Sherlock Holmes

If yours is to be the meeting place agreed upon beforehand, celebrate the first adventure in the Holmes-Watson partnership with this typically heavy English dinner. Take care not to nibble in the afternoon; you might want to start this meal at tea time (4 o'clock) so to be able to linger over the dishes late into the evening. As Holmes referred to Lestrade and Gregson as "the pick of a bad lot," so too is this meal.

"Rache" Fruit Cup

Grapes, small, seedless, 1 bunch

Sherry, 1 oz. per serving (other wine may be substituted)

Wash small seedless grapes, remove stems, and cut in half. Place crushed ice in bottom of each sherbert glass or stemmed goblet. Fill the glass with grapes. Pour about 1 hearty jigger of sherry (or another white wine of your choosing) into each portion; serve immediately.

Note: Melon balls may be substituted for grapes, or many varieties may be combined for a colorful display.

Follow this with:

Lestrade and Gregson Kidney Pie

One beef kidney
Water boiling, 6 cups
Flour, ¼ cup
Water, cold, ⅓ cup
Salt, 1½ teaspoons

Pepper, ⅛ teaspoon
Butter, 3 tablespoons
Egg, hard-boiled, chopped, 1

Remove membrane from kidney, split in half, lengthwise; remove fat and white veins. Slice crosswise, ¼-inch thick; cut slices in pieces and cover with cold water. Let stand for 1 hour; drain. Repeat this process once more to be sure you've removed all impurities. Place kidney pieces in 2-quart saucepan. Add boiling water and simmer 1 hour. Cover and simmer ½ hour longer, or until liquid is reduced by half. Mix flour and water to a smooth paste. Add to stew slowly, stirring constantly; simmer until thickened. Add remaining ingredients and simmer for a few minutes. Serve on toast, or pour into a 1-quart casserole and top with pastry; bake in hot oven (425°F) for 15 minutes, or until pastry is golden brown. *Serves 4.*

There are a great many pastries knocking about and if you are familiar with one, by all means use it. Or you might want to use the rich biscuit topping found in "The Adventure of Shoscombe Old Place."

Should you be in need of a dessert, try this:

Holy Four Chocolate Chiffon Pie

Gelatin, unflavored, 1 tablespoon	Eggs, separated, 4
Water, cold, ¼ cup	Sugar, 1 cup
Water, boiling, ½ cup	Salt, a pinch
Chocolate, 2 squares (2 oz.)	Vanilla, 1 teaspoon
	Vanilla wafer pie shell, 1
Whipped cream, for topping	

Soften gelatin in cold water 5 minutes. Mix boiling water and chocolate until smooth. Add gelatin to chocolate mixture and stir until dissolved. Add slightly beaten egg yolks, ½ cup sugar, salt, and vanilla. Beat thoroughly. Cool until mixture begins to thicken. Beat egg whites until foamy, beat in remaining sugar gradually, then fold into gelatin mixture. Pour into pie shell and chill until firm. Spread with whipped cream just before serving. *Makes one 9-inch pie.*

THE REIGATE SQUIRES
Thursday, 14 March-Tuesday, 26 March
1887

"Ah, you must give us a little time."
—Sherlock Holmes

Holmes has gone to Reigate, near Surrey, to rest after having outmaneuvered the colossal schemes of Baron Maupertuis, and succeeded where the police of three nations had failed. Europe was ringing with his name, but the exertions were too much for him. Watson prescribed a vacation with his old friend Colonel Hayter, whom he had known in Afghanistan. While there, a puzzling series of burglaries and a murder rouse Holmes from his rest. He finds the solution of the case, although the Cunninghams, father and son, try to murder him by bodily assault. Holmes being unable to fend for himself in his weakened condition needed Watson, Inspector Forester, and Colonel Hayter to drag the two men from their attack.

For a tea, use the following:

Reigate Rolled Sandwiches

Variation #1

Bread, 8 slices

Chili sauce, 2½ tablespoons

Onion, medium, minced, 1

Olives, ripe, diced, 2-3

Cheese spread, sharp, ¼
  cup

Bacon, crumbled, 3-4 slices

Cut crusts from bread slices, spread with chili sauce, onion, olives, and a sharp and snappy cheese spread. Top with crumbled, crisp bacon. Roll the bread, fasten with toothpicks, and cut in half; then place rolls under broiler and lightly toast on all sides. Serve with a heated bean-dip. *Makes 16 small sandwiches.*

Variation #2

Bread, unsliced, 1 loaf

Pimiento cheese spread, 1
  cup

Olives, chopped, 9

Salami or pepperoni, diced,
  ¼ lb.

Bacon, 9 slices

Remove crust from standard-size loaf of unsliced bread. Sice lengthwise into long ⅓-inch thick pieces. Spread each slice generously with pimiento cheese spread, chopped olives, salami or pepperoni slices. Roll each slice gently from the short end; wrap each roll with a partially-cooked slice of bacon and fasten with toothpick. Toast under broiler, turning frequently; serve not. See other adventures with tea recipes for other ideas.

THE ADVENTURE OF THE DEVIL'S FOOT
Tuesday, 16 March-Saturday, 20 March
1897

"We are devil-ridden, Mr. Holmes!"
—The Reverend Mr. Roundhay, Vicar of Tredannick Wollas

The following recipes might be used for Halloween, the birthday of that foul and dread Napleon of Crime, ex-Professor Moriarty—the devil. They are ideal for a picnic lunch also, and, if the weather permits, you should take a romp in the country and recall that this case occurred while Holmes and Watson were vacationing in Cornwall and mucking about the countryside there. Cornish game hen and Cornish pasty recipes were considered, but I found them too tedious for a quick getaway. The following dishes are easy and simple. Pack them up and have fun.

Note: On principle, I am not including a Devil's Foot Root Cake or Devil's Foot Root Ham. I'm sure that I've included enough devil's foot root recipes of other types for the edification of my readers.

Crab Stearndale, à la Devil's Foot

Butter, 3 tablespoons	Pepper, a dash
Onion, finely chopped, 2 tablespoons	Milk, 1 cup
	Cream, ½ cup
Flour, 3 tablespoons	Crabmeat, fresh-cooked or
Mustard, dry, 1 teaspoon	canned, 3 cups
Paprika, ½ teaspoon	Bread crumbs, buttered, ½
Salt, ¾ teaspoon	cup

Cheese, grated, ½ cup

Heat butter and add onion; cook over low heat until soft but not browned. Blend in flour and seasonings. Slowly add milk and cook, stirring constantly over low flame until thickened. Add cream. Pick over crabmeat to remove any cartilege; add to heated sauce. Fill crab shell, scallop shell or ramekin with the mixture. Sprinkle with buttered crumbs and grated cheese. Bake in a moderate oven (375°F.) 20-25 minutes or until browned. *Makes about 6 servings.*

Note: *If, after you throw the completed mixture onto a roaring fire or place some on the smoke-guard (or talc-shield) of a kerosene lamp, thick, black clouds of smoke result, get out of the room immediately!*

Radish Pedis Diaboli Salad

Any tossed, green salad with a plenitude of radishes, hence its name.

Note: The author could not resist the temptation—oops, there's another one. In the future I will *try* not to be guilty of too much leg pulling. But just for the hell of it, see the next recipe:

Crazy Brothers' Devil's Root Foot Sauce

This is a general recipe for use on any deviled food:

Durham mustard, 1 heaping tablespoon

Chili vinegar, ¼ cup

Horseradish, grated, 1 tablespoon

Shallots, bruised, 2

Salt, 1 teaspoon

Cayenne, as much as you dare, a dash for the sane

Black pepper, ½ teaspoon

Sugar, 1 teaspoon

Chilies, chopped, 2 (optional)

Egg yolks, raw, 2 (optional)

Combine all ingredients and rub on any deviled meat. Broil slowly as near as possible to the flame.

Radix Pedis Diaboli Eggs*

Eggs, hard-boiled, 8

Vinegar or pickle juice, 1 teaspoon

Mustard, dry, ¼ teaspoon

Salt, ½ teaspoon

Pepper, ⅛ teaspoon

Cayenne, a dash

Onion, grated, 1 tablespoon

Bacon, crisply-cooked, diced, 5 strips

Mayonnaise, 5 tablespoons

Worcesstershire sauce, ½ teaspoon

Radishes, enough for garnishing

Carefully cut eggs in half lengthwise; remove the yolks. Mash the yolks, add vinegar, seasonings, and enough of the mayonnaise to moisten to a firm, creamy consistency. Pile yolk mixture into the sliced egg whites; sprinkle with paprika, garnish with radishes. For a sandwich mixture, mash whites along with yolks and increase mustard to ½ teaspoon. *Makes 4 sandwiches.*

If you need a translation of the title, turn in your deerstalker!

Deviled Mortimer's Foot Root Sandwich

Meat, ground, cooked, 1 cup

Ketchup or chili sauce, 2 tablespoons

Cayenne, a dash

Pepper, a dash

Worcestershire sauce, ½ teaspoon

Paprika, ¼ teaspoon

Onion juice, ½ teaspoon

Salt, ½ teaspoon

Mayonnaise, 2-3 tablespoons

Combine all ingredients and mix well. Serve on any type of bread; corn rye would be the best choice under the circumstances. *Makes 4 sandwiches.*

Serve this sandwich with any good beer or ale. Lemonade or soft drinks for the youngsters, iced tea for the nonalcoholic.

THE ADVENTURE OF WISTERIA LODGE
Monday, 24 March-Saturday, 29 March
1890

"My first idea was that I had been the victim of some absurd practical joke."   —John Scott Eccles

This quote sounds as though Mr. Eccles read the recipies for the preceding case. Actually, he was referring to the unique disappearance of the foreign gentlemen who had stayed at Wisteria Lodge. Should you have friends who appear as suddenly as the Tiger of San Pedro and his servants disappear, try:

Tiger of San Pedro Chili à la William Terence

Beef, chopped, 1 lb.

Onion, chopped, 1

Chili, kidney, or pinto beans, 2 no. 2 cans.

Tomato soup, condensed, 1 can

Salt, 1 teaspoon

Chili powder, 1 tablespoon (or more, to taste)

Ripe olives, 1 can

Drain the beans before adding other ingredients. Brown the meat and the onion in a little butter or oil and cook until the meat is browned (about 10 minutes). Add the liquid reserved from the beans to the meat and simmer. Add everything else, then let it simmer covered for a half hour. *Serves 6-8.*

Oxshott Mystery Garlic Toast

Bread, French or Italian, 1
  loaf
Butter, ½ cup

Garlic, 1 clove
Cheese, Cheddar or Swiss,
  grated, ¼ cup

Cut a long loaf of French or Italian bread into slices about 1½-inches thick. Melt the butter; add the garlic, cut in several pieces; let the garlic stand in the butter in a warm place for about 15 minutes. (You may also use 1½ teaspoons of garlic powder or 1 teaspoon of garlic oil in the same amount of butter.) Spread the butter lightly over the cut surfaces of the bread. Sprinkle the grated cheese over the surface of the bread. Place in a hot oven (400°F) for about 10 minutes, or until well heated throughout. If cooking under a broiler, place bread 3-4 inches below the flame, until golden brown. It would do well to remember that broiler heat varies from stove to stove; therefore, don't take your eye off the bread for very long, or your toast will take on absolutely too dark a hue!

For a larger group, you might want to try:

Don Murillo's Tostada Trifle ã la Helen Lee

Beef, ground, 2 lbs.
Onions, large, chopped, 2
Garlic, chopped, 2 cloves
Chili beans, 2 no. 4 cans
Tortillas, 1 dozen
Lettuce, ½ head
Tomatoes, stewed, 1 no. 2
  can

Green chili salsa, 1 can
Onion, small, 1
The condiments: Cheese,
  grated, Olives, sliced,
  Sour cream

Sauté the onions and garlic in a small skillet and brown over low heat. Drain the juice from the beans and save it; mash the beans with a potato masher. Place mashed beans in heavy skillet and heat over moderate heat for about 20 minutes. In another skillet, crumble the meat and brown for about 20 minutes, stirring occasionally. Combine about one-half of the onion and garlic mixture into the beans and the other half into the meat, after draining the grease. Pour the bean juice into the meat and let simmer over a low heat for about 10 minutes. Place beans and meat into two separate bowls for serving. In a clean skillet, pour enough oil to cover the bottom about ½-1 inch and heat. Fry the tortillas about ½-1 minute on each side. Be sure that the oil is very hot. Chop the lettuce coarsely, and leave on a serving plate to be added to taste. Do the same with grated cheese, olives, and sour cream. Mix the stewed tomatoes and salsa, also to be served separately and added to taste. Serve all ingredients separately and allow your guests to serve themselves. This meal is excellent when served with beer or ale (or iced tea for those people who are on the wagon). *Serves 12.*

THE ADVENTURE OF THE EMPTY HOUSE
Thursday, 5 April
1894

"Sit down, and tell me how you came alive out of that dreadful chasm."
—Dr. Watson

Sherlock Holmes returned from the fearsome abyss at Reichenbach and the world was overjoyed. This is such a momentous anniversary that I shall give recipes for meals to be eaten throughout the day.

Some Poor Bibliophile's Breakfast

Ham, sliced, smoked or un-cooked, thick (or thin as you will), 1½ lbs.	Flour, 1½ tablespoons
	Cream, thin, (light), 2 cups

Salt and pepper, to taste

Brown tenderized ham on both sides in a skillet in its own fat. Remove it to a hot platter. To the fat in the skillet, add flour and cream, stirring constantly and quickly. Cook it until slightly reduced in quantity and thickened. Add salt and pepper and pour sauce over ham resting on toast. *Makes 6 portions.*

Serve with:

Cavendish Club Corn Fritters

Corn, cooked or raw, 2 cups	Baking powder, 1 teaspoon
Flour, ½ cup	Salt, 1 teaspoon

Eggs, 2

Combine corn, flour, baking powder, salt, and eggs, beating until thick. Fry, by the tablespoon in hot bacon drippings, or butter, letting the fritters turn brown on both sides. *Makes 6 portions.*

Watson has still not yet met Holmes. But he has a hearty lunch as usual, not expecting to do very much for the rest of the day. Use any one, or a combination of these club sandwiches for your luncheon. Actually, club sandwiches may be made with any filling you desire. I shall give you some to practice with, afterward you may experiment on your own. General directions for making club sandwiches are as follows:

Preparation of fillings

Toast bread (optional), remove crusts if desired, and butter lightly. Spread filling on first layer; cover with lettuce (optional) and second slice of toast. Repeat this step for any successive layers. You can of course go as high as you wish. Fasten layers together with toothpicks; cut in triangles for easier handling— especially if they have grown to any gargantuan proportions. The following recipes will make enough for 4 servings.

Chicken and Mushroom Club à la Ronald Adair

Chicken Filling

Chicken, chopped, 1 cup   Mayonnaise, 3 tablespoons
Celery, chopped, ¼ cup   Salt and pepper, to taste

Combine all ingredients and mix well.

Mushroom Filling

Mushrooms, raw, chopped,
   1 cup
Butter, 2 tablespoons
Salt and pepper, to taste

Sauté mushrooms in butter for 5 minutes; add salt and pepper to taste, cool. Garnish sandwiches with stuffed green olives and tomato slices on lettuce.

Shakiri Hunter Sandwich

On the first slice of toast place sliced hard-boiled eggs and chopped ripe olives (or green, stuffed olives); spread with mayonnaise (and mustard) and top with shredded lettuce. On second layer, arrange thin slices of peeled tomato and crisp, cooked bacon. Top with a third slice of toast.

Now that you've got the hang of it, you can go onto your own creations with pride in knowing that you can do something with a reasonable amount of surety in the success of its completion.

Bagatelle Card Club Sandwich

Bread, thin-sliced, 1 loaf
Butter, softened, 1 cup
(about 1 quarter lb.)
Salmon, smoked, 8 slices
Cream cheese, 3 oz.
(approximately, more if
you want)
Lettuce, chopped, ½ head
Eggs, hard-boiled,
chopped, 4
Mayonnaise, ¼ cup

Russian dressing, ¼ cup
Mustard, with horseradish,
¼ cup
Cucumber, pared and
sliced, 1
Salt, ¼ teaspoon
Pepper, ⅛ teaspoon
Tomatoes, peeled and
sliced, 2
Anchovies, rolled, 8
(optional)

Olives, chopped, ½ cup

For each sandwich, cut five slices of bread into rounds varying in diameter from 1-4 inches; spread each round with butter. Cover the largest rounds with salmon, then with cream cheese. Cover the next smaller rounds with lettuce and a mixture of hard-boiled eggs, mayonnaise, salt, and pepper. Place this round on the first. Cover the third round with a slice of tomatoe, a slice of cucumber, and Russian dressing. Spread the next rounds with a mixture of cream cheese and olives and place on top of the growing sandwich; add the smallest buttered round, place a rolled anchovy on top, fastened with a toothpick. *Makes 8 sandwiches.*

It is now 6 o'clock and poor Watson has run into an old bibliophile, knocking some of his books out of his hands. He then goes to Park Lane to see what he might discover about Ronald Adair's murder. Retracing his steps to his office at Kensington, he again meets the old bookseller who comes to apologize. Watson looks away a moment then turns back. Holmes stands where the old man had been. Watson faints. After reviving him, the friends have a quiet discussion and proceed to Camden House, across the road from 221B Baker Street. Colonel

Sabastian Moran is captured, Lestrade takes him off to jail, and Holmes and Watson have a bite to eat.

Oscar Meunière Shrimp of Grenoble

Butter, ½ cup

Shrimp, cooked or canned, 3-4 cups

Lemon juice, 2 tablespoons

Parsley, finely-chopped, 1 tablespoon

Salt and pepper, to taste.

Heat butter and shrimp; cook just long enough to heat thoroughly. Remove shrimp to hot platter. To remaining butter, add lemon juice and chopped parsley; season to taste. Pour lemon mixture over shrimp. *Makes 6 portions.*

Follow this with:

1894 London Broil

Preheat broiler and place 2-3 lb. flank steak on a greased rack. Be sure that you broil the meat about 2-3 inches from the flame—the hotter the better—for no more than 5 minutes on each side. Be sure that the meat is kept rare. If a flank steak gets cooked medium or well-done, the meat becomes extremely tough. Serve with:

Bordelaise Sauce

Red wine, ½ cup

Black peppercorns, crushed, 4-5

Brown sauce (as made for "The Adventure of the Copper Beeches," but without the addition of chestnuts), 1 cup

Diced beef marrow, ¼ cup

Lemon juice, ½ teaspoon

Parsley, ½ teaspoon (optional)

Cook wine and peppercorns together in a saucepan until slightly reduced, then add brown sauce and simmer for 15 minutes. Poach bone marrow for a few minutes then drain and (just before serving) add it to the sauce with the lemon juice and parsley.

Note: Carve the steak by cutting across or against the grain, which will make it the more tender.

Serve with vegetables and beverages to your taste.

It is late in the evening; the two friends have separated, Holmes to stay in Baker Street, Watson to his dig in Kensington. Watson might be too excited to do so, but it's not unlikely that he had a small snack before drifting off to sleep. As for instance:

A.C.D.'s Reluctant Ambrosia

Valencia oranges, large, 2
Bananas, ripe, 3
Cherries, strawberries, or
    mint (optional)

Sugar, confectioner's, ¼ cup
Coconut, shredded, 1½
    cups (optional)
Brandy, 1 healthy jigger

Peel the oranges carefully, removing all the membrane. Peel the bananas and cut into thin slices. Add other fruits now, if you desire, then combine and stir the coconut and sugar. Arrange alternate layers of oranges and bananas (and any other fruit that you added), sprinkling each layer with the coconut-sugar mixture, reserving some for the top. Chill well before serving. Add brandy just before serving. *Makes 4 portions.*

Note: Instead of coconut, you might want to try crushed mint between the layers.

It has been an eventful day for Holmes and Watson and hopefully for you also. Now go to bed. It's going to be eventful tomorrow as well.

THE ADVENTURE OF THE COPPER BEECHES
Friday, 5 April-Saturday, 20 April
1889

"Is Toller still drunk?"
—Sherlock Holmes

The best drink that I can think of imparting to my readers is made of gin. I can see the eyebrows lift and the lips begin to sneer. Gin has a distinctively bad reputation. Most Victorian novelists assumed that only the lower classes— scullery maids, footmen, tweenies, and the like—had a taste for it. However that may be, it is one of the finest mixing bases ever invented. And the best of all the types of gin is the dry London variety which may be found in most, if not all, liquor stores. These adventure's dishes will be found useful for small gatherings of intimate friends, and may be expanded for larger open-house parties.

Toller's Gin Alexanders

Cream, 1 cup   Gin, 1 cup

Creme de cacao, ⅓ cup

In a shaker with 4-5 ice cubes, or ¾ cup crushed ice, pour cream, gin, and absolutely no more than ⅓ cup creme de cacao. Shake briskly for a full 5 minutes; pour into chilled glasses.

If there are any molly-coddles who ask for "brandy alexanders" in your home, this is the time to ask them to turn in their calabash and depart for other regions.

Note: April is rather pushing what I consider the alexander season; the best time is at Christmas and New Year's.

Rucastle's Roast Beef Sandwich

This is simply an open-faced hot sandwich made with cold (or at least, not piping hot) roast beef slices covered with:

Violet's Chestnut-Brown Sauce

Chestnuts, shelled, cooked, chopped, 2 cups

Butter or meat drippings, ¼ cup

Onion, grated, 2 tablespoons

Carrot, grated, 2 tablespoons

Bay leaf, 1

Cloves, whole, 4

Flour, 4½ tablespoons

Stock, meat or consomme, 2 cups

Salt and pepper, to taste

Heat butter or drippings in a heavy skillet, add onion, carrot, bay leaf, and cloves. Simmer over low heat until browned. Add flour, stirring constantly over low heat until flour browns. Remove from heat and gradually stir in stock or consomme. Season to taste and return to heat. Cook until thick and smooth, stirring constantly. Strain before serving. *Makes about 1⅔ cups.* To the hot strained sauce, add the chestnuts, coarsely chopped. Ladle the sauce over beef slices and bread enough for 4 sandwiches. Try a thick sour dough in an unsliced loaf. Add your own salad and serve.

If a larger party is expected, double the recipe . . . and the alexanders!

THE ADVENTURE OF THE THREE STUDENTS

Friday, 5 April-Saturday, 6 April
1895

"Let us see in the future how high you can rise."
—Sherlock Holmes

I thought that this would be the time to have a high tea. The case is amenable to the possibilities of one. So that the recipes will be ready for your company, start early. Discuss the students who are the suspects in the case and suggest that Picasso's work entitled "The Three Students" was inspired by his reading of this adventure.

For those of you not familiar with any tea, let alone a high tea, let me explain that it is a meal eaten in the mid-afternoon, at approximately 4 o'clock. It could possibly take the place of dinner if there is a sufficient quantity of food. Start with:

Soames' Scones

Flour, 2 cups
Baking powder, 3
  teaspoons
Salt, ½ teaspoon

Sugar, 2 tablespoons
Shortening, ⅓ cup
Milk or water, about ¼ cup
Eggs, slightly beaten, 2

Milk or cream, about ½ cup

Sift flour; add baking powder, salt, and sugar and sift again. Cut shortening with a pastry blender or two knives; add enough water or milk to make a stiff dough. Knead thoroughly; place on a wooden bread board and beat with a heavy mallet or the end of a rolling pin, 20-30 minutes or until dough blisters and is creamy smooth. Fold the dough over continuously during beating, keeping it in a small round ball. Turn out on a lightly floured board; knead lightly for about ½ minute. Pat or roll the dough out to about ½ inch thickness; cut into 4-inch squares; cut each square diagonally to make triangles. Brush with milk or cream, or lightly beaten egg whites or yolks diluted with 2 tablespoons of water; sprinkle with sugar. Place on a greased baking sheet and bake in a hot oven (425°F.) for 12-15 minutes. *Makes 10-12 scones.*

Bannister's Beef Olives and Sausages

Stewing beef, lean, 1 lb.
Herb stuffing (see below)
Flour, 2 tablespoons
Salt, ½ teaspoon
Pepper, ½ teaspoon
Beef drippings, 1
  tablespoon

Beef sausages, ½ lb.
Parsley, chopped, 1
  teaspoon
Beef stock or water, about
  1½ cups

Stuffing for Beef Olives

Garlic, cut, 1 clove
Onion, medium, chopped, 1
Butter, 1 tablespoon
Celery, chopped, 1 cup
Beef stock, 1 cup

Bread crumbs, dried and
  sieved, 1 cup
Parsley, chopped, 1
  teaspoon
Thyme, crushed, ½ teaspoon

Rub the mixing bowl with the cut clove of garlic; fry chopped onion in butter until clear. Stir in celery and beef stock and pour into the mixing bowl. Add bread crumbs, parsley, and thyme, and mix well. Turn into saucepan. Stir until mixture leaves sides of pan cleanly; cool slightly. Cut beef into thin slices about 3 inches long and 1½ inches wide. Divide stuffing between strips, placing a portion at one end of each, then roll up. Tie together with string, or pierce with skewers all the way through. Mix flour with salt and pepper. Dip olives in seasoned flour and fry in drippings until brown. Scald and cold-dip sausages; dry them and remove the skin. Divide each in three equal portions. Arange half the olives in the bottom of a greased casserole. Cover with the pieces of sausage, then with the remaining olives. Sprinkle with remaining flour and parsley. Cover with beef stock or water flavored with meat extract, covering tightly. Cook in a slow oven (300°F.) for about 2½ hours. *Serves 4-5.*

If you wish, serve small cakes, tarts, and cookies, the more the better. And at high tea, the *only* beverage is—tea!

THE ADVENTURE OF THE SPECKLED BAND
Friday, 6 April
1883

"Pray be precise as to details."
—Sherlock Holmes

Holmes and Watson have left Helen Stoner at the Crown Inn to await the final results of their enquiry into the case of the speckled band. As English inns were well known for their sideboard spreads, this in one adventure for which I advise a buffet meal, laid-out upon your own sideboard, containing the following ingredients for your investigation.

Grimesby's Gripe

Butter, 2 tablespoons
Flour, 3 tablespoons
Bouillon, chicken, 2 cups
 (or 1 cup bouillon and 1
 cup cream)
Parsley, minced, 1
 tablespoon

Bread crumbs, grated,
 untoasted, ½ cup
Eggs, separated, 4
Lobster meat, boiled, diced,
 2 cups
Salt and pepper, to taste
Mushroom sauce (see
 below for preparation)

Preheat oven to 325°F. Melt butter in a skillet, stir in flour until blended. Stir in bouillon (and/or cream) gradually; add parsley, bread crumbs, egg yolks, lobster meat, salt, and pepper. Whip egg whites until stiff but not dry, then fold them into the other ingredients. Bake the lobster mixture in a well-oiled 9-inch ring mold until firm, about 20 minutes. Unmold and serve with mushroom sauce, made as follows:

Mushroom Sauce

Mushrooms, sliced, ¼ lb.
Butter, 2 tablespoons

Brown sauce (see recipe
 given in "The Adventure
 of the Copper Beeches")

Sauté mushrooms in butter, then remove from skillet. Add to the drippings left therein, 1 cup *Violet's Chestnut-Brown Sauce*, excluding the chestnuts. When the sauce is heated, add the mushrooms. *Serves 5-6.*

Helen's Potato Fluff à la Roylott

Mashed potatoes, 3 cups   Egg yolks, well-beaten, 2
                         Egg whites, 2

To hot mashed potatoes, add the egg yolks. Beat the egg whites until stiff; fold into potato mixture. Place in a greased casserole and bake in a moderate oven (375°F) for about 20 minutes or until lightly browned.

Serve the above with a cold, sliced ham to convey an air of plentitude upon your table. For a dessert use this:

Crocus Crullers (that promise well)

Eggs, 4   Milk, ⅓ cup
Sugar, ⅔ cup   Flour, sifted, 3½ cups
Lemon rind, ¾ teaspoon   Cream of tartar, ½ teaspoon
Shortening, melted, ⅓ cup   Baking soda, ½ teaspoon
                         Salt, ¼ teaspoon

Heat deep fat to (370°F.). Sift sugar beat the eggs until light. Add sugar gradually, blending until the mixture is creamy. Add lemon rind, shortening, and milk, and stir. Sift flour (once more) with cream of tartar, soda, and salt. Stir sifted ingredients into the egg mixture. Roll the dough to the thickness of ¼ inch. Cut it into strips of about ½ × 2½ inches with a pie jagger. To make a fancier shape, twist the strips slightly into several convolutions. Begin to deep fry, taking care to not fry too many at one time (this will lower the temperature of the fat). Alexandre Dumas, a very wise gourmet, once said that the food must be "surprised" by the fat, to give it the crusty golden coating so characteristic and desirable. Be sure to use a bland oil, of the "all-purpose" variety. Do not let the fat smoke, as this means that it is breaking down and will affect the flavor of the food fried. Be sure also, to dip your utensils (slotted spoon, tongs or fry-basket) into the fat first, so that the food will release quickly from them once immersed. Always immerse gently, to avoid splashing. Skim out crumbs that collect while frying, as they will induce foaming in the fat and affect the flavor of the food. When the fat has become dark and thickish looking, discard it as its smoking temperature has become too low and the absorption rate becomes higher. For such a recipe as the crullers it is important that the fat be as bland as possible, to avoid contributing its taste to the food. Also allow a seven minute period between fryings to allow the fat's temperature to rise. But be sure to bring the heat of the fat down to 330°F.

between cookings. Drain on absorbent paper. Serve on the buffet-board dusted with powdered sugar.

THE YELLOW FACE
Saturday, 7 April
1888

In the event you've had a spat or misunderstanding with someone you love, such as the misunderstanding between Jack and Effie Munro, and you wish for as happy a reconciliation, get up early and fix this breakfast for him or her. You might be pleasantly surprised to find your mate up also, readying the same meal. I certainly hope so. I want to think that this book is being read by someone other than the author's families.

Yellow Face Potato Omelet

Bacon slices, diced, 6
Bacon slices, crisply cooked, 4-5
Onion, chopped, ¾ cup
Potatoes, pared, sliced, 3 cups

Eggs, moderately-beaten, 6
Cayenne, the slightest dash
Salt and pepper, to taste

Cook all the bacon slightly in a heavy skillet; add the onions and continue cooking until bacon is crisp and onion soft, but not browned. Remove 4-5 bacon slices. Add uncooked potatoes and season to taste. Cover and cook about 15 minutes, or until almost tender; uncover and brown on both sides, turning potatoes to brown evenly. Beat the eggs. Just as potatoes become tender add ⅓ of the eggs. Continue cooking over low heat without stirring until the eggs are firm. Turn over the whole potato cake with a wide spatula, or two narrow ones. Add another ⅓ of eggs, repeat turning. When the last ⅓ is cooked through, the omelet is ready to serve. Fry the strips of bacon and then place them on omelet to suggest a face. *Makes 3 portions.*

Serve with:

Whispered Norbury Beefers

Bacon, 6 strips
Dried beef (or beef jerky), shredded, 1 cup

Cheese, American, sharp or mild, grated, ¾ cup
Salt and pepper, to taste

Pimientos, chopped, ⅓ cup   Paprika, for show

Tomatoes, finely-chopped,
  ½ cup

Fry bacon until crisp, then drain. Pour excess fat from pan; add dried beef (or jerky) and cook 5 minutes. Add pimientos and tomatoes, blend well. Add cheese and seasonings to taste, and stir until cheese is melted. Spread on buttered bread or rolls, top with 2-3 additional strips of cooked bacon for each serving. *Serves 4.* Whisper a loving "Norbury" when serving.

For later on during the day, say for tea, you might wish to try this dip:

Late Afternoon Yellow Face Dip á la Sharon

Onions, 1½ cups   Cheese, Cheddar, sharp,

Garlic, 1 clove   grated, 2 cups

Oil, ¼ cup   Worchestershire sauce, 1

Tomatoes, whole, 1   tablespoon

  no. 4 can   Chillies, green, diced, 4-oz.

Cornstarch, 2 tablespoons   can, 1

Processed cheese spread,

  Cheddar, 1½ cups

In a skillet, brown onions and garlic. Press the tomatoes through a strainer. Add tomato pieces and liquid to onions with cornstarch. Stir and bring to a boil; turn down heat and let simmer. Stir until mixture begins to thicken, about 5 minutes. Blend in cheese spread. Then add the grated Cheddar cheese. Stir until all is melted. Add Worcestershire sauce and drained, diced green chilies. Stir over low temperature and serve. Mixture may be refrigerated and reheated at will.

THE ADVENTURE OF THE SOLITARY CYCLIST
Saturday, 13 April-Saturday, 20 April
1895

"It may be a mere fancy of mine..."
—Miss Violet Smith

Should you have awakened this morning finding yourself alone, have a quick breakfast (should you require one). But when lunchtime comes around, have a nice leisurely meal, perhaps using the Surrey recipe below. Should you have been cycling around and have found another solitary cyclist, invite the person for lunch and choose from any of the following.

Violet's Solitary St. Germaine Soup Quicky

Salt pork, lean, diced, ½ lb.
Pea soup, condensed, 1 can
Bouillon, 2 cups

Thyme and cayenne, to
taste

Cook salt pork until crisp. Add pea (or split pea) soup and bouillon. Add a few grains of thyme and cayenne to taste; stir. Heat and serve. *Makes 4 portions.*

Surrey Sandwich

Combine ¾ cup of peanut butter and 6 slices crisp bacon, chopped. Mix well and moisten with a little chili sauce. Spread on bread. *Makes 6 sandwiches.*

Straight Left Ham Loaf

Gelatine, clear, 1
   tablespoon
Bouillon or soup stock, well-
   seasoned, 1¾ cups
Onion, grated, 2 teaspoons
Vinegar, 2 tablespoons

Celery, thinly-sliced, ½ cup
Radishes, thinly-sliced, ¼
   cup
Ham, diced, 2 cups
Pickle, chopped, ¼ cup
Mayonnaise, ½ cup

Mustard, dry, 1 teaspoon

Soften gelatin in ¼ cup of cold bouillon or soup stock. Heat the remaining stock to a boil; add softened gelatin and stir until dissolved; add grated onion. Add vinegar and chill until partially set. Fold in the celery, radishes, pickles, ham, mayonnaise, and mustard; turn into a mold or loaf pan, first rinsed with cold water. Chill till firm. Unmold on a bed of chicory, escarole, or lettuce. Garnish with pickle fans and halves of hard-boiled eggs. *Makes 6 portions.*
Serve with:

Unecclesiastical Williamson Sauce

Mustard, Grey Poupon or
   white wine, 1 cup

Mayonnaise, ¼ cup
Worcestershire sauce, 1
   teaspoon

Onion, diced, 2-3 tablespoons	Olives, ripe, chopped

To the Worcestershire sauce, add mayonnaise, diced onion, and olives. Spread on *Straight Left Ham Loaf.*

Should you wish something a bit less filling, try:

Woodley's Worry

Combine ½ cup cream cheese and ½ cup cooked, diced ham. On the slices of bread to be used, spread half with butter, and remaining halves with ham and cheese mixture. Put sandwiches together; spread tops and bottoms lightly with butter and place in a hot waffle iron; bake until browned. Serve at once. There will be enough spread for 8 sandwiches, in case you meet more than one solitary cyclist. You can also substitute sliced Cheddar or Swiss cheese per sandwich and sliced, cooked ham, should you desire.

THE FINAL PROBLEM
Saturday, 24 May-Monday, 4 May
1891

"You must drop it, Mr. Holmes, you really must, you know."
—ex-Professor James Moriarty

Holmes and Watson are together for what seems to be the last time. Let us go back to that afternoon before the tragedy, in the peacefully lovely country of Switzerland. Is it not possible that there in the *Englischer Hof* of Peter Steiler the elder, the world's foremost consulting detective and that most faithful of companions spent a few pleasant hours dipping their beef in a fondue bowl and eating salmon from the village of Interlaken?

Meiringen Fondue Bourguignonne

Beef, fillet, 3-4 lbs.	Peanut oil, 1 cup (or 2 cups
Butter, clarified, 1 cup	peanut oil and no butter)

Cut beef into 1-inch cubes (allow about ½ lb. beef for each guest). If you're expecting more than 6-8 guests, prepare another heat source and divide the number of guests about the two fondue dishes (or you may substitute an electric skillet). Arm each guest with two forks: one, a long handled fire-proof fondue fork, with which he will cook his pieces of meat (no more than two at a time on one fork) to his own taste, and the other with which to eat it without getting burned. Allow each guest to dip his meat around in the butter and oil until done to this own liking. Be sure that there is a constant heat under the pot or skillet during cooking time. This is a tremendous help to the host and/or hostess, who has most of the food preparation and cooking work done by his or her guests. After each guest has cooked his meat to suit him, sauces must be made available for dipping the meat. Sauces may include a Béarnaise or Bordelaise, barbeque, mustard with capers, thickened tomato, mayonnaise with garlic and herbs, or any that suits your fancy to concoct. Prepare at least 1 cup of each kind of sauce per heat source. Serve with crusty French bread and a tossed salad with green grapes or avocado slices. Have plenty of beer, ale, and iced tea or soft drinks on hand.

Now for the main course:

Salmon ā la Interlaken

Onions, medium, thinly-sliced, 2	Flour, 2 tablespoons
Butter (or oil), 6 tablespoons	Salt and pepper, to taste
	Juice of ½ lemon
Salmon steaks, 4	Sherry
	Lemon slices

Sauté onions in 4 tablespoons of butter until evenly browned. Remove onions and keep warm. Add remaining butter. Lightly flour both sides of the salmon steaks, season, and brown evenly on both sides in hot butter. Cook until fish flakes easily when tested with a fork. Add lemon juice and transfer fish to hot platter. After cooking, add a little sherry to the pan to rinse it. Spoon onion on salmon steaks and pour sauce over all. Garnish with lemon slices. Serve 1 salmon steak to each person.

For dessert have a pudding such as:

Englischer Hof Butterscotch Custard

Brown sugar, 1 cup	Salt, ¼ teaspoon
Flour, ¼ cup	Milk, scalded, 2¼ cups
Butter, 3 tablespoons	Eggs, separated, 4
	Vanilla, ½ teaspoon

Combine in a double boiler, over but not in hot water, the sugar, flour, butter, and salt. Stir and cook ingredients until blended, add milk. Beat the egg yolks until light, then pour a little of the milk mixture over them; beat well and place it into the double boiler. Stir and cook until yolks thicken slightly, then add vanilla. Beat custard until smooth; cool. *Serves 6-8.*

For a different main dish that is easy and economical for the party, try:

Decrepit Italian Noodle-Cheese Custard

Noodles, 5 cups

Cheese, sharp, grated, 1 lb.

Bread crumbs, dry, 1½ cups

Butter, melted, ¼ cup

Eggs, beaten, 7

Milk, 1¾ cups

Onion, grated, 3
   tablespoons

Pimiento, chopped, ⅓ cup

Green peppers, chopped,
   membranes removed, ⅓
   cup

Salt, 1 teaspoon

Pepper

Qlives, sliced, stuffed, ½ cup

Preheat oven (325°F.). Cook the noodles and drain them. Have half the cheese and bread crumbs ready to mix with the butter. Mix the rest of the crumbs and cheese with the eggs, milk, onion, pimiento, green peppers, salt, pepper, and olivessThen divide the mixture into two parts and place each part in a 9 × 9 inch baking pan. Cover each with the cheese, butter, and crumb mixture. Bake about 25 minutes or until the custard sets and the top is golden brown. Serve with a savory creole sauce. (See "The Hound of the Baskervilles.") *Serves 18.*

For something to drink try this:

Moriarty's Mulled Cider

Cider, 2 quarts

Brown sugar, ⅔ cups

Salt, ¼ teaspoon

Cloves, whole, 6

Allspice, whole, 6

Cinnamon, 4 sticks

Combine all ingredients in saucepan; place over low heat. Bring to boiling point and simmer for about 5 minutes. Strain. Serve hot in cups or earthenware mugs. *Makes 10 to 12 servings.*

For parties, you might try:

Mulled Cider Punch, à la Moriarty.

Follow the preceding recipe, decreasing cider to 1 quart and adding 1 cup granulated sugar; simmer as directed; strain. Add 2 quarts orange juice and 2 cups lemon juice; heat to boiling point. Pour into heated bowl or pitcher. Float thin slices of orange and lemon on top. *Makes 25-30 servings.*

THE ADVENTURE OF SHOSCOMBE OLD PLACE
Tuesday, 6 May-Wednesday, 7 May
1902

"Those brown blobs in the center are undoubtedly glue."
—Sherlock Holmes

With its imagery of a Saxon-Norman graveyard, leaden coffins, and the like, this case lends itself to the macabre. Celebrate it accordingly. After sending out invitations, greet your guests at the door with a lighted candle and pre-arranged countersign (for this case an excellent example would be: "What was found in the furnace?" "The upper condyle of a human femur." Should the guest wish a double-countersign: "When was it found and by whom?" "In the morning by Harvey; enter my home."). You might request them to wear only black and perhaps carry in some part of the meal with them (if you wish to have a dinner by committee).

After greeting them, lead them to a darkened room to await the other guests. Some slight lighting may be used, but keep it to the absolute minimum. A candle or two will be sufficient. Request that everyone speak in hushed tones. After all the guests have arrived, lead them to the dining room, which should have no other illumination save that from the table, which should be ablaze with candles. Have the meal all ready to be served so that there is no extraneous getting up and moving about. Should your abode not allow guests to be led to a dining room, give each guest a candle and ask him to light it when everyone has arrived and is ready to be seated.

Begin by serving a soup or salad. Follow with the main course:

Brown Blob Chicken Pie

Chicken fat or butter, 5
   tablespoons

Salt and pepper, to taste
Chicken, cooked, cut in
   pieces, 2-3 cups

Onion, sliced, ½ cup
Flour, 4 tablespoons
Stock, chicken, 2 cups (use
chicken bouillon if
necessary)

Peas, cooked, (may be
canned), 1 cup
Carrots, cooked, diced, 1
cup

Heat fat. Add onion and cook over low heat for about 10 minutes, or until soft and slightly browned. Add flour and stir over low flame until thick and smooth. Season to taste (cream may be substituted for up to 1 cup of stock). Add celery salt and onion salt if desired. Arrange chicken meat and vegetables in layers in a large casserole or 6 individual ramekins. Cover with sauce. Top with rich biscuit topping.

Rich Biscuit Topping

Flour, sifted, 2 cups
Baking powder, 2
teaspoons

Salt, 1 teaspoon
Egg, slightly-beaten, 1
Shortening, ½ cup

Milk, about ¼ cup

Sift flour, baking powder, and salt. Add egg. Cut in the shortening with a pastry blender or two knives, blending it until the mixture resembles coarse corn meal. Stirring in with fork, add enough milk to make a dough soft. With a rolling pin, roll dough to ½-inch thick for large casserole, or ¼-inch thick for small pies. Using a cooky cutter, cut out 1-inch diameter circles for small pies and 1½-2-inch diameter circles for 1½-2 quart sized casserole. Place biscuits close together on top of the casserole; brush with milk, cream, or diluted egg yolk. Any leftover dough may be placed on a separate pan and made into additional biscuits. Bake in a hot oven (400°F.) for 25-30 minutes. *Makes 5-6 portions.* Make another one if necessary.

If pressed for time use this quick topping instead of the biscuit.

Toast Topping

Cut thin slices of bread into cubes, crescents, rounds, or any fancy shape desired. Brush each piece with melted butter. Arrange close together or overlapping on pie. Bake in hot oven (400°F.) for about 20 minutes, or until browned.

For dessert prepare:

Chocolate Coffins

Marshmallows, regular-
    sized, 20
Milk, 1 cup
Cocoa, 5 tablespoons

Sugar, 2 tablespoons
Cream, heavy, whipped, 1
    cup
Salt, a few grains
Vanilla, 1 teaspoon

Heat marshmallows in milk until melted. Mix cocoa and sugar together and add to hot mixture. Stir until blended; cool. Combine whipped cream with salt and vanilla and fold in chilled marshmallow mixture. Pour a half-inch layer in a refrigerator tray after lining it with heavy waxed paper or foil. Sprinkle with finely crushed cookie crumbs. Repeat the recipe omitting the cocoa and sugar, but following all other directions. Pour this onto the cookie crumbs, and then top the vanilla layer with cookie crumbs. Top the whole thing with the remaining chocolate mixture. Freeze it all until firm. Lift out and cut into slices. *Serves 6-8.*

Note: into one part of the vanilla, hide a chocolate-covered wafer cookie to represent the "charred femur" of the story. Arrange a prize, or some reward for the person who finds the "femur" in his coffin.

THE ADVENTURE OF THE PRIORY SCHOOL
Thursday, 16 May-Saturday, 18 May
1901

"What is it, Watson?"
"Absolute exhaustion — possibly mere hunger and fatigue."
—Sherlock Holmes and Dr. Watson

To prevent hunger and fatigue from overtaking your friends, this is a plan for a tea that Dr. Thorneycroft Huxtable would have enjoyed very much during that day on which he so dramatically made his appearance at 221B Baker Street.

Thorneycroft's Thoracic Thrill

Onion, chopped, 2
    tablespoons

Cheese, American or
    Cheddar, grated, ½ lb.

Mustard, prepared, 1
  tablespoon
Mayonnaise, 1 tablespoon
Green pepper, chopped, 2
  tablespoons
Dill pickles, chopped, 2
  tablespoons

Devilled ham, 3 oz. (or ½
  cup finely-cut cooked
  ham)
Cream, melted butter, or oil,
  ¼ cup

Combine all the ingredients and serve in hollowed-out hard and crusty rolls.
Fills about 12 rolls.

Saltire's Sardine Savoury

Sardines, skinless and bone-
  less, 12
Worcestershrie sauce, ½
  teaspoon
Tomato ketchup, ½
  teaspoon

Celery or onion, finely cut, 1
  tablespoon
Olives, stuffed (green),
  chopped, 1 tablespoon
Mayonnaise
Bread, white, thinly sliced,
  slices

Mash the sardines with a fork; add Worcestershire sauce, ketchup, celery or
onion, and olives. Moisten ingredients with mayonnaise or French dressing to a
good spreading consistency. Season with salt and pepper. Cut crusts from thin
slices of white bread. Spread the sardine mixture on the bread. Roll slices and
secure them with toothpicks. Toast the savouries in a 400°F. oven and serve hot.
Makes sandwiches.

Holderness Herring and Onions

Herring fillets, marinated
Toast, small rounds or
  squares

Mustard, prepared
Onion, Bermuda, sliced
Salt and pepper, to taste

Drain the herring and place fillets on toast. Spread with prepared mustard
and cover with thin slices of onion. Season with salt and pepper. Heat for about
5-10 minutes in a slow (325°F.) preheated oven. *Makes as many canapes as you
have herring fillets.*

Fighting Cock Canapes

Chicken, creamed, 1-2 cups   Toast, cut into rounds
Mushrooms, ½ cup   Butter
Cayenne, a dash   Paprika, to garnish

Sauté the mushrooms, and add the creamed chicken and a few grains of cayenne. Heat thoroughly. Toast rounds of bread in the broiler and butter lightly; place a piece of coated chicken on each round. Sprinkle with paprika; serve at once. Makes as many canapes as you have chicken pieces.

A rich-flavored tea completes this menu.

A SCANDAL IN BOHEMIA
Thursday, 19 May-Saturday, 21 May
1887

"This account of you we have from all quarters received."
—a unsigned note written by the King of Bohemia

Count Von Kramm, a Bohemian nobleman of extravagant tastes, removes his special masque and reveals himself to be Wilhelm Gottsreich Sigismond von Ormstein, Grand Duke of Cassel-Felstein and hereditary king of Bohemia—but not before Holmes has languidly referred to him as "Majesty," thus blowing Willy's cover. The king wishes to marry and requests Holmes to purloin a photograph from a famous operatic prima donna from New Jersey with whom he's carried on a questionable liaison. No ordinary photo, mind you, but one in which the king and she both appear. Such a photo would scandalize the young convent-bred princess, so it seemed necessary to Holmes to return it before the opera diva shows her the photo or tries to blackmail the king into buying it back. Enter our Sherlock disguised as a drunk, unkempt groom and as a noncomformist minister who gets soundly trounced by the lady who forever after is referred to by him as *the* woman—Irene Adler!

Wicked Willey's Soup Columbines
(known as Svitek Do Polévky in Bohemian)

Butter, 2 tablespoons   Salt and pepper, to taste

Salt

Eggs, separated, 2

Liver, ground, ⅔ cup

Bread crumbs, 1 cup

Milk, ¼ cup

Majoram, a pinch (or ½
  clove mashed garlic

Butter, 1 tablespoon

Bread crumbs, 2
  tablespoons

Note: This is but one variation that can be worked out of this recipe. You may add any finely chopped or crumbled meat.

Blend butter thoroughly with salt and egg yolks. Add finely ground liver. Fold in stiffly-beaten egg whites and bread crumbs mixed with milk, until smooth. Grease a cake pan with butter, dust well with bread crumbs, and fill with batter. Bake in a preheated moderate oven for 10 minutes, or until done. Let cool, cut into strips, and place them into:

Clotilde's Caraway Soup
(known as Kmínová Polévka in Bohemian)

Butter, ¼ cup

Flour, ¼ cup

Stock, beef (or water), 5
  cups

Salt, to taste

Caraway seed, 1 teaspoon

Macaroni, cooked

Brown butter in flour. Add water or stock, salt, and caraway seeds. Let simmer for 20-30 minutes. Add noodles just before serving. After the colombines have been cut into strips, serve them on a platter and allow each person to take strips for their soup.

Follow with:

Imperial Opera Pop-Open Oysters a la Ardis

It is possible to grill western oysters right on the coals of your barbeque without toughening them. If, however, you have the eastern variety, it is best to place the oysters on foil in which holes have been punched, before placing them on the coals. Be sure to scrub the unopened oysters in the shells. Grill until the shells pop open. Serve with lemon slices and individual cups of melted butter for dipping.

And for dessert:

Irene's New Jersey Junket

Milk, 2 cups
Sugar, 2 teaspoons
Essence of rennet, 2
  teaspoons (or prepared
  rennet, 1 teaspoon)

Brandy, 2 teaspoons (or any
  fruit or candy flavoring), 1
  teaspoon
Cinnamon or nutmeg, to
  taste

This is a very tricky pudding to make; the least wrong move and the pudding will not coagulate, so be on your toes. Warm the milk to precisely 98°F. and put it into the bowl in which it will be served. Then add sugar and stir in rennet and brandy (and fruit or candy flavoring). Let the pudding stand about 1½ hours until it coagulates. Sprinkle with cinnamon or nutmeg and serve cold. *Makes 4 portions.*

The pudding may also be made in individual ramekins or dessert cups. After adding all ingredients, pour into 4 ramekins; sprinkle with cinnamon or nutmeg. Let stand 1½ hours, chill, and serve.

THE ADVENTURE OF THE THREE GABLES
Tuesday, 26 May-Wednesday, 27 May
1903

"Good-bye Susan. Paregoric is the stuff."
—Sherlock Holmes

This is a rather confused tale of scandal concerning a pround and haughty woman, "betrayed" by her former lover who has written a book "with the names changed" but with all details intact. She hires common ruffians to beat him up and that is about all there is to it; Holmes has very little to do. A luncheon meal follows:

Steve's Dixie Sandwich-Meal*

Toast, large slices, 4
Bacon slices, sautéed, 8

French dressing, ½ cup
Mustard, prepared, ½ cup

Tomatoes, large, skinned, sliced, 4

Onion, sliced, 1 (optional)

Cream sauce, 1 cup

Cheese, grated, 1 cup

Eggs, 4

Place the toast on a baking sheet and cover each slice with one strip of bacon, tomato slices, and onion slices if desired. Spread mustard and dressing on each slice. Poach the 4 eggs and place one on each slice of the garnished toast. Cover each serving with one-fourth of the cream sauce (as made for "The Adventure of the Blanched Soldier," reducing flour and butter to 2 tablespoons each) and one-fourth of the grated cheese. Place toast under broiler until cheese melts. Serve the sandwiches piping hot. This should serve 4, but don't be surprised if it's eaten by 2.

For tea, at 4 o'clock prepare the following with other sandwich, canape, and dip recipes for tea time.

*Have all your ingredients ready before you poach the eggs.

Susan's Paregoric Braids

Milk, scalded, 2 cups

Shortening (part or all butter), ¼ cup

Sugar, ¼ cup

Salt, 1½ teaspoons

Compressed yeast, 2 cakes

Water, lukewarm, ¼ cup

Flour, sifted, 5-6 cups

Combine scalded milk, shortening, sugar, and salt; cool to lukewarm. Soften yeast in lukewarm water; stir and combine with cooled milk mixture, adding about half the flour. Beat well. Add enough of the remaining flour to make a soft dough; mix thoroughly. Turn out on a lightly floured board and knead for about 10 minutes, until smooth and satiny. Place dough in a warm, greased bowl; brush surface lightly with melted shortening. Cover and let rise in a warm place (80°-85°F.) for about 2 hours, or until doubled in bulk. Turn out on a board and shape by rolling pieces of dough into slender ropes about ¼-inch in diameter and 12-14 inches long. Braid 3 ropes together, cutting off into desired lengths. Press all 3 ropes firmly together. If unable to sprinkle with "paregoric" substitute poppy seeds. Place braids on a greased baking sheet; cover and let rise ½-¾ hour, or until doubled in bulk. Brush with milk, melted shortening, diluted egg white, or diluted egg yolk. Bake in moderate oven (375°F.) for 15-20 minutes.

THE ADVENTURE OF THE SIX NAPOLEONS
Friday, 8 June-Sunday, 10 June
1900

"We're not jealous of you at Scotland Yard. No sir, we are very proud of you. . . . "
                                                      —Inspector Lestrade

To celebrate this occasion, I elected to have this case represented by a costume party or, if you wish to do this up in a big way, a masquerade ball. Request that each person come costumed as a character in the adventure, as one of the Napoleons. If a very large assemblage is planned, allow everyone a choice of any character in the Canon. This invitation should go out in as flamboyant a manner as you feel is called for by the occasion. Be sure to disallow anyone to come as Holmes or Watson. I feel that the host and/or hostess should fight it out between themselves as to whom should portray which. Such a measure will eliminate a bumper crop of duplicate Holmeses and Watsons. Hide a black colored pearl or bead in some part of your home or yard and fix up some kind of treasure map for a pearl hunt. Later in the evening, you might want to have everyone try to guess characters, etc. There are any number of possibilities. To get back to what I should be doing, begin by serving:

Inspector Lestrade's Scotland Yard Punch*

Sugar syrup, 1 cup   Dark rum, 1 bottle
Lemon juice, 1 cup   Brandy, 1 bottle
Light rum, 1 bottle   Strong tea, 8 cups

Apricot brandy, 1 cup

By bottle, I mean a fifth of a gallon or 25 oz. This recipe will serve approximately 5 quarts for 20 people, assuming that everyone will have two 4-oz. cups. You may also wish to use peach liqueur or peach brandy instead of apricot brandy. If so, reduce its use to taste, rather than a set amount.

To serve this punch and keep it cold at the same time, I hasten to tell you a novel way to go about it. Purchase a 50-lb. cube of ice, and place it in your kitchen sink. After chipping out a small depression in the center of the ice block, place a metal bowl of at least a 3-quart capacity over the depression. Fill the bowl

*After enough of this, no one will care what they're doing, so go easy until all have had a chance to get into the spirit.

with boiling water, being careful not to spill any underneath it. As the water cools, which will occur every 15-25 minutes, empty and refill the bowl, stirring occasionally. Bail out the depression in the ice until the desired depth has been reached—no more than half the depth of the ice. Place the ice on a lipped tray, a few inches larger around than the ice block. Be sure that the tray is covered with aluminum foil, arranged so that a gutter is formed, allowing the water to run off into a bucket, or some convenient place. Turn the edges of the foil all around the ice in any case. Any cruderies about the edges of the ice may be masqued by greenery, flowers, or some other decorations. Just pour the punch into the depression of the ice and serve.

Any of the canapes, hors d'oeuvres or party sandwiches mentioned in The Three Students," "The Final Problem," "The Priory School," etc., can be used to good effect here.

The following recipe seems like a must at such a proceeding:

More Than Six Napoleons

Flour, sifted, 2 cups   Shortening (at least half
Cream of tartar, ½ teaspoon   butter), 1 cup (½ lb.)
                    Ice water, ⅔ cup

Sift flour and cream of tartar. If shortening is very hard, pound it with a wooden mallet or rolling pin to make it more plastic. Break or cut the shortening into 1½-inch cubes. Toss the cubes around in the flour until well coated with flour. Do not blend with flour. Add all but 2 tablespoons of the water all at once. Mix gently with a wooden spoon, using a folding motion until the paste forms a ball. Do not break up cubes of shortening any more than necessary. Pour the remaining water over the crumbs in the bottom of the bowl, and pat into the ball of paste. Flour a board well. Toss the paste, which is very sticky at this point, in the flour just until it can be handled. Pat it into a square 1½ to 2 inches thick. Roll paste out into a square about ¼ inch thick, keeping corners square. Brush off excess flour with a soft pastry brush. Work quickly and in a cool place to keep pastry as firm as possible. Fold pastry in thirds; roll a little to seal the layers; fold in thirds again. Repeat rolling and folding 4 times. After each time, cover with a damp cloth or waxed paper and chill for a short period in the refrigerator. This makes the dough easy to roll and the pastry extra flaky. Roll out pastry to ¼ inch thick, and cut into 2 oblongs, 8 inches wide. Cut crosswise into 2 oblongs of the same size. Transfer onto a baking sheet lined with ungreased brown paper. Bake in a hot oven (425°F.) for 20-25 minutes. Cool thoroughly.

Filling

Sugar, ⅔ cup
Flour, 5 tablespoons
Salt, ¼ teaspoon
Milk, 2 cups

Vanilla, 1 teaspoon
Eggs, 2 (or egg yolks, 4,
  slightly-beaten

Combine dry ingredients in top of double boiler; stir in milk gradually. Cook over boiling water until thickened, stirring constantly. Cover and cook 10 minutes longer, stirring occasionally. Stir a little of the hot mixture into slightly beaten eggs or egg yolks and slowly stir into remaining hot mixture. Cook over hot (not boiling) water for 2 minutes, stirring constantly. Add vanilla and chill. Cream ¾ cup butter; gradually beat in the cream filling, adding a small amount at a time; beat thoroughly; chill thoroughly. Spread one oblong thickly with the chilled filling. Cut other oblong into strips about 2 × 4 inches. Lay on top of filling; cut through filling and lower half. Sprinkle with confectioner's sugar or spread with confectioner's frosting.

Now, if you've finished everything before your guests arrive, greet them in your usual warm and effusive manner. And have fun!

THE BOSCOMBE VALLEY MYSTERY
Saturday, 8 June-Sunday, 9 June
1889

"Circumstantial evidence is a very tricky thing."
—Sherlock Holmes

This case, with its touch of Australia, and the tramping of Holmes and Watson in the west of England at Hatherly Farm and Boscombe Pool lends itself to a picnic lunch. If going to your favorite area to "get away from it all" for an afternoon or a weekend, pack your bag with these delectables:

Ballarat Beef and Cheese Sandwiches

Cheese, American or Cheddar, diced finely, ¼ cup
Mayonnaise, 2 tablespoons
Corned beef or any dried beef, shredded, canned, 4 oz.

Onion, grated, 1 tablespoon
Celery, minced, 2 tablespoons
Salt and pepper, to taste
Curry powder, to taste

Dill pickles, diced, ¼ cup

Bread, 12 slices

Mustard, or Worcestershire
sauce, to taste

Cream the cheese with mayonnaise. Add shredded beef and chop until fine. Add pickles, onion, and celery, stirring until consistency is spreadable. Season with salt, pepper, mustard, curry powder, or Worcestershire sauce. Spread it on the bread (toast it if you desire) and wrap up. *Makes 6 sandwiches.*

Australian Calico Salad

Elbow macaroni, 1 cup

Lemon juice, 1½
tablespoons

Oil, 1 tablespoon

Onion, grated, 1 teaspoon

Celery stalks, diced, 1 cup

Olives, green, stuffed, ½ cup

Salt, 1 scant teaspoon

Pepper, coarsely ground, ½
teaspoon

Sour cream, 3 tablespoons

Pimiento, chopped, 2
tablespoons

Hot sauce, a dash

Exact proportions are unimportant for this salad. Prepare the elbow macaroni. While it drains, combine the lemon juice and salad oil beating it well. Toss this in together with the macaroni. After chilling the mixture for 1-2 hours, add onion, olives, black pepper, sour cream, pimiento, and a dash of hot sauce. Chill. *Serves 5-6.*

Serve with a hearty red wine, or if you wish, a more robust, full-bodied ale or beer.

If you wish, make up this light dessert, and transport it in your picnic basket:

Cooee Cookies

Flour, sifted 3½ cups

Salt, ¼ teaspoon

Baking powder, 1 teaspoon

Baking soda, ½ teaspoon

Cream of tartar, 1 teaspoon

Shortening, 1 cup

Brown sugar, 2 cups

Egg, well-beaten, 1

Evaporated milk, 3
tablespoons

Vanilla, 1 teaspoon

Sift flour, salt, baking powder, soda, and cream of tartar. Cream shortening and add sugar gradually. Continue beating until light. Add the egg and blend well. Add the dry ingredients, thinning the mixture with evaporated milk. Add vanilla, mix well. Shape the dough into a long roll, 3 inches in diameter. Wrap in waxed paper and store in refrigerator for 24 hours. When you are ready to bake, cut the roll into thin slices with a sharp knife. Place on an ungreased baking sheet and if desired, press chopped nuts on each cookie. Bake in a hot oven (400°F.) 6-10 minutes, depending on the thickness of the cookies. *Makes 4-5 dozen cookies.*

THE STOCKBROKER'S CLERK
Saturday, 15 June
1889

"It's only a question of time now."
—Dr. Watson

Tea time once more. Time to enjoy another crop of sandwiches and canapes with a full-bodied tea at 4 o'clock. These may also be used to brighten up everyday lunches and those luncheons that feed nothing but ennui. With your permission, I present the following:

Pycroft's Pinwheels

Purchase a loaf of unsliced bread; remove all crusts except the bottom one, and be sure that it is a close-textured loaf. (The bottom crust is left on to give firmness while cutting.) Heat a very sharp knife and cut the bread lengthwise ⅛ to ¼ inch thick, using a sawing motion. Spread each length with any smooth, soft sandwich filling. At one end lay small, sweet pickles or a few stuffed olives. Beginning at the end on which the olives or pickles were placed, roll the bread, as you would a jelly roll. Spread a little soft butter on the last lap of the bread to make it stick, which it will do when chilled. For variety, instead of pickles or olives, lay alternating strips of green pepper and pimiento crosswise, 1 inch apart, over entire slice of bread and spread filling with horseradish mustard or other condiments, but take care that they are not spread on too thickly. Wrap each roll in waxed paper and place in refrigerator. When ready to serve, cut into slices, about ¼ inch thick. If desired, after slicing, cover each pinwheel with a small slice of cheese and place upon a baking sheet at a low temperature (325°F.) for 5-8 min. Serve immediately either way.

Stockbroker's Shrimp Sandwiches

Shrimp, cooked and
  cleaned, 1½ cups
Butter, 2 tablespoons

Onion, grated, 1 tablespoon
Pimiento, sliced, 1
Toast, 12 slices

Olives, green, 24

Melt the butter and add the grated onion and pimiento. Stir in shrimp and keep stirring over a low heat for 1 minute. Prepare 12 slices of toast; heap shrimp mixture on 6 slices of toast, cover with the other 6 slices. Cut each unit into 4 quarters and fasten a stuffed green olive to the top of each quarter by means of toothpicks. Serve at once. *Makes 24 portions.*

Franco-Midland Fruit Sticks

Bread, white, sliced
Apricots, canned, sliced,

Cinnamon
Brown sugar
Butter

Cut slices of white bread into strips about 2 inches wide. Toast all strips on one side in the broiler, then place them on a baking sheet with the untoasted side up. Drain apricot slices and place them on the untoasted sides. Sprinkle well with a mixture of cinnamon and brown sugar. Dot with butter and brown under the broiler once more. Remove and serve immediately.

THE MAN WITH THE TWISTED LIP
Saturday, 18 June-Sunday, 19 June
1887

"I think, Watson, that you are now standing in the presence of one of the most absolute fools in Europe. I deserve to be kicked from here to Charing Cross."

—Sherlock Holmes

Neville St. Clair is supposed dead by everyone, including Sherlock Holmes. Holmes has met Dr. Watson in an opium den run by a "rascally Lascar" while try- ing to gather evidence that will convict his suspected murderer, a beggar named

Hugh Boone, who has a hideous scar curling his mouth into a loathsome convolution. To find out how Holmes met Watson in an opium den and to learn precisely what happened to St. Claire, you might want to read this case, one of the most ingenious of the Holmes adventures, during your breakfast. Holmes and Watson most likely were back from the Bow Street Police Station in time for their morning meal of perhaps:

Hugh Boone Egg Scramble

Butter, 1 tablespoon
Eggs, 4
Salt, ⅛ teaspoon
Pepper, ⅛ teaspoon

Paprika (optional), ⅛
teaspoon
Milk or cream, about 4-5
tablespoons

Note: One beaten egg white may be added to whole eggs in the proportion of one additional white to 4 whole eggs.

Beat eggs, salt, pepper, milk or cream, and pour into a greased skillet or double boiler. A well-buttered double boiler, over not in, hot water, is best. As the egg mixture thickens, break apart with a fork or stir with a wooden spoon. When thickened, serve on toast, buttered or spread with fish-paste, deviled ham, or liver sausage. *Serves 2.*

An extra touch is to pour the eggs in individual well-buttered ring molds, fill the center, and let set. Or on occasions, pour into ring molds while still rather creamy in consistency (storage heat will finish them up and set them). Foods with which you can fill the center of such ring molds are: grated cheese, crisp bacon bits, chopped sautéed onion, finely chopped ham (à la Denver egg), chopped sardines (or almost any flaked, chopped, or sliced meat or fish), various vegetables. Experiment for yourself.

THE ADVENTURE OF THE THREE GARRIDEBS
Thursday, 26 June - Friday, 27 June
1902

"They degenerated greatly toward the end."
—Mr. Nathan Garrideb

This case, with its "element of comedy," seemed to lend itself to a backyard-type of affair, so effective on weekends. We hope that your gathering will "greatly degenerate toward the end" into a warm glow that stays with you until your next soiree.

Killer Evans Kabobs

This dish can be made with a high-grade top round meat, or any tender steak cut 2 inches thick, or it may also use something as diverse as fish, chicken, liver, etc. The possibilities are endless. For this particular kabob you might want to use meat and fish together, after having been steeped for at least three hours in different marinades. Alternate with mushroom caps, cherry tomatoes, green pepper, hot peppers, and ripe olives. When kabobing delicate meats such as liver, which cooks quickly, wrap each morsel in bacon. A bacon wrapping over the fish is also tasty. Conversely, should the meat be one that requires a long cooking time, skewer the alternates (tomato, mushroom, etc.) separately and mingle meat and vegetables in serving. Brush with melted butter and barbeque (or broil), turning at given times to ensure browning evenly. Brush with melted butter several times while broiling.

Marinades are also important, more important than some people know. They not only flavor, but also tenderize, to a large extent, the meat or fish that is to be consumed. Try these two marinade recipes:

Waterloo Road Marinade

For fish:

Beer, 1½ cups

Oil, ½ cup

Garlic, 1 clove

Lemon juice, 2 tablespoons

Sugar, 1 tablespoon

Salt, 1 teaspoon

Cloves, whole, 3

Combine beer, and salad oil, stirring in the oil slowly. Add the remaining ingredients and stir. *Will marinate 5 lbs. of fish.*

A more pungent variation for beef or pork:

Beer, 1½ cups

Salt, ½ teaspoon

Mustard, dry, 1 tablespoon

Ginger, ground, 1 teaspoon

Soy sauce, 3 tablespoons

Hot pepper sauce, ⅛ teaspoon

Sugar, 2 tablespoons

Marmalade, 4 tablespoons

Garlic, minced, 2 cloves

Combine all ingredients. Stir well: allow meat at least 3 hours to steep, and 4 or 5 wouldn't hurt. *Will marinate 4 lbs. of meat.*

Garrideb Marinade à la Benjamin

Wine, red, 2 cups
Liquid smoke, 3
 tablespoons
Juice of 1 lemon

Garlic salt, ½ teaspoon
Pepper, 1 tablespoon
Worcestershire sauce, 3
 tablespoons

Combine all ingredients. Mix well and stir thoroughly. *Will marinate 6 lbs. of beef.*

Note: If broiling in the kitchen, save the marinade that collects and mix some water with it for a savoury gravy.

For barbeques such as this, beer and ale are the only things to serve.

THE ADVENTURE OF BLACK PETER
Wednesday, 3 July-Friday, 5 July
1895

> *"Well, well, we all learn by experience. . . .*
> —Sherlock Holmes

Tonight's dinner is an informal affair for a single person, or to be shared with a loved one or friend. The food was inspired by that foul and loathsome sea-captain, Black Peter Carey, the meanest, ugliest . . . I'd better stop there, or you'll start thinking that the meal will be foul and loathsome also!

John Hopley Neligan Rarebit

Tomato soup, condensed, 1
 can (1⅓ cups)
Cheese, American, Old
 English, or Cheddar,
 grated, ½ lb. (about 3
 cups)

Mustard, dry, ½ teaspoon
Fish, coarsely flaked,
 (home-cooked or
 canned, any kind of
 fish), 1 cup

To the hot soup, add cheese and mustard; stir over very low heat until cheese is melted and mixture is smooth. Add fish to rarebit and heat, stirring gently to avoid mashing the fish. Serve on toast. *Makes 6 portions.*

Black Peter Salad

Section 1 orange and 1 small grapefruit for each serving. Arrange on shredded lettuce (or chicory), petal fashion, alternating the sections. Fill the center with mayonnaise; top with diced, sliced or whole ripe olives (according to your preference). A clever finishing touch would be to skewer each section with a tooth-pick or stir-stick that looks like a miniature harpoon.

Sea Unicorn Sandwiches

Variation #1 (Very good with the *John Hopley Neligan Rarebit*)

Spread cream cheese on two slices of a bagel, top with smoked salmon, sliced very thin. Cover and eat. For a very elegant touch, on the cream cheese, spread red caviar, then top with the salmon, cover and eat.

Variation #2

Shrimp, cooked and cleaned, 12	Salt, ⅛ teaspoon
Egg white, 1	Paprika, ⅛ teaspoon
Cheese, grated, ¼ cup	Red pepper, a dash
	Mayonnaise, ½ cup

Coarsely chop the shrimp. Whip the white egg until stiff. Fold in grated cheese, salt, paprika, a few grains of red pepper, mayonnaise. Blend in the shrimp and spread the concoction on bread or toast. Place in a pre-heated broiler until light brown.

Variation #3

Lobster meat, ½ lb. (or crabmeat)	Curry powder, ¼ teaspoon
Mushrooms, ½ lb.	Worcestershire sauce, 1 teaspoon
Cream sauce, 1 cup	Wine, white, dry, 3 tablespoons
Green pepper, finely chopped, 1 tablespoon	Salt and pepper, to taste
Pimiento, chopped, 1 tablespoon	Bread crumbs, dry, ¼ cup
	Butter, 3 tablespoons

Sauté the mushrooms, and combine with lobster or crabmeat. Add cream sauce, green pepper, pimiento, curry powder, Worcestershire sauce, wine, salt, and pepper. Heap the mixture on toast rounds and sprinkle the top with a covering of dry bread crumbs and dots of butter, enough to make a thorough but light covering. Bake 5 inches from heat source, until golden brown, or a little longer for a crispy crust.

To finish up the evening properly, for dessert, serve black walnut cookies, black walnut or blackberry ice cream, blackberry cream pie, etc.Festoon the walls of your den with fishnets, and lower away!

THE GLORIA SCOTT
Sunday, 12 July-Tuesday, 4 August-Tuesday, 22 September 1874

"I have some papers here."
—Sherlock Holmes

It is merely a trick of chronology that the nautical "Adventure of Black Peter" should be followed by the maritime drama of "The Gloria Scott." You have three dates on which to celebrate the case, Holmes' very first. A luncheon menu follows:

Hotspur Ham Balls

Ham, ground, 1 lb.	Egg, beaten, 1
Pork, ground, ¾ lb.	Milk, ¼ cup
	Pepper, ⅛ teaspoon

Mix all ingredients and shape into 2½-inch balls. Brown slowly in a shallow pan with a small amount of fat. Add enough water to just cover the bottom of the pan. Cover tightly and simmer gently for 45 minutes. Serve with chili sauce. *Makes 8 balls.*

Justice of the Peace Pilaff

Shrimp, 17 oz. can	Consommé, chicken, 1 can,
Rice, raw, 1 cup	diluted with ½ can water
Butter, 4 tablespoons	(or 2 chicken bouillon
Onion, chopped, 1	cubes dissolved in 2 cups
teaspoon	hot water)

In a heavy oven proof skillet, cook the rice in the butter until golden brown. Add the onion and consommé, and cover the skillet. Bake for 35 minutes in a slow (325°F.) oven. Drain the shrimp, and pour into skillet mixture. (If you can afford two cans of shrimp, so much the better.) Bake for 10 more minutes. *Serves 3-4.*

THE DISAPPEARANCE OF LADY FRANCES CARFAX
Tuesday, 15 July-Friday, 18 July
1902

"It can only be as an example of that temporary eclipse to which even the best balanced mind may be exposed."

—Dr. Watson

The most mentioned meal in the Canon is breakfast. I have been remiss in not including more, I think. This case concerns a maiden lady who falls in with a bad crowd. To get at her money, they try to dispose of her by burying her along with another corpse. Fortunately, Holmes is able to prevent this grave situation. (And that pun is sent tomb it may concern.) Had enough? Go on to the recipes:

Holy Peter's Poached Eggs in Wine

Wine, red, 1 cup
Garlic, crushed, 1 clove
Onions, minced, 2 table-
  spoons (or garlic powder,
  ⅛ teaspoon)

Salt, ¼ teaspoon
Pepper, ⅛ teaspoon
Eggs, 6
Toast, 6 slices
Butter, 2 tablespoons

Flour, 2 tablespoons

Combine wine, garlic, onion, salt, and pepper in a skillet; heat to a boil, then reduce heat and simmer for 3 minutes. Break the eggs onto a saucer, one at a time, and slide them into the skillet. Poach until the whites are firm. Remove and put them on slices of toast or fried bread, rubbed with garlic before frying. Strain the wine, put back into skillet with kneaded butter, which is made by rubbing in your fingers 2 tablespoons butter and 2 tablespoons flour. Form this into small balls and drop them into the simmering wine mixture. Simmer only long enough to dispel the floury taste. This butter is excellent for thickening any number of thin gravies. This amount is used for 1 cup of a thin liquid. Pour the gravy over the poached eggs and serve. *Serves 6.*

Lady Frances Hidden Body Soufflé

Milk, ¼ cup

Eggs, separated, 4

Baking powder, 1 teaspoon

Onion or chives, grated, 1
  teaspoon

Chervil

Butter, 1 tablespoon

Oysters, poached and
  chopped

Combine and beat with a fork the milk, egg yolks, and baking powder. If you have 1 or 2 more egg whites, add these and omit the baking powder. Then beat until stiff, but not dry, the egg whites. Add the onion or chives, and chervil before cooking. Melt butter in a heavy skillet over a slow heat. Fold the yolk mixture into the egg white. Pour batter into skillet. Cover. As the omelet cooks, remove the lid and slash it several times with a knife, to permit the heat to penetrate the lower crust. When the omelet is half done (about 5 minutes), it may be placed uncovered on the center rack of a moderate (325°F.) oven until the top is set. Then move it quickly out of the oven, as the top collapses in a hurry. Place poached chopped oysters into the middle of the souffle. Serve it cut into pie-shaped wedges. Everyone should have his own "Hidden Corpse" concealed within.
Serves 4 portions.

THE ADVENTURE OF THE LION'S MANE
Tuesday, 27 July-Thursday, 3 August
1909

> *"I see no reason for mystery."*
> —Maid Bellamy

For anything less than a high tea, which yet might supplant the evening meal, I suggest the following recipes. I was happy to find names that were so felicitous to transform into reminders of the day's case—one which was written by Holmes himself after his retirement from active practice to his apiaran studies in Sussex.

Lime's Mane Ginger Jelly

Gelatin, lime-flavored, 1
  package

Boiling water, 1 cup

Ginger ale, 1 cup

Fruits, for garnish

Whipped cream, or topping

Dissolve gelatin in boiling water; chill. As mixture thickens, beat with egg beater until frothy and stir in ginger ale. Turn into mold and place in refrigerator. To dress up this mold, surround with canned fruits and serve with whipped cream. Apricot on slices of pineapple will give it a glamorous touch.

Sherlock's Potato Beehives

Potaotes, mashed   Onion, Bermuda, large, 1

                                   Butter

Use a mashed fairly dry potato mixture. Shape into mounds, beehive fashion, and place on greased baking pan. Slice a large Bermuda (red) onion and separate into rings; fry in butter about 5 minutes or until soft, but not browned. Place 3 or 4 rings over each mound of potato, choosing slices to fit, starting with a large ring at the bottom of the mound to correspondingly smaller ones spaced toward the top. Brush with melted butter. Bake in a hot (400°F.) oven about 15 minutes, or until browned. If you wish, you may add some leftover or ground meat in the interior of each potato hive.

THE ADVENTURE OF THE DANCING MEN
Wednesday, 27 July-Wednesday, 10 August-Saturday, 13 August
1898

"I suppose that you are the detectives from London."
—An unidentified station master in North Walsham

When reading of the journey of Holmes and Watson to Riding Thorpe Manor in Norfolk, the memories of that district of beautifully green countryside always gives me a light-headed feeling, something that many of my friends say is a permanent fixture. It is my opinion that a brisk walk out-of-doors on a warm day is something one should always strive for. Therefore, another picnic lunch is indicated. Have your conveyance close by to carry a portable grill (or hibachi), which will be necessary for the dishes I'm about to list. Should you be somewhat pressed for cash, you will appreciate the title of this meal's entreé.

Locked-Up Chequebook Beefsteak

Use beefsteak, any cut, about 1 inch in thickness and 1 lb. in weight. Marinate the meat overnight in *Waterloo Marinade* ("The Adventure of the Three Garridebs"). Rub 2 tablespoons of English mustard into the steak, or spread a thin layer of prepared mustard over it before broiling. If using the dry mustard, rub the steak with garlic first. Cook approximately 5-7 minutes on each side for rare steak, 10 minutes each side for medium steak, and I don't care how long you take if you can eat it well-done. Have the frying pan or grill sizzling hot, and if using the former, one tablespoon bacon drippings before throwing in steak. Sear both sides quickly (30 seconds to 1 minute), then cook to desired state. Remove to a hot plate and season to taste with salt and pepper. Serve with fried or grilled potato slices or grilled corn-on-the-cob. Then write a message with the "dancing men" code, inviting someone to go with you on an evening excursion, or plan a weekend rendezvous. You'd best send the code solution also—or the book containing the case so that the person can decipher your message.

THE ADVENTURE OF THE RETIRED COLOURMAN
Thursday, 28 July-Saturday, 30 July
1898

"I find your narrative most arresting."
—Sherlock Holmes

Josiah Amberly, the retired colourman of the title, was so smug as to believe that he could outwit Scotland Yard and even Sherlock Holmes. That Holmes caught him, in the end proved that even those with "the mark of a cunning mind" were no match for Holmes' "indelible" powers of observation. I believe it safe to say that Holmes cracked the case, and the culprit was apprehended by mid-morning, which leads me to surmise that Holmes and Watson were back in Baker Street by noon, allowing them to partake of Mrs. Hudson's fine cuisine. A luncheon meal is called for.

Little Purlington Pancake Roll-ups

Flour, 1 cup
Salt, ½ teaspoon
Milk, 1 cup
Eggs, 2
Drippings, or butter or oil,
   1 tablespoon, plus 1
   teaspoon
Meat, fish, or poultry,
   ground or minced,
   cooked, 2 cups

Celery, minced, 1 cup
Cream of mushroom soup,
   ¾ cup
Pimiento, chopped, 2
   tablespoons
Salt and pepper, to taste

Mix the flour and salt; add in milk and beat until smooth. Add the eggs, beating the mixture thoroughly; then add drippings or oil. Heat 1 teaspoon of butter or drippings in a skillet. Pour in just enough batter to cover the pan and tilt the skillet so the mixture spreads evenly, as in making crepes. Turn and cook the other side; remove and make the remaining pancakes. Mix the remaining ingredients and place some of the mixture in the center of each pancake, roll up, and place close together in a shallow baking dish. Place in moderately preheated (350°F.) oven for 20 minutes. While they are heating, make cheese sauce:

Cheese Sauce

Butter, 2 tablespoons
Flour, 2 tablespoons
Flour, 2 tablespoons
Mustard, dry, ½ teaspoon

Milk, 1 cup
Cheddar cheese, sharp, grated, ⅓ cup

Melt the butter in skillet, blending in flour and mustard. Add milk gradually and cook, stirring until thickened. Stir in cheese until it is melted and add salt and pepper to taste. Pour sauce over pancakes, sprinkle with toasted almonds and paprika. Serve with tea or coffee.

Follow this with the succeeding recipe for dessert.

Retired Colourman Coffee Blancmange

Cornstarch, 4-5 tablespoons
  (see Note below)
Sugar, ½ cup

Salt, ⅛ teaspoon
Milk, 1½ cups
Coffee, 1½ cups
Vanilla, 1 teaspoon

Mix cornstarch, sugar, and salt in the top of a double boiler. Slowly stir in milk and coffee. Place over boiling water and stir constantly until thick and smooth. Cover and cook 15 minutes longer, stirring occasionally. Add vanilla and turn into molds. Chill. Unmold and serve with chocolate sauce, any fruit sauce, caramel or butterscotch sauce (any of which recipes you'll have to find elsewhere, if you want to make them from scratch), or surround with fresh or canned fruits or berries and top with whipped cream.

Note: Use 4 tablespoons cornstarch for an unmolded pudding, 5 tablespoons for a molded pudding. Flour (5-7½ tablespoons) may be used instead of cornstarch.

THE NAVAL TREATY
Thursday, 30 July-Saturday, 1 August
1889

"Oh, come! Try the dish before you."
—Sherlock Holmes

Percy Phelps, an old friend of Watson's during his school days and now a public servant, has lost a document of immense value from the foreign office. Enlisting Holmes' aid, all is set right in a few pages and before the end of the story, we find that the thief is someone close to Phelps, a person of a dark and deeply dangerous nature. Breakfast is served and beneath the covered dish is a surprise for Phelps—and for you, I hope. The Canonical breakfast is either curried chicken or ham and eggs. I have opted for the latter.

Undercover Ham and Eggs

Ham, cooked, ground, 1 cup	Pepper, ⅛ teaspoon
	Paprika, ⅛ teaspoon
Egg, 1	Eggs, 4
Water, 1 tablespoon	Toast, buttered, 4 slices

Chervil, for garnish

Preheat oven to 325°F. Combine ham, egg, water, pepper, and paprika. Place the mixture into 4 (or more for a large breakfast) muffin tins. Leave a large hollow in each one. Drop 1 egg into the hollows of each muffin tin. Bake the ham cakes until the eggs are firm, then turn the cakes out onto rounds of buttered toast. Garnish with chopped chervil. Be sure, of course, to serve this on a covered plate. This would be an excellent way to commemorate an occasion for one you love, by placing your "important document" in the covered dish also. Serve with a fruit juice of your choice.

HIS LAST BOW
Sunday, 2 August
1914

"Might I trouble you to open the window, for chloroform vapour does not help the palate."

—Sherlock Holmes

Having picked up his old friend Dr. Watson to act as his chauffeur, Holmes apprehended the notorious German spy, Count Von Bork, while still impersonating an Irish-American counterspy named Altamont. This event brought to a close the last of Holmes' recorded cases. It is not too unlikely that Holmes and Watson, after depositing the vengeful German in London had a late night snack or cup of tea before the next day's activities. I recommend for your late night snack the following.

Altamousse

Gelatin, unflavored, 1 envelope
Bouillon, or soup stock, well-seasoned, 1¾ cups
Onion, grated, 2 teaspoons
Ham, cooked, ground, 2 cups
Celery, finely chopped, ¼ cup
Green pepper, finely chopped, ¼ cup

Pimiento, 2 tablespoons
Hard-boiled eggs, diced, 2 (optional)
Pepper, ⅛ teaspoon
Paprika, ⅛ teaspoon
Mustard, dry, 1 teaspoon
Heavy cream, ½ cup, whipped

Soften the gelatin in ¼ cup of cold bouillon or soup stock. Bring the remaining stock to a boil; add softened gelatine and stir until dissolved; add onion. Chill until partially set. Add ham, celery, green pepper, pimiento, and eggs. Add pepper, paprika, and mustard to whipped cream and fold into gelatin mixture. Turn mixture into a loaf pan or mold first rinsed in cold water. Chill until firm. Unmold on a bed of salad greens. Garnish with pickle fans and radish roses. Serve with a tart dressing. *Makes 4-6 servings.*

And, of course, you should really not drink anything else but Imperial Tokay Wine with this!

THE ADVENTURE OF THE MAZARIN STONE
Monday, 9 August
1903

"The faculties become refined when you starve them."
—Sherlock Holmes

While listening to Holmes play the Bacarolle from "Tales of Hoffman" on his violin (and later on his gramophone) in his bedroom, Count Negretto Sylvius and Sam Merton discuss the disposition of the fabulous Mazarin Stone. They had stolen this gem thinking themselves safe from detection. Holmes, outwitting them, has them carted off to the pokey, and having retrieved the stone, takes the great liberty of dropping it into the coat pocket of Lord Cantlemere, who is in charge of its safety. After commenting on Holmes' "perverse sense of humour" ("My old friend here will tell you that I have an impish habit of practical joking."), he departs and Holmes rings for dinner. What else could Mrs. Hudson serve but:

Stewed Negretto (or Troubled Sylvius)

Veal breast, 3 lbs., or	Thyme, ⅛ teaspoon
shoulder cut, 2 lbs.	Onions, medium, sliced, 2
Boiling water, 4 cups	Carrots, sliced or diced, 3
Bay leaf, 1	Parsley, 2 sprigs
Salt, 1½ teaspoons	Celery, thinly sliced, 1 cup
Peppercorns, 5 or 6	Flour, 1-3 tablespoons

Have the veal cut in 2-inch pieces. Wipe with a damp cloth. Put meat in a heavy pot and pour boiling water over it. Add bay leaf and seasonings. Cover and gently simmer for 45 minutes. Add vegetables; cover and continue cooking about ½ hour, or until meat and vegetables are tender. Remove meat and vegetables to a hot platter. Thicken gravy if desired by stirring 2 tablespoons of flour for each cup of liquid in the pot. (Blend the flour with cold water to make a thin paste first—1½ tablespoons of water to each tablespoon of flour.) Pour the flour paste gradually into the stew liquid, stirring briskly to prevent lumping. Bring to a boil, stirring constantly; cook until smooth and thickened. Serve the gravy either in a separate bowl or poured around the meat and vegetables on the platter. *Serves 6.*

Serve the following with the meat and gravy:

Mazarin Stones

Flour, sifted, 1½ cups	Salt, ½ teaspoon
Baking powder, 2	Shortening, 1 tablespoon
teaspoons	Milk, ¾ cup

Cheese, grated, ¼ cup

Sift flour, baking powder, and salt. Blend the shortening with a fork; add milk, alternately with cheese. Drop by tablespoonfuls into gently boiling stew, allowing dough to rest on meat and vegetables. Cover closely and steam for about 15 minutes. *Makes about 12 medium dumplings.*

Add light red wine to round out the service and your meal is complete.

THE ADVENTURE OF THE NORWOOD BUILDER
Tuesday, 20 August-Wednesday, 21 August
1895

"I think there will be no difficulty in clearing it up."
                                  —Inspector Lestrade

Hoping that your thumbprints will not cause you as much trouble as John Hector MacFarlane's caused him, I will now give you a couple of dishes that will involve your hands a great deal, but with ample reward in their satisfactory results. This breakfast begins with:

An Oldacre of Waffles

Flour, 2 cups
Baking powder, 3
   teaspoons
Salt, 1 teaspoon
Cinnamon, ground, ¼
   teaspoon
Eggs, separated, 3

Milk, 1½ cups
Sweet potatoes, cooked
   and mashed, ¾ cup
Melted butter, ¼ cup
Chopped nuts, ⅓ cup
   (optional)

Sift together flour, baking powder, salt, and cinnamon. Beat egg whites until stiff. Beat egg yolks; add milk and potatoes and beat until blended. Add butter to dry ingredients and mix well. Fold in egg whites and nuts (if you're using them). Bake and serve hot, with syrup (if you use it). These waffles can also be used for desserts and can be served à la mode or with a fruit sherbet. *Makes 4-6 servings.*

After hiding the fact that there is an unusual ingredient in this recipe, in true Jonas Oldacre fashion, let us continue with another "Norwood" recipe.

MacFarlane's Scotch Woodcock

Butter, 3 tablespoons
Anchovy paste, 2 teaspoons
Egg yolks, 2 or 3

Cream, ½ cup
Pepper, ⅛ teaspoon
Salt, ⅛ teaspoon

If you use *An Oldacre of Waffles*, omit the cinnamon when preparing them. Butter the waffles and spread each with a thin layer of anchovy paste. Beat together the egg yolks, cream, pepper, and salt. Then melt the remaining butter (2 tablespoons) in a double boiler; add the egg mixture and scramble unitl creamy, but not at all dry. Arrange the waffles on a hot dish and cover with the egg mixture. Toast may be substituted for the waffles. *Makes 2 servings.*

THE CARDBOARD BOX
Saturday, 31 August–Monday, 2 September
1889

"I yearned for the glades of the New Forest or the shingle of Southsea."
—Dr. Watson

Although this is rather a tragic case, it need not be celebrated in a tragic manner. As the story opens, Holmes seems to be able to read Watson's mind (an incident that was later lifted in toto the beginning of "The Reigate Squires"). This leads into a case brought around by Lestrade concerning a pair of ears sent to a maiden lady. So much for the story. Noting the date, you may be yearning for a stroll in the woods or a day at the beach. When you return, invite your friends over and have a party. If you plan to celebrate this day's adventure, these recipes should work out nicely.

Susan Cushing's Crabmeat

Crabmeat, flaked, 1 can
  (6½ oz.)
Mayonnaise, ⅓ cup
Mustard, prepared, 1
  teaspoon
Salt, ⅛ teaspoon
Cayenne, a dash
Juice of ½ lemon

Parsley, chopped, a few
  sprigs
Bread, 6 slices
Cheese, Parmesan or
  Romano, ¼ cup
Bread crumbs, fine, very
  dry, 2 tablespoons

Mix all ingredients but the last three. Toast bread (after trimming crusts) and spread with crab mixture. Mix cheese and crumbs; sprinkle on top of crab mixture. Cut each slice into four triangles; broil until lightly browned. *Makes 24.*

A little more substantial is the following:

Shadwell Police Station Sandwiches

Cream cheese, 12-oz.
  package
Bread slices, 24
Butter, 3 tablespoons
Chicken, one 6-oz. can

Almonds, blanched,
  chopped, ¼ cup
Salad dressing, ⅓ cup
Salt and pepper, to taste
Ham, devilled, 4½-oz. can

Get out cream cheese and let reach room temperature. Cut bread into rounds using a 3-4 inch cookie cutter; butter each round. Spread 8 rounds with a chicken salad filling, made by combining a finely chopped can of chicken, almonds, and salad dressing. Season to taste with salt and pepper. Top with 8 rounds of bread; spread those with devilled ham. Top with remaining 8 rounds of bread. Cream the cream cheese well, adding enough milk to make a good spreading consistency. Frost top and sides of sandwiches with cream cheese spread. You can put a border of parsley around the edge of each sandwich (although the police at Shadwell certainly do not!). Garnish with radish slices and carrot curls (if you want, but again the Shadwell police would laugh at such goings-on. *Makes 8 sandwiches.*

Gruesome Packet Punch

Boiling water, 3 cups
Tea leaves, 4 tablespoons
Sugar, 3 cups
Water, cold, 1½ quarts
Orange juice, 3 cups
Lemon juice, 1½ cups

Strawberries, sliced and
  sweetened, 3 cups
Ginger ale, 1½ quarts
Marshmallows, large,
  several
Pipe cleaners, a few

Pour boiling water over tea leaves; steep for 5 minutes; strain. Pour hot tea over sugar and stir until sugar is dissolved. Add cold water and let cool. Add orange and lemon juice and strawberries. Pour over ice in a punch bowl and just before serving, add ginger ale. Something stronger may be added in place of the ginger ale if so desired. Garnish with thin slices of orange and lemon and, should you wish, fresh mint. Bend the pipe cleaners in the shape of ears and thread the marshmallows on them so that they'll float in the punch, creating the contents of "gruesome packet," as noted in the story. To create more of a packet-looking affair, use the ice block punch bowl method of serving, as noted in "The Adventure of the Six Napoleons." *Serves 12.*

THE ADVENTURE OF THE ILLUSTRIOUS CLIENT
Wednesday, 3 September-Tuesday, 16 September 1902

"My knowledge on these subjects may be second only to your own...."
—Dr. Watson

This is one of the most sordid of the cases handled by Sherlock Holmes. It concerns his efforts to block the advances of one Baron Gruner, to the beautiful, but cold Violet de Merville. Watson goes to great lengths in picturing Gruner as a foul and loathsome debauchee, a person lacking any decent feelings whatsoever. Referring to this low individual, I think it appropriate to start with this dessert recipe.

Gruner's Gravel Pie

Cake or cookie crumbs, 1
  cup
Baked pie shell, 1
Raisins, ½ cup
Brown sugar, mild
  molasses, or honey, 1 cup

Water, hot, ½ cup
Eggs, 3
Flour, ⅓ cup
Cinnamon, 1 teaspoon
Nutmeg, ¼ teaspoon
Ginger, ⅛ teaspoon

Butter, soft, ⅓ cup

Preheat oven to 325°F. Sprinkle bottom of pie shell with raisins; then combine and cook in a double boiler sugar (molasses or honey), hot water, and beaten eggs until thick. Cool and pour ingredients into pie shell. Then sprinkle with cake or cookie crumbs. Combine the rest of the ingredients except for the butter. Alternate sprinkling these ingredients with the crumbs over the top of the pie. Dot with butter before the addition of crumbs, which should be sprinkled last.

An alternate pie is one named after one of the most interesting of murderers, a greatly inventive genius who took out several patents before his apprehension. Holmes referred to him as, "my old friend."

Charlie Peace Peach Cream Pie

Pastry

Flour, sifted, 2 cups
Salt, 1 teaspoon
Shortening, chilled, ⅔ cup

Water, cold, about 6
  tablespoons
Butter, 2½ tablespoons

Sift flour and salt. Using a pastry blender or 2 knives, coarsely cut in half the remaining shortening until particles are about the size of peas. Sprinkle water, 1 tablespoon at a time, over the small portions of the mixture; with a fork, press the flour particles together as they absorb the water. Do not stir. Toss aside pieces of dough as formed and sprinkle remaining water over dry portions. Use only enough water to hold the pastry together. It should not be wet or slippery. Press all together lightly with the fingers, or wrap dough in waxed paper and press together gently. Bear in mind that the less the dough is handled, the more tender and flakey the pastry will be. Chill dough. Roll pastry into an oblong ⅛ inch thick.

Dot surface with butter. Roll up as for jelly roll. Roll out again into an oblong and fold in sides to make three layers. Fold in ends the same way, making in all nine layers. Wrap in waxed paper and chill thoroughly. When ready to use, roll out into an oblong about ⅛ inch thick again. *Makes two 9-inch pastry shells, one 9-inch 2-crust pie, or 8-10 4-inch tart shells.*

Filling

Sugar, ⅔ cup

Cornstarch, 3½ tablespoons

   (or flour, 5 tablespoons)

Salt, ½ teaspoon

Milk, 2½ cups

Egg yolks, slightly-beaten, 3

Vanilla, 1 teaspoon

Peaches, sliced, fresh or

   canned, 12-15 slices

Use one-half above pastry recipe, making one 9-inch pastry shell. Combine sugar, cornstarch or flour, and salt in the top of a double boiler; stir in cold milk. Cook over boiling water until thickened, stirring constantly. Cover and cook 15 minutes longer. Stir in a little of the hot mixture into lightly-beaten eggs; add to remaining mixture in double boiler and cook for 2 minutes over hot, not boiling, water, stirring constantly. Cool and add vanilla. Arrange peaches in pastry shell. Pour in cream filling. (You may alternately place fruit on top of filling.) Top with whipped cream, if desired.

THE ADVENTURE OF THE CREEPING MAN
Sunday, 6 September-Monday, 14 September-
Tuesday, 22 September
1903

"In all our adventures, I don't know that I have seen a more strange sight."

—Dr. Watson

In this adventure, Professor Presbury injects serum that is purported to be a rejuvenant. For it seems that he has fallen in love with a lady young enough to be his daughter. In his enthusiastic infatuation with her, his desire gets the best of his sense, and he uses an experimental solution made from monkey hormones. According to Holmes, the serum has given the man ape-like characteristics. Therefore, he creeps about, climbs trees in reckless abandon, and teases his faithful dog, who smells the monkey in the professor and finally attacks him. As has been pointed out by Mr. D. Martin Dakin, this story smacks more of a curiosity of Robert Louis Stevenson than a true adventure of Sherlock Holmes.

More than likely, Watson made up the case to fill in a slack time in his friend's career and then sold it to a gullible story editor. If, however, Holmes was beginning to believe that an injection of monkey hormones could make so drastic a change in human nature, it is indeed time that he "disappeared into that little farm" of his dreams.

Creeping Man Crêpes

Flour, sifted, ½ cup	Milk, ⅔ cup
Salt, ¼ teaspoon	Shortening, melted, 1
Eggs, well-beaten, 2	tablespoon

Sift flour and salt. Combine beaten egg, milk, and shortening; add flour and salt and beat until smooth. Pour enough batter to cover the bottom of a hot greased skillet; tip pan to make the crêpe as thin as possible. Fry until browned on both sides. Keep hot until all crêpes are baked. You will have noted, I hope, that this is not the sweet-freak's recipe with sugar and jelly oozing over the crêpes. This is a truly English recipe in outlook. Instead of jelly, try some gravy (poultry or meat) over the crêpes and roll them up. For the appreciative pallet, substitute ⅔ cup buttermilk and ¼ teaspoon of baking soda for the milk. The crêpes will then take on a most handsome flavor that will not, I am confident, cause you to creep about and be afflicted with ape-like tendencies.

THE ADVENTURE OF THE ENGINEER'S THUMB
Saturday, 7, September-Sunday, 8 September
1889

"Between your brandy and your bandage, I feel a new man."
—Victor Hatherly

Excluding the figure of ex-Professor Moriarty, with sunken eyes and an oscillating, reptilian-like head, one is hard put to find a more nightmarishly drawn character than Colonel Lysander Stark, of infamous memory. Sidney Paget never equalled the dark and brooding, sinister features in any other of his portraitures or characters in the Holmes' cases. Hatherly's thrilling story of entrapment and escape, sans thumb, chills the reader. I have always wondered about the tantalizing reference to the other case brought around by Watson to Holmes called:

Colonel Warburton's Madness

Oil, ½ cup	Tobasco, dash
Onion, chopped, 1	Chili powder
Garlic, minced, 1 clove	Cornmeal, 1 cup
Beef, ground, 1 lb.	Milk,
Salt, 2½ teaspoons	Corn, creamstyle, 1 no. 2½
Tomatoes, no. 2½ can	can

Olives, ripe, pitted, 1 cup

Sauté the onion and garlic in the oil for 5 minutes then add the beef and brown it. Next, add the salt, tomatoes, chili powder and Tabasco. Cover and cook for 15 minutes. Stir in the cornmeal and milk and cook another 15 minutes; stir constantly. Add corn and olives. Pack all this into two greased loaf pans, brush tops with oil and bake in a slow (325°F.) oven for 1 hour. *Serves 8.*

Have a loaf of French bread on hand (make that two loaves) for a nice dinner party, doing this to them:

Conversational Thumb Loaves

Bread, sour dough, 2 loaves	Onion soup mix, dry, 1 package
Butter, softened, ½ lb.	

Split loaves in half, lengthwise; cream the onion soup mix and butter together. Spread this concoction on each cut side of the bread and put the halves back together. Wrap in foil and place in medium (350°F.) oven for 20 minutes. Serve with brandy for everyone.

You might want to substitute the following for the *Colonel Warburton's Madness.*

Hatherly's Herring

This must be made with freshly-caught herring only, split down the back and boned. Cut off head, tail, and fins. Roll in a medium-ground, seasoned Scotch oatmeal (Quaker's will do), pressing a little to make it stick. Fry the herring on both sides in bacon drippings. Serve on portions of *Conversational Thumb Loaves.* Pour over the herring:

Stark's Sauce

Butter, 2 tablespoons
Flour, 2 tablespoons
Stock, fish or chicken, 2
  cups
Mushrooms, chopped, ¼
  cup
Stock, chicken, strong, ¾
  cup

Egg yolk, 1
Cream, 2 tablespoons
Mustard, dry ½ teaspoon (or
  prepared mustard, 1
  teaspoon)
Salt, ¼ teaspoon
Pepper, freshly-ground, ½
  teaspoon

Lemon juice, 1 tablespoon

Melt in top of doubler boiler (not an aluminium one—it will discolor) butter, flour, fish or chicken stock, and stir over low heat until thickened. Add mushrooms and stir in strong chicken stock, then remove from heat. Add egg yolk, mix well with cream. Add mustard, salt, pepper, and lemon juice just before serving.

Another dish on which to use *Stark's Sauce*, for a more informal backyard affair would be:

Lysander's Liver (or He's Got His Gall)

Liver, calf, ¾ lb.
Onions, medium, 4
Bacon, 6 rashers (strips)

Green peppers, 2
Olives, stuffed, as many as
  necessary

If not to be barbequed, preheat broiler. Simmer the liver in boiling water until nearly tender; drain, cut into inch-sized cubes. Quarter the onions and place them in water to separate the sections. Cut the bacon into 1-inch pieces, and also the peppers, after removing seeds and membrane. Alternate on skewers pieces of liver, onion, pepper, bacon, and stuffed olives. Heat a few bacon scraps or butter in a large skillet. Add the filled skewers, move them about while cooking for about 3 minutes. Place them under broiler or on barbeque until bacon is crisp and liver tender. Serve *Stark's Sauce* in individual cups in which to dip the contents of the skewers.

THE CROOKED MAN
Wednesday, 11 September-Thursday, 12 September
1889

"That was the state of things, Watson."
—Sherlock Holmes

Suspected murder in a locked room is a favorite theme of detective writers and it would be expected then, that at least one such case present itself to Sherlock Holmes. There are few other cases that match Watson's verbal portraiture. Prepare your guests for an evening meal which will include the following.

Nancy's Friday-Night Gumbo

Butter, 1 tablespoon
Onion, chopped, ¼ cup
Flour, 2 tablespoons
Tomatoes, strained, 1½ cups
Stock, fish, 4 cups

Okra, thinly sliced, 1 quart
Shrimp, raw, shelled, cleaned, ½ lb.
Crabmeat, raw, cleaned, ½ lb.
Oysters, shelled, 16

Seasoning, to taste

Melt butter in pot, stir in onion and cook until golden. Stir in flour until blended, then add tomatoes, stock, and okra. Break the shrimp and crab into small pieces and add; simmer until okra is tender. Add oysters and seasoning. Serve when oysters are plump. *Serves 8.*

With the soup, serve:

Crooked Man Cracker Crumb Dumplings

Egg, slightly-beaten, 1
Salt, ⅛ teaspoon
Pepper, few grains

Garlic, onion, or celery salt, few grains
Cracker crumbs

To slightly-beaten egg, add seasonings and enough cracker crumbs to make a mixture that will hold its shape. Form into tiny balls; drop into rapidly boiling soup and poach for 10 minutes. Garnish each serving of soup with 3 or 4 dumplings. These can be used in any stew, thick soup, or broth. *Makes about 20-24 dumplings, or enough for 8 servings of soup.*

Color-Sergeant Devoy's Darnes

Preheat broiler and allow ½ lb. salmon steaks or darne, ¾-1 inch thick, per serving. Brush the steaks well with clarified butter. Place rack 6 inches from flame and broil 5 minutes. Baste, turn, baste again, and continue to broil 5-8 minutes. To test the steaks for doneness, see if you can lift out the central bone without bringing any flesh with it. Serve with freshly-grated horseradish. Fill the hollow (from which you have removed the bone) with your choice of a stuffed tomato, a mound of vegetables, or potatoes garnished with parsley.

For dessert, include on your menu:

Royal Mallows Pudding

Sugar, 1 cup
Gelatin, unflavored, 1½
   tablespoons
Water, cold, ½ cup
Boiling water, ½ cup

Egg whites, 4
Vanilla, 1 teaspoon
Crushed sweetened fruit or
   Cointreau

Sift sugar. Soak gelatin in cold water; dissolve it in boiling water. Cool ingredients; whip egg whites and add gelatin to them in a slow stream. Whip the pudding constantly. Add sugar ½ cup at a time. Whip well after each addition; whip in vanilla, and continue to whip until the pudding thickens. Chill at least 4 hours and flavor the custard when it is cold with Cointreau, or serve with crushed fruit.

THE GREEK INTERPRETER
Wednesday, 12 September
1888

"Somehow this case attracts me."
—Mycroft Holmes

This case introduced the exceptionally gifted brother of Sherlock, Mycroft Holmes, who in turn introduced one of the strangest cases ever tackled by his brother. Although Sherlock is superior in mental capacity, Mycroft declines working on cases that take him from his armchair, where the portly genius spends his time at the Diogenes Club or at his post with the government. These dishes would be enjoyed by Mycroft since they are planned to give the cook plenty of time to enjoy a "leisured ease."

Mycroftburgers

Make thin patties of seasoned ground beef. It's best to roll them out between sheets of waxed paper. Between 2 patties, place a slice of your favorite cheese and a slice of onion (red onion works delightfully well here), then pinch the edges together, making sure that they are together quite well. Fry or broil as usual, keeping an eye out for any melted cheese escaping from the patties.

Should the burgers be too "elementary" for your culinary tastes try:

Kratides' Krab Kasserole

Butter, 4 tablespoons
Flour, 4 tablespoons
Milk, 2 cups
Mustard, prepared, 2
  teaspoons
Salt and pepper, to taste
Worcestershire sauce, a
  dash

Egg yolks, unbeaten, 4
Crabmeat, 1 lb.
Mushrooms, browned in
  butter, 1 cup
Lemon juice, 2 teaspoons
Lemon, ½
Bread crumbs
Cheese, Parmesan, grated

Cream the butter, flour, and milk. When thickened, add seasonings. Gradually stir in the egg yolks and crabmeat, then the mushrooms. Pour into individual casseroles or ramekins. Sprinkle crumbs and cheese on top, baking in a moderate (375°F.) oven for 15 minutes. Just before serving, squeeze half of lemon so that some juice is sprinkled on each ramekin. Serve with a light white wine. *Makes 4 servings.*

For dessert:

Sophy's Sand Tarts

Brown sugar, 1¼ cups
Butter, ¾ cup
Egg, 1
Egg yolk, 1
Vanilla, 1 teaspoon
Lemon rind, grated, 1
  teaspoon

Flour, sifted, 3 cups
Salt, ¼ teaspoon
Egg white, 1
Sugar
Almonds, split, blanched

Sift sugar, beat butter until soft, and combine with sugar until soft and creamy. Beat in egg, egg yolk, vanilla, and lemon rind. Sift flour and salt. Sift the flour and salt gradually into the butter mixture until the ingredients are well blended. The last of the flour may have to be kneaded by hand. Chill dough for several hours. Preheat oven to 400°F. Roll the dough until extremely thin. Cut into rounds and brush the tops of cookies with egg white. Sprinkle generously with sugar and garnish with almonds. Bake on greased sheets for about 8 minutes.

THE SIGN OF FOUR
Tuesday, 7 February-Friday, 10 February
1888

"Sherlock Holmes was never at fault, however."
—Dr. Watson

We are introduced to Dr. Watson's (first? second?) wife, Miss Mary Morstan, who brings to his and to Sherlock Holmes' attention the strange affair of the Sholto family and all its strange and detailed convolutions. This day we will celebrate with a tea.

Jonathan's Small Dip

Cheese, Cheddar, ¾ lb.
Cheese, Roquefort or
  Gouda, ¼ lb.
Butter, 2 tablespoons
Worcestershire sauce, ½
  teaspoon

Mustard, dry, ½ teaspoon
  (or prepared mustard, 1
  tablespoon)
Salt, ¼ teaspoon
Garlic, crushed, ½ clove
Beer or ale, 1 cup

Combine all ingredients and melt together over heat. *Makes 3 cups.*

Serve to accompany the dip:

Tonga's Toasted Sticks in Rings

Bread, sliced
Butter, melted
Egg, beaten, 1

Cheese, grated, 1½ cups
Chili sauce, 1 tablespoon
Cayenne, a dash
Sesame seeds (optional)

Cut very soft slices of fresh bread in narrow strips, the length of the slice after trimming the crust. Using a donut cutter, cut other slices in rings. Fit two or three strips of bread into each ring, as the hole allows; brush with melted butter. To the beaten egg add the cheese, chili sauce, and cayenne pepper. Spread mixture on the sticks and rings of bread. If desired, sesame seeds may be sprinkled at this point. Bake in a moderate (375°F.) oven until lightly browned, about 10 minutes.

You might also serve this:

Hot Sign of the Four-Cross Buns

Milk, scalded, 1 cup	Cinnamon, ¾ teaspoon
Shortening, part or all	Compressed yeast, 2 cakes
butter, ⅓ cup	Water, lukewarm, ¼ cup
Sugar, ½ cup	Flour, sifted, about 5 cups
Salt, 1½ teaspoons	Eggs, beaten, 2

Raisins or currants, ½ cup

Combine scalded milk, shortening, sugar, salt, and cinnamon; cool to lukewarm. Soften yeast in lukewarm water, add a pinch of sugar to the yeast to develop the culture; stir and combine with cooled milk mixture; add about half the flour; add the beaten eggs and beat well. Add enough of the remaining flour to make a soft dough; mix thoroughly. Turn out on a lightly-floured board and knead about 10 minutes, or until smooth and satiny. Place dough in a warm, greased bowl; brush surface very lightly with melted shortening; cover and let rise in a warm room for about 2 hours or until doubled in bulk. When the dough is light, turn out on lightly-floured board; lightly knead in raisins or currants. Shape into balls about 2 inches in diameter, or a little smaller; place in a greased square pan (8 × 8 × 2 inches). Brush with diluted egg yolk; cover and let rise about ¾ hour, or until doubled in bulk. Bake in a moderate (375°F.) oven about 30 minutes.

Confectioner's Frosting

Sugar, confectioner's, 1 cup	Vanilla or almond flavoring,
Water, hot, or milk, about 1	½ teaspoon
tablespoon	

Gradually add hot water to confectioner's sugar, or milk, until the frosting has a good spreading consistency; add flavoring. For a bit more flavor, add 2 teaspoons of rum instead of vanilla or almond extract. When buns are cool, spread four crosses of frosting on each bun. Sprinkle lightly with confectioner's sugar, if desired.

THE ADVENTURE OF THE RED CIRCLE
Wednesday, 24 September-Thursday, 25 September 1902

"Dear me, Watson, this is certainly a little unusual."
—Sherlock Holmes

The fearsome Neapolitan secret society of the "Red Circle" is brought to New York by the brute Giuseppe Gorgiano, and Gennaro and Emilia Lucca become fugitives from its grasp. Living in London, they are followed by the licentious Gorgiano who is under contract to kill them both for fleeing without committing a murder. For the final results of the case, read the rest of the story on your own. As for what concerns us now, read on.

Attenta Antipasto

On platters to be passed around, or on individual plates serve any combination of the following: anchovies, salami slices, cotto slices, cucumber and green pepper sticks, sardines, smoked salmon, smoked herring, bologna, pepperoni, Canadian bacon, linguini, cheese-stuffed celery sticks, stuffed leeks, *Radix Pedis Diaboli Eggs* (see "The Adventure of the Devil's Foot"), pickled oysters, smoked oysters. Almost any vegetable, fish, or meat that can be eaten cold is suitable for the antipasto course. Follow it with:

Pericolo Pepper Pot

Honeycomb tripe, 1 lb.
Veal knuckle, 2 lbs.
Water, cold, 3 quarts
Peppercorns, ½ teaspoon
Thyme, ⅛ teaspoon
Salad oil, 1 tablespoon
Onion, sliced, ¾ cup
Carrots, diced, 1 cup
Celery, diced, ⅓ cup

Green pepper, diced, ½ cup
Flour, 2 tablespoons
Salt, 1 tablespoon
Macaroni, broken in small
   pieces, ½ cup
Parsley, minced, ¼ cup
Condensed tomato soup, 1
   can (1⅓ cups)

Cut tripe into tiny cubes, then place it with veal knuckle and water in kettle. Cover and bring slowly to a boil; remove scum that forms at the top, then reduce heat. Add peppercorns and thyme; cover and simmer genlty for 3 hours; strain, saving tripe and veal knuckle for later. Return stock to the kettle. Boil uncovered until reduced to 2 quarts. Melt oil in skillet, add onion, carrots, celery, and green pepper; cook about 5 minutes or until vegetables are soft but not browned. Add flour, stirring until well-blended. Stir into stock. Add salt, macaroni, and parsley; cook gently about 15 minutes or until vegetables and macaroni are tender. Remove meat from veal knuckle, dice and return with tripe to stock. Add tomato soup. For a more peppery flavor add ¼ teaspoon pepper. *Makes 6 servings.*

Serve with crusty long loaves of French sour dough bread spread with garlic butter.

Note: ½ cup cream may be substituted for the tomato soup.

For dessert serve:

Red Circle Wine Gelatin

Gelatin, unflavored, 3
   tablespoons
Water, cold, ½ cup
Boiling water, ¼ cup
Sugar, ½ cup
Orange juice, 1¾ cup

Lemon juice, 6 tablespoons
Wine, heartily flavored, 1
   cup
Red food coloring, a few
   drops (optional)
Whipped cream

Soak gelatin in cold water and then dissolve in boiling water. Stir until sugar is dissolved; taste and stir in additional sugar if needed. Cool, then add orange juice, lemon juice, wine. Add food coloring if desired. Pour into a round ring mold; chill until firm and serve with whipped cream.

Note: If the wine is not strong, use less water and increase the amount of wine accordingly.

SILVER BLAZE
Saturday, 25 September-Tuesday, 30 September
1890

"Is there any other point to which you wish to direct my attention?"
—Inspector Gregory

This is one of two cases in which is found a great example of what has been termed "the Sherlockismus," showing that Holmes knew the advantages of negative evidence. In this adventure which takes us near the vicinity of the Great Grimpen Mire and its echoes of the Hound of Hell, Holmes solves the disappearance of the race horse, "Silver Blaze" in a somewhat dubious manner that has found him accused of fixing a race to his own profit. Now you can race and fix an easy and tasty dessert.

Dog in the Nighttime Chocolate-Chip Droppings

Butter, ½ cup
Brown sugar, ½ cup
Sugar, ½ cup
Egg, 1
Vanilla, ½ teaspoon

Flour, 1 cup plus 2
 tablespoons
Salt, ½ teaspoon
Baking soda, ½ teaspoon
Semi-sweet chocolate chips, ½ cup

Preheat a moderate (375°F.) oven. Cream butter, add sugars, and beat until creamy. Beat in egg and vanilla. Sift flour, soda, and salt; stir into mixture. Stir chocolate-chips into the batter, then drop the batter from a teaspoon well apart, on a greased cookie sheet. Bake for about 10 minutes. *Makes 45 cookies.*

THE HOUND OF THE BASKERVILLES
Tuesday, 25 September-Saturday, 20 October
1888

"Really Watson you excell yourself."
—Sherlock Holmes

The most famous of all the adventures of the Sacred Writings deserves a special celebration. You might proceed with a large party or perhaps a more intimate dinner for a few people. Proceed with the plans you desire and raise a toast to that good old s.o.b., the hound of the Baskervilles! A punch for a party celebration might be in this:

Hellish Hound Punch

Mix in a punch bowl:

Rum, light, 2½ bottles	Vermouth, dry, 2½ cups
	Creme de cassis, 2½ cups

Add block of ice then add over the ice 2 quarts carbonated water.

Note: Remember that the word "bottle" here means a fifth or 25 oz.

For your dinner, try these:

Baskerville Creole

Kidneys, beef, 2	Onions, small, chopped, 4
Flour, ¼ cup	Green peppers, chopped, 2
Salt, ½ teaspoon	Tomato juice, 2 cups
Pepper, ⅓ teaspoon	Salt, 1 teaspoon
Bacon, chopped, 12 rashers	Pepper, ¼ teaspoon
(strips)	Bay leaf, small piece

Prepare kidneys by washing them thoroughly, removing the membrane; split through center and remove fat and large tubules. Soak in salted water for ½-1 hour, or marinate in well-seasoned French dressing. Combine flour, ½ teaspoon salt and ⅓ teaspoon pepper. Cut kidneys in ½-inch slices and roll in the seasoned flour. Brown bacon slightly in heavy skillet. Pushing bacon to one side, add kidney slices and cook until meat is browned on all sides. Add onions and green peppers and continue cooking until lightly browned. Add the tomato juice and salt, pepper, and bay leaf. Cover tightly and simmer about 30 minutes. Serve on toast. *Makes about 6 servings.*

Stapleton's Stuffed Steak

Flank steak, 2 lb.	Bread crumbs, soft, as
Salt, 1 teaspoon	needed
Pepper, ¼ teaspoon	Water, stock, or tomato
Bacon, diced, ¼ lb.	juice, ½ cup
Onions, medium, finely	Milk, enough to moisten
chopped, 2	ingredients

Score steak; wipe with cloth; sprinkle with salt and pepper. Prepare stuffing by sautéing bacon and onions until lightly browned; remove fat; add crumbs. Spread thin layer of stuffing on steak. Roll lightly, fasten with skewers or tie with string. Brown meat on all sides in fat or in hot (400°F.) oven. Place on a rack in a roasting pan; add liquid; cover tightly and roast in slow (300°F.) oven for about 2 hours, or until tender. *Serves 4.*

THE FIVE ORANGE PIPS
Thursday, 29 September-Friday, 30 September 1887

"I think Watson, . . . that of all our cases we have had none more fantastic than this."

—Sherlock Holmes

The Ku Klux Klan raised its ugly head in London with the introduction of John Openshaw in the sitting room at 221B. His narrative of the singular occurrences at his home directs Holmes to the ship *Lone Star.* Unfortunately, the ship was lost at sea before Holmes could catch up with the culprits and another swift justice was left to deal with the murderers. John Openshaw arrived after 6 P.M. so we may surmise he might have been offered something on the order of:

Clark Russell's Fine Sea Clam Canapes

Clams, fresh or canned, 1 cup

Mayonnaise, about 1 tablespoon

Salt and pepper, to taste

Chili sauce, drained, 2 teaspoons

Bread, cut in rounds, 18-24 slices

Cheese, mild, grated, 4 tablespoons

Pimiento, diced, for garnish (or paprika)

Drain the clams and chop. Add enough mayonnaise to hold together; season with salt, pepper, chili sauce. Toast rounds of bread on one side; spread clam mixture on untoasted side. Sprinkle with cheese and garnish with bits of pimiento or a dash of paprika. Heat under broiler until cheese is melted and lightly browned. Serve hot. *Makes 1½-2 dozens canapes.*

After John Openshaw left, we can assume that Holmes and Watson sat down to a supper of perhaps the following:

Crisscrossed K.K.K. Potatoes

Cut medium-sized baking potatoes in half, lengthwise. With a knife score the underside in a crisscross fashion, about a quarter of an inch deep. Mix a little salt and dry mustard with butter, allowing 1 tablespoon for each potato-half you use. Spread this on the potatoes, baking them as usual, anywhere between 350°-475°F., for 1 hour until they turn a crisp brown color.

Lone Star Stuffed Ham Steaks

Sweet potatoes, cooked, mashed, 1 cup

Bread cubes, toasted, 3 cups

Celery, finely-chopped, ⅓ cup

Onion, finely-chopped, ¼ cup

Sausage links, 4

Salt, ¾ teaspoon

Poultry seasoning, ¾ teaspoon

Butter, melted, 1½ tablespoons

Center cut ham steaks, fully cut, ½ inch thick, 2

Combine sweet potatoes, bread cubes, celery, and onion. Cut sausage links into ½-inch pieces; brown and add to the mixture. Blend in salt, poultry seasoning, and butter. Slash butter around ham steaks to prevent curling and place 1 steak in a greased baking dish. Spread with stuffing. Top with remaining steak. Cover and bake in preheated slow (325°F.) oven for 30 minutes. Remove cover and bake for 30 minutes longer. *Makes 6 portions.*

Orange Pips Sauce

Sugar, 1 cup

Salt, ¼ teaspoon

Cornstarch, 2 tablespoons

Flour, 1 tablespoon

Orange juice, 1¼ cup

Lemon juice, ½ cup

Water, ½ cup

Butter, melted, 1 tablespoon

Orange rind, grated, 1 teaspoon

Lemon rind, grated, 1 teaspoon

In a saucepan, combine sugar, salt, cornstarch, and flour; then stir in orange and lemon juices and water. Cook over a low flame, stirring constantly unitl boiling. Boil for 3 minutes; remove from flame. Sitr in butter and orange and lemon rinds just before serving. Pour over steaks.

Put 5 orange pips in an envelope, mark it with a K.K.K. and send it to some one you are not too fond of.

THE MUSGRAVE RITUAL
Thursday, 2 October
1879

"I have taken to living by my wits."
—Sherlock Holmes

The Musgraves are an old family, dating back some hundreds of years in England. The scion of the house, an old school-fellow of Holmes' named Reginald, called upon him for professional advice concerning odd occurrences of late at his home. His butler, Brunton was missing, the second housemaid Rachel Howells had lost her sanity, and tied up in all of it seemed to be an old family observance called the Musgrave Ritual. Holmes rode out with Musgrave and ultimately solved the third case of his career with some startling results.

Prepare a picnic lunch to include the following:

Brunton's Burger Banquet

Press ground beef into ⅛-pound patties. Grease a hot skillet with bacon fat. On each of 4 patties, place 2 strips crisply cooked bacon, crumbled smoked oysters, minced onions, and a slice of cheese. Place another pattie on top and bind with a strip of partially cooked bacon, fastened with a toothpick. After cooking, place on bread, hamburger roll, or muffins (described below) spread with horseradish mustard, mayonnaise, or French dressing. *Makes 4 sandwiches.*

Musgrave's English Muffins

Water, hot, 1 cup	Water at 85°F., 2
Milk, scalded, ½ cup	tablespoons
Sugar, 2 teaspoons	Flour, 4 cups
Salt, 1 teaspoon	Butter, softened, 3
Compressed yeast, 1 cake	tablespoons

Start with all ingredients at 75°F., then combine hot water, milk, sugar, and salt in a mixing bowl. Let the yeast cake dissolve in 85°F. water for 10 minutes.

Combine the two mixtures and add 2 cups of the flour (sift before measuring). Beat flour gradually into yeast mixture, then cover bowl with a damp cloth and permit the dough to rise in a warm place (about 85°F.) for about 1½ hours, or until it has collapsed back into the bowl. Beat the butter into the dough and beat or knead in the remaining 2 cups flour. Let the dough rise again until it has doubled in bulk. If you desire, you may put dough in greased 3-4 inch rings for final rising, filling them half-full. If not using rings, place the dough on a lightly floured bread board and pat it until it is ¾-1 inch thick. Cut into 3-4 inch diameter rounds, and let stand until doubled in bulk. Cook until light brown on a fairly hot, well buttered griddle (one made of heavy aluminum will needs little greasing). Turn once while cooking, using a pancake turner. Use a rack to cool muffins slightly. Cut, or use 2 forks to pry apart the muffins to butter, and toast under the broiler about 2-3 inches from flame, about 1 minute, or until lightly browned. Served with hamburgers, or for breakfast with a poached egg. *Makes about twenty 3-inch muffins.*

THE PROBLEM OF THOR BRIDGE
Thursday, 4 October-Friday, 5 October
1900

"The faculty of deduction is certainly contagious, Watson."
—Sherlock Holmes

Sherlock Holmes is visited by J. Neil Gibson, the former American Senator and well-known Gold King. Gibson asks Mr. Holmes' assistance to secure the release of a Miss Grace Dunbar, accused of murdering the wife of Mr. Gibson. Watson descends to breakfast to find that Holmes is nearly finished with his meal, which included two hard-boiled eggs and perhaps the following:

Thor Bridge French Toast

Vanilla, ½ teaspoon	Salt, ½ teaspoon (or rum, 1
Eggs, 2	tablespoon)
Milk, 1 cup	Bread, 8 slices
	Cheese sauce, see below

Beat eggs, combine with milk, salt, and vanilla (or rum). Preheat oven to 350°F. Soak bread in egg mixture and then toast on a buttered, ovenproof plate for about 5 minutes. Top with:

Cheese Sauce

Milk, ¼ cup

Cheese, minced or grated,
 ½ lb.

Salt, ½ teaspoon

Cayenne, a dash

Butter, 3 tablespoons

Stir over low heat until smooth. Spread on toast, then return to oven to brown lightly. *Makes 4 portions*, but you may have to make more.

THE ADVENTURE OF THE VEILED LODGER
Monday, 5 October
1896

"Let us renew our energies before we make a fresh call upon them."
—Sherlock Holmes

This story actually only involves Holmes' listening to the story of Eugenia Ronder, a former circus belle, whose face was hideously scarred by a lion, Sahara King, several years before. After counselling her to not contemplate suicide as an alternative to living with so grisly a souvenior of her past indiscretion, he receives a bottle of prussic acid by post, evidence of the woman's resolve to live. Now he can eat in peace. A lucheon meal follows.

Eugenia Ronder's Rarebit

Onion soup, condensed, 1
 can

Cheese, grated, ½ lb. (about
 3 cups)

Mustard, dry, ½ teaspoon

Beer, ⅓ cup (optional)

Cayenne, a dash

To the hot onion soup, add cheese, beer, mustard, and cayenne. Stir over a very low heat until cheese is melted and mixture is smooth. *Makes 4-6 servings*.

Follow it with:

Sahara King Soufflé

Thick White Sauce, 1 cup
Meat, finely chopped, 1 cup

Eggs, separated, 3 or 4

| Carrot, celery, and parsley, raw, finely chopped, ¼ cup | Salt, paprika, nutmeg, lemon juice, Worcestershire sauce, to taste |

Prepare *Thick White Sauce* (see "The Adventure of the Blanched Soldier"). Preheat oven to 325°F. When sauce is smooth and hot, stir in meat and vegetables. When these ingredients are hot, remove from stove and add 3 egg yolks. Season to taste. Let cool slightly. Whip 3-4 egg whites until stiff, but not dry. Fold them lightly into the mixture. Bake in a greased 7-inch soufflé dish until firm, about 40 minutes. Serve a light, dry white wine, or possibly a rosé. *Serves 4.*

THE RESIDENT PATIENT
Wednesday, 6 October-Thursday, 7 October
1886

"This really grows outrageous, Mr. Blessington."
—Dr. Percy Trevalyan

On the morning of 7 October, Dr. Watson was awakened by Sherlock Holmes at half past seven with the news that there was a brougham awaiting to take them to Brook Street to solve the strange affair that had been brought to their attention the day before by Dr. Trevalyan. After finding Mr. Blessington's body hanging from a hook, an apparent suicide, Holmes and Watson go home to breakfast, one that very likely included:

Baker Street Kippers, à la Mrs. Hudson

Preheat broiler; place kippers, skin side down on a hot oiled grill. (Do not try to grill canned kippers, as they are much too wet.) Dot fish with butter and grill 5-7 minutes. They may also be baked in a 350°F. oven for 10 minutes. Season with lemon juice and pepper and serve on *Musgrave's English Muffins* (see "The Musgrave Ritual) or on:

Norah Creina Crumpets

These are essentially the same as the *English Muffins* of "The *Musgrave's* Ritual." The batter is, more liquid, using 2⅔ cups milk in place of the water and milk in the recipe. Greased muffin rings must be used in this preparation. Otherwise follow the same recipe, in all other particulars. This is a typically English breakfast at its best!

THE ADVENTURE OF THE NOBLE BACHELOR
Friday, 8 October
1886

"American slang is very expressive sometimes."
—Sherlock Holmes

Everyone will expect me to include a recipe containing a couple of brace of woodcock and pheasant. However, my co-author has already included a selection of such fowl. Curses! I suppose I can try something else. See below.

Hatty's Herring

Score kippered herring, remove bones, and spread with horseradish mustard (the best U.S. brand is Best Foods in the West, and Hellman's in the East). Sprinkle with buttered bread crumbs or cracker crumbs; heat under the broiler until lightly browned, or add a little milk or cream and bake in a hot (400°F.) oven until liquid is absorbed. Allow 1 kippered herring per serving.

Frisco Frittered Onion Rings

Flour, 1⅓ cups
Salt, 1 teaspoon
Butter, melted, or cooking
   oil, 1 tablespoon
Egg yolks, 2
Flat beer, ¾ cup
Onions, separated into
   rings, 2 cups
Egg whites, 2

Mix in a bowl the flour, salt, butter or oil, and egg yolks. Then add gradually, stirring constantly, the flat beer. Allow the batter to rest covered and refrigerated for at least 3-12 hours or overnight if possible. Add the stiffly beaten egg whites just before using. Dip the onions in the batter; be sure that the surface of the onion rings is as dry as possible for the better adherance of the dough. The resting period is most important for fermentation of the beer into the rest of the batter. The rings may be deep fried or pan fried, with no less than 1½ inch of hot cooking oil.

St. Simon's Cinnamon Snails

Compressed yeast, 1 cake
Sugar, 2 teaspoons
Milk, scalded, 1 cup
Flour, 4½ cups
Butter, melted
Cinnamon

Lard, 7 tablespoons
Sugar, 7 tablespoons
Eggs, beaten, 3

Brown sugar
Dried fruits or raisins
(optional)

Salt, 1 teaspoon

Have all ingredients at 75°F. when working with them. Combine a crumbled cake of yeast with sugar dissolved in milk after scalding it for about 10 minutes. Add lard and stir until melted. Cool. Then combine sugar, eggs, and salt. Stir in the milk mixture and cool to about 85°F. Stir in the yeast mixture and flour. Beat the dough about 5 minutes. Place in a foil covered bowl in the refrigerator overnight. Take out just before baking. When the dough has doubled in bulk, roll it on a floured board to the thickness of ¼ inch. Spread generously with melted butter, sprinkle with cinnamon and brown sugar. If desired, you can add seedless raisins, chopped citron and/or grated lemon rind. Roll the dough like a jelly roll; cut into 1-inch slices. Rub muffin tins generously with butter and sprinkle well with brown sugar. Place each roll firmly on bottom of muffin tin. Permit to rise in a warm place for ½ hour. Bake in a preheated oven (350°F.) for about ½ hour. *Makes 12 muffins.* If there is any left over, you can freeze it.

THE ADVENTURE OF THE SECOND STAIN
Tuesday, 12 October-Friday, 15 October
1886

"What you say is perfectly logical, Mr. Holmes."
—Lord Bellinger, Prime Minister of Great Britain

A greatly secret document of state has disappeared. The Premier and the European Secretary have come to Holmes to beg his assistance in trying to locate it before a state of war breaks out among the nations of Europe. Holmes finds it, naturally, except that it had been purloined by a party whom one would not expect to have taken it. Holmes refers to this case as being "the crowning glory of my career, and it must be conceded that his deductive powers are very much in evidence as he traces the culprit and returns the pivotal letter to the safekeeping of the government. It is believed because of the facts given by Watson who tries to disguise the date and year of this adventure, that the only possible time it could have taken place was during the primiership of Lord Salisbury. Therefore we can discount the name used by Watson as "Bellinger" and read "Salisbury" throughout.

That is providential, for the entrée for dinner tonight is:

Lord Salisbury's Steak

Beef, ground, 1 lb.	Butter, 2 tablespoons
Salt, 1 teaspoon	Flour, 2 tablespoons
Pepper, ¼ teaspoon	Curry powder, 1 teaspoon
Mushrooms, chopped,	Water, 1 cup
drained, one 4 oz. can	Bouillon, beef, 1 cube

Mix meat, salt, and pepper, shape into 4 patties. Pan fry in lightly greased skillet until of desired doneness. Remove from skillet and keep hot. Cook mushrooms in butter for 2 or 3 minutes. Blend in flour and curry powder. Add water and bouillon cube, cook until smooth and thickened. Pour over meat patties and serve. *Makes 4 portions.*

Try meat covered with this sauce:

Second Stain Savoury Sauce

Bacon, diced, ½ lb.	Tomatoes, whole, pack
Onion, ½ cup	style, no. 3 can, (3-4 cups)
Celery, ½ cup	Tomato paste, 1 can
Garlic, finely-chopped, 2	Salt, 2 teaspoons
cloves (optional)	Pepper, ¼ teaspoon
Green pepper, chopped, ½	Bay leaf, small piece
cup	Cayenne, dash

Brown bacon; remove from skillet, reserving fat; drain. To bacon fat, add onion, celery, garlic, and green pepper. Cook until lightly browned, stirring frequently. Add salad oil for additional fat if needed. Add tomatoes, tomato paste, seasonings, and cooked bacon. Simmer over low heat about 1½ hours or until thickened. One-half cup of red wine may be added to the sauce just before serving.

For the sake of the hostess (or whomever is doing the wash) I hope that there is not a first stain, so that there will be no second stain on any of the good house linen. A full-bodied bread with a fine crustiness should be served with this entrée (French or sour dough). A hearty red wine is to be served with the meal. A sparkling burgundy or a Bordeaux would be excellent. For dessert:

Lady Hilda's Coffee-Chocolate Custard

Chocolate, ½-1 oz.

Coffee, strong, hot, 1 cup

Milk, scalded, 1 cup

Salt, ⅛ teaspoon

Egg yolks, 2 (or whole eggs, 3)

Sugar, 4-6 tablespoons

This may be done in your blender. Place in blender chocolate, finely cut-up, and coffee; then add milk, sugar, salt, and eggs. Blend this mixture until smooth. To cook, bake in a slow (325°F.) oven for about 20-30 minutes (with homogenized milk, add 10 minutes). To test for doneness, near the edge of the baking dish, insert a knife. If the blade comes out clean, the custard will be solid all the way through when cooled. There is sufficient storage heat in the baking dish to finish the cooking process. Remove from oven and place on a rack to cool.

Note: Should you test custard in center and find it as done as that about the edges, set the dish in ice water at once to arrest any further cooking. If milk is pasteurized, it is not necessary to scald it, but scalding shortens the cooking time. Before placing baking dish in oven, or the individual cups for cooking custard, place them in a pan containing about an inch of hot, but not boiling water.

A CASE OF IDENTITY
Tuesday, 18 October-Wednesday, 19 October
1887

"A certain selection and discretion must be used in producing a realistic effect.

—Sherlock Holmes

The case to be celebrated today is one of the more outré that were brought to the attention of Sherlock Holmes. Though no actual crime was committed, a slight case of selfishness compounded by greed was ended satisfactorily by Holmes' timely interference.

Watson's Waffles

	4 Waffles	6 Waffles
Egg(s) separated,	1⅓	2
Milk, cups,	2	3
Shortening, melted, tablespoons,	½	1
Flour, cups,	1	1½
Baking powder, teaspoons,	1	2
Salt, teaspoons,	1	1½
Sugar, tablespoons.	4	6

Beat egg yolks; add milk and melted shortening; pour into combined dry ingredients stir just enough to moisten. Fold in egg whites which have been beaten stiff, but not dry. (If using buttermilk, reduce baking powder to ½ and 1 teaspoon (respectively) and add ½ baking soda to dry ingredients.) Bake 4-5 minutes in a moderately hot waffle baker. Serve hot, with melted butter and syrup or any other desired accompaniment.

Note: For those with a slightly sweet tooth, for 6 waffles, add 1 teaspoon sifted cinnamon, ½ teaspoon allspice, ½ teaspoon ground cloves, and ½ teaspoon nutmeg to dry ingredients. Increase sugar to ¼ cup; increase milk by 2 tablespoons.

If you don't have a sweet tooth, but would like something different with your waffles, try cutting lean strips of bacon to fit sections of the grids. Place one piece on each section of grid. Close cover and bake for 1 minute before adding batter. Serve with scrambled eggs, if so desired.

After breakfast, for lunch, or a midafternoon snack, try:

Hosmer Angels on Horseback

Wrap strips of bacon around small oysters; fasten with toothpicks. Place in a shallow baking pan and bake in a hot (400°F.) oven until bacon is crisp. Serve hot.

THE RED-HEADED LEAGUE
Saturday, 19 October-Sunday, 20 October
1889

" . . . you are, as I understand, richer by some £30 to say nothing of the minute knowledge which you have gained on every subject which comes under the letter A."

—Sherlock Holmes

The pawnbroker, Jabez Wilson, has come to Baker Street with a problem vastly different from the usual. The league of Red-Headed Men had employed him for eight weeks, when with no warning, he found nailed on the door of his office this placard:

The Red-Headed League

is

Dissolved

October 9, 1890*

After Holmes and Watson read this and burst out laughing, they agreed to take the case and find out that Wilson's assistant is an old adversary with whom Holmes had had two little affairs and skirmishes. A lunch before Holmes asks Watson back in the evening to stand vigil for John Clay is in order.

The Red-Herring Leek Sandwich
(official lunch of the Red-Headed League)

Drain marinated red herring and place the fillets on a square of toast. Cover with thin slices of leek (or of Bermuda onion). Spread mustard and ketchup (or any other sandwich-spread you wish) and serve with a special beverage:

The Jabez Julep
(official drink of the Red-Headed League)

Mint, fresh, 1 sprig	Angostura bitters, a dash
Sugar, powdered	Mint leaves, medium, 6
Grenadine, 2 teaspoons	Bourbon, 2 oz.

Whiskey, a scant oz.

If you find this date at odds with the date up top it is because Watson or his proofreader mixed up his dates, as usual.

Chill a 14-16 oz. glass or silver mug. Wash and partially dry a long sprig of fresh mint, and dip it in powdered sugar. In a bar glass combine grenadine, angostura bitters, and mint leaves. Bruise the leaves and blend all ingredients. Pour in bourbon and stir again. Remove glass from chilling, pack it with ice, and strain the mixture into the glass. With a bar spoon, churn ice and add whiskey and a dash more grenadine for color. Top with a cherry or two. *Makes 2 drinks.*

Then enjoy:

John Clay's Cherry Custard
(official dessert of the Red-Headed League)

Egg yolks, beaten, 4   Maraschino cherry juice,
Sugar, ⅔ cup   1 cup
Cherry halves, for garnish

Preheat oven to 300°-325°F. Mix egg yolks, sugar, and cherry juice. Bake as directed in "The Adventure of the Second Stain" for *Lady Hilda's Coffee Chocolate Custard.* You might want to add, before baking, ½ teaspoon vanilla and grate nutmeg over the top. After removing from oven, garnish with cherry halves and serve. *Makes 4 portions.*

THE ADVENTURE OF THE GOLEDEN PINCE-NEZ
Wednesday, 14 November-Thursday, 15 November
1894

> *"By George, it's marvelous!"*
> —Inspector Stanley Hopkins
> (in an ecstasy of admiration)

More an affair of the heart than the murder case it begins with, this adventure is another in which the deductive prowess of Sherlock Holmes is brought to fore with the remarkable analysis of the pince-nez spectacles that were snatched from the face of the woman who accidentally killed the young assistant of Professor Coram. Holmes and Watson would have returned to Baker Street in time for dinner.

Yoxsley Old Place Leftover Meat Surprise

French bread (sour dough,
  if possible), 1 loaf
Processed cheese spread,
  mild, 1 jar
Leftover meat, sliced or
  chopped (fried crumbled
  hamburger works)

Mushrooms, sliced, 2 small
  cans
Oregano, 1½ teaspoons
Green onion, chopped, ¾
  cup
Olive (or salad) oil, 4
  tablespoons

Tomato sauce, 1½ cans

Spread a large sheet of aluminum foil on a cookie sheet, cupping the edges
so the juice won't run out, or use a shallow baking pan. Slice loaf of bread
lengthwise and place the two halves, cut side up, in the pan. Spread the next five
ingredients, in order listed above, on bread, being sure to spread the cheese clear
to the edge all over, so that the bread will be prevented from becoming soggy.
Spoon tomato sauce on top, dribble the oil over all, place in slow (325°F.) oven
for 20 minutes. *Serves 6.*

Mrs. Hudson is apparently not going to very much trouble tonight, so then,
neither should you. Serve the preceding recipe with easy to fix vegetables and:

Professor Coram's Leftover Potatoes

Bacon drippings, 2
  tablespoons or more
Potatoes, boiled, sliced,
  cold, 2 cups

Salt and pepper, to taste
Paprika, ¼ teaspoon
Onion, minced, 1 teaspoon
  or more

Melt bacon drippings in a skillet, adding potatoes, salt, ground pepper,
paprika, and onion. Sauté the potatoes slowly until they become light brown.
Turn frequently, until done and serve. *Makes about 4 portions.*

THE ADVENTURE OF THE DYING DETECTIVE
Saturday, 19 November
1887

"Three days of absolute fast does not improve one's beauty, Watson."
Sherlock Holmes

If you are familiar with this adventure, you know that Holmes runs on deliriously about oysters, recipes for which I do not need any prodding to relate. Those for whom oysters hold no mystery, may turn to the next page. The walruses and carpenters among you may read and salivate. Cook them up and enjoy!

1796 Scalloped Diseased Coolie Oysters à la DeForeest

Oysters, 1 pint
Saltines, or Ritz crackers,
   crushed, 2 cups
Crackers, whole, about 18

Salt, to taste
Cayenne, to taste
Oyster liquor and milk,
   about ½-¾ cup

Butter, ¼ lb.

Drain and reserve liquor from oysters. If oysters are large, cut in two or more pieces. Crush saltines and melt the butter (slowly), mixing in cracker crumbs. Thickly butter a baking dish (about 9" × 9" × 2"), laying whole crackers over the bottom. Lay all the oysters on top of this and sprinkle with salt and cayenne. Cover with crushed crumb mixture and add liquor (add milk if necessary) to cover bottom of pan to ¼ inch deep. Bake about 20 minutes in 350°F. oven. *Serves 4-6.*

Shall the World Be Overrun by Oysters Pie

Oysters, 1½ pints
Oyster liquor and milk, 1½
   cups
Butter, 3 tablespoons
Celery, thinly-sliced, ½ cup
Onion, grated, 2
   tablespoons
Flour, 3 tablespoons

Carrots, cooked, diced, 1
   cup
Parsley, finely-chopped, 2
   tablespoons
Salt, 1 teaspoon
Pepper, ½ teaspoon
Rich Biscuit Topping,
   1 recipe

Drain oysters, reserving liquor. To the liquor, add enough milk to measure. Heat butter, add celery and onion. Cook over low heat for about 5 minutes; blend in flour. Slowly add milk and liquor; cook over low heat, stirring constantly until thickened. Add carrots, parsley, oysters, and seasonings pouring mixture into greased casserole (about 1½ quart-capacity). Cover with biscuit topping (see "The Adventure of Shoscombe Old Place"). Bake in hot (400°F.) oven 25-30 minutes or until browned. *Makes about 6 servings.*

Note: Plain pastry cut in fancy shapes may be substituted for biscuit topping.

Serve with a dry white Rhine wine, whichever of the above recipes you decide using. Serve with scalloped potatoes and vegetables of your choice.

THE ADVENTURE OF THE SUSSEX VAMPIRE
Thursday, 19 November-Saturday, 21 November 1896

"Such things do not happen in criminal practice in England."
—Sherlock Holmes

A man finds his wife bending over the crib in which their newly born baby is sleeping. She looks up at him horrified, and he then sees blood on her lips. Looking down at his son, he sees two tiny pricks in the boy's neck, surrounded by blood. So then we begin supper with:

Stuffed Vampire Peppers

Beef, or other ground meat, 1 lb.
Onion, grated, 1 tablespoon
Celery, finely-chopped, ⅓ cup

Cooked rice, 1½ cups
Salt and pepper, to taste
Green peppers, 6

Brown beef slightly, stirring to keep meat in separate particles. If the meat is lean with very little fat, add oil. Add onion and celery; cook about 5 minutes longer, or until vegetables are soft. Add rice and season to taste. Moisten with a little *Bloody Sauce* (described below). Wash green peppers, cut a slice from the top, clean out seeds and white seed parts, leaving a clean shell. Place peppers in boiling salted water and boil 5-8 minutes, or until almost tender. Drain. Stuff each pepper, not too full, so that the stuffing will not break through the shell. Before baking, cover with *Bloody Sauce* (described below), although the sauce is optional. Place peppers in shallow baking dish containing enough water to cover bottom of dish about ¼ inch. Bake in moderate (375°F.) oven for 25-30 minutes, or until browned. *Serves 6.*

Bloody Sauce

Salad oil, 3 tablespoons

Onion, finely-chopped, ½ cup

Garlic, finely-chopped, 1 clove

Tomatoes, canned or stewed, 2½ cups (no. 2 can)

Chili powder, 1 teaspoon

Sugar, 1 teaspoon

Bay leaf, small piece

Cloves, ground, ⅛ teaspoon

Salt, 1 teaspoon

Pepper, ¼ teaspoon

Heat oil in heavy skillet; add onion and garlic. Simmer about 5 minutes or until soft, but not browned. Add remaining ingredients and continue cooking over low heat 40-50 minutes, or until thick. *Makes about 2 cups.*

It is in this case that mention is made of the case of the Giant Rat of Sumatra. So in honor of my sister Helen, who was born on the anniversary of that adventure (a story for which the world is not yet prepared, according to Dr. Watson), I suggest the following to serve with the *Vampire Peppers:*

Giant Rat Peppered Rare Roast Beef

Thoroughly rub soy sauce over entire suface of beef about 1 hour before roasting. Place beef in deep pan or baking dish and pour Worcestershire sauce over it, then sprinkle onion bits, garlic powder, and coarse, freshly-ground pepper on it. Cook as usual for a rare roast, at 325°F., allowing 30 minutes per pound when under 5 pounds. If over 5 pounds, cook at 335°F., allowing 20 minutes per pound.

Serve a sparkling burgundy with this dinner, and expect to have a bloody good time.

THE ADVENTURE OF THE BRUCE-PARTINGTON PLANS
Saturday, 21 November-Monday, 23 November
1895

"In all your career you have never had so great a chance to serve your country."

—Mycroft Holmes

With all Europe an armed camp, the vital plans to a submersible boat fall into the hands of Oberstein, a top German spy. Mycroft Holmes rushes to his brother's flat on Baker Street to tell him of the disappearance, not only of the plans but of a junior agent for the government, Cadogan West. Sherlock discovers the answer to the mystery in the underground, the English subway system. When Mycroft arrives, breakfast is served in his honor with:

Eggs Mycroft

Eggs, hard-boiled, 6
Butter, 3 tablespoons
Flour, 1 teaspoon
Salt, ½ teaspoon
Paprika, ¼ teaspoon
Parsley, finely-chopped, 1
   tablespoon

Chives, finely-chopped, 1
   teaspoon
Lemon juice, ½ teaspoon
Water, 2 tablespoons
Boiled ham, broiled, 6 slices
Toast, buttered, 6 slices

Remove whites from eggs, taking care to keep the yolks whole; chop whites. Melt butter; add flour, salt, and paprika and stir 'til smooth. Add chopped egg whites, parsley, chives, lemon juice, and water; stir over low heat until well blended and heated throughout. Place each slice of broiled ham on a slice of crisp buttered toast; top with one of the whole egg yolks; surround yolks with egg white mixture. *Serves 6.*

Baker Street Underground Kippers

Kippers, poached or
   steamed, 2-3 cups
Potatoes, boiled, thinly
   sliced, 2-3 cups
White sauce, 2 cups

Lemon juice, 2 tablespoons
Thick sour cream, ½ cup
Bread crumbs, buttered, ½
   cup
Cheese, grated, ½ cup

Flake fish coarsely; arrange fish and potatoes in layers in a greased casserole. Prepare white sauce (see "The Adventures of the Blanched Soldier") and combine with lemon juice and sour cream; pour over potatoes and fish. Sprinkle with grated cheese and buttered crumbs. Bake in moderate (375°F.) oven for about 25 minutes, or until browned. *Makes about 6 servings.*

THE ADVENTURE OF THE MISSING THREE-QUARTER
Tuesday, 8 December-Thursday, 10 December
1896

"Excellent Watson! You are scintillating this morning."
—Sherlock Holmes

A young college man named Cyril Overton asks Holmes to find three-quarters of his rugby team who have disappeared, before the big game. Holmes and Watson are a bit befuddled when Overton expects that they know the lad to whom he was refering, but they both get over that and trace the missing team captain to . . . well read the story and find the solution for yourself. To start the day before starting on the case, Holmes begins with:

Cyril Pop-Overtons

Flour, sifted, 1 cup   Milk, 1 cup
Salt, ½ teaspoon   Shortening, melted, 1
Eggs, 2 (if small, use 3)   tablespoon

Popovers are not as hard to make as many people had thought awhile back. This recipe is streamlined to fit some simplified ideas. Sift flour and salt. Beat eggs with a rotary beater until light and thick. Add flour and salt and 1 cup of the milk; continue to beat slowly until all the flour is moistened—about 30 seconds. Gradually add remaining milk and melted shortening, beating until the mixture is free from lumps—1-2 minutes. Fill greased custard cups, or muffin tins, a little less than half full. Bake in a hot (425°F.) oven for about 40 minutes. Serve at once. *Makes 6-8 large popovers.*

To add a bit of something special, try these variations: Place diced crisp bacon in pans which have been greased with bacon drippings, before adding batter. Bake as directed. Bits of sausage (cooked of course) may also be used.

With either of the above ideas, you may try this: After preparing popovers as directed, fill the baked popovers with creamed eggs, vegetables, fish, chicken, or ham.

If you plan to have the *Pop-Overtons* according to the standard recipe, serve them with:

Finnan Haddie à la Mrs. Martha Hudson

Finnan haddie, 1 (for sauce)
Milk, to cover fish
Thick White Sauce, ⅔ cup
Egg, hard-boiled, 1
Green pepper, finely
   chopped, 1

Pimiento, chopped, 1
   teaspoon
Finnan haddie, 2 lbs.
Cream, 1 cup
Butter, 4 tablespoons
Onions, chopped, ½ cup

Paprika, ½ teaspoon

In a skillet, barely cover the finnan haddie (smoked haddock) with milk and soak for 1 hour. Bring slowly to a boil, then simmer for 20 minutes and drain. Flake and remove skins and bones and place the fish in very hot *Thick White Sauce* (see "The Adventure of the Blanched Soldier," reducing flour to 2½ tablespoons and butter to 2 tablespoons). If, after flaking, there is 1 cup of fish, use ⅔ cup cream sauce, adjust according to the amount of fish you have after flaking. Add hard-boiled egg, green pepper, pepper, and pimiento for each cup of flaked fish (or any portion of a cup). Stir and blend well. Set sauce aside and keep warm. Preheat oven to 350°F. Soak the haddock in warm water for ½ hour, skin side down. Pour off water. Place fish on greased, ovenproof pan, cover with cream; dot generously with butter, sprinkle with onions and paprika. Bake for 40 minutes. (If cream evaporates, use more.) After removing from oven cover with cream sauce and serve. *Makes 6 portions.*

Note: If you desire, delete the haddock flakes from the sauce (along with the accompanying steps involved), but serve the sauce and other ingredients over the fish.

THE ADVENTURE OF THE BERYL CORONET
Friday, 19 December-Saturday, 20 December 1890

> *"Holmes, here is a madman coming along."*
> —Dr. Watson

Thus begins the case of the missing coronet, thought by the person to whose care it was entrusted, one Mr. Alexander Holder, to have been taken by his son Arthur. The man had burst upon Watson and Holmes in the morning of a very cold winter day, with the snow lying all about the area. It is from that very snow that Holmes got one of the deciding clues as to who did take the noble diadem and to where it was taken. This cold, blistery morning, let us begin with:

Coronested Eggs

Variation # *1*

In a greased muffin pan line each cavity with very soft bread. Place in the broiler for about 2 minutes, until it turns golden brown. Remove from heat and break 1 egg into each cavity, add salt, and 1 teaspoon of milk to each egg. Dot with butter and garnish with chopped chives. Bake for 8-10 minutes in a moderate oven (350°F.). After removing, set circular strips of bacon on each; place a dark grape inside bacon ring, and serve.

Variation # *2*

Beat 2 egg whites until very stiff. Heap them into a greased ovenproof dish. Make two cavities an equal distance apart, not too near the edge. Slip into each cavity 2 unbroken egg yolks. Bake for 10 minutes or until the eggs are set, at 350°F. Season with salt and white pepper, garnish with chopped chives, and fasten strips of bacon around with toothpicks set on top as above. *Makes 1 or 2 servings.*

Variation # *3*

Preheat oven to 325°F. Sauté or broil as many strips of bacon as you will need per eggs cooked. Grease the bottom of muffin pans and line the sides, in a circular fashion, with bacon. Place 1 tablespoon chili sauce into each pan; then drop in 1 egg and pour 1 teaspoon melted butter over each egg. Sprinkle with salt and paprika, then bake for 10 minutes or until the eggs are set. Carefully turn them out onto rounds of toast. You might try a ring of pineapple with a dark grape in the middle.

Note: You might try adding cooked mushrooms, chopped tomato, small bits of leftover meat or hash, sausage, or anchovy. Actually, you can be as creative as you want with any of these recipes, so don't be afraid to experiment.

THE ADVENTURE OF THE BLUE CARBUNCLE
Tuesday, 27 December
1887

"I am not retained by the police to supply their deficiencies."
—Sherlock Holmes

The battered billycock brought 'round by Peterson, the commissionaire, provides the basis for some of Sherlock Holmes' most extraordinary deductions, including how he can tell that the wife of Henry Baker (to whom he deduced ownership of the hat) has ceased to love him, how Mr. Baker was once well off, but has come down in life, and how the gas has been turned off at Mr. Baker's home, among others. The Countess of Morcar's fabulously rare blue carbuncle has been stolen and found by the same commissionaire in the goose he found lying next to the hat. Holmes traces the real culprit and lets him go after scaring him half to death, since he realizes that he was not cut out to be a thief and that once inside prison, he would more than likely become a jailbird for life. "Besides, it is the season of forgiveness."

Roasted, Stuffed Goose

Any good cookbook has a recipe for roast goose, even this one. (You'll find it in the first section of this book on page 46.) To give it a particularly Sherlockian aspect, however, you might want to hide a blue marble in the stuffing and award a prize to the person who breaks his tooth on discovering it. I shall, however, give you recipes for something else that can be served with your fowl. Be sure to ask the butcher if it was a bar-tailed goose and accept no substitutes!
Serve with these delights:

Countess Crescents

Milk, scalded, 2 cups
Shortening (part or all
    butter), ¼ cup
Sugar, ¼ cup

Salt, 1½ teaspoons
Compressed yeast, 2 cakes
Water, lukewarm, ¼ cup
Flour, sifted, 5-6 cups

Combine scalded milk, shortening, sugar, and salt; cool to lukewarm. Soften yeast in lukewarm water; stir and combine with cooled milk mixture; add about half the flour; beat well. Add enough of the remaining flour to make a soft dough. Mix thoroughly. Turn out on a lightly-floured board and knead about 10 minutes, until smooth and satiny. Place dough in warm, greased bowl; brush surface very lightly with melted shortening. Cover, let rise in warm place (80-85°F.) until doubled (about 2 hours). Turn out and shape one-fourth of the mixture into circles about 9 inches in diameter. (Mark with cake or pie tin to obtain an exact circle.) Cut into 10 or 12 wedge-shaped pieces and roll each, jelly roll fashion, beginning at round edge. Place on greased baking sheet with point of dough on the bottom, curving each roll into a crescent shape on the baking sheet. Brush with milk, melted shortening (butter), diluted egg whites, or yolks. Bake in moderate (375°F.) oven for 15-20 minutes.

Serve with vegetables and salad of your choice, and cranberry sauce, relish plate (including a variety of pickings), and the following:

Commissionaire Peterson's Plum Pudding

Bread crumbs, fine, dry, 5½ cups

Salt, 2 teaspoons

Brown sugar, 1½ cups

Cloves, ground, ½ teaspoon

Nutmeg, 1 teaspoon

Milk, scalded, 1½ cups

Eggs, well-beaten, 12

Beef suet, ground, 1 lb.

Raisins, seedless, 2 cups

Currants, 2 cups

Apples, chopped, 1½ cups

Lemon peel, candied, chopped or thinly sliced, ½ cup

Orange peel, candied, chopped or thinly sliced, ½ cup

Citron, candied, chopped or thinly sliced, ½ cup

Cherries, candied, chopped or thinly sliced, ½ lb.

Orange rind, grated, 2 tablespoons

Cider, or brandy, ½ cup

Combine bread crumbs, salt, brown sugar, and spices. Stir in the hot milk; cool. Add suet, fruits, and cider or brandy. Mix well. Turn into 2 greased 2-quart molds. Cover and steam 6 hours, putting 1 inch water in a steamer or covered roasting pan or kettle. Place the mold on a rack and cover the steamer. Use medium or high heat until steam escapes, then reduce to low. Steaming should be steady, but light.

Serve a deep Rhine wine, or a light Sherlockian Chablis, to be daringly different; Champagne might be welcome also.

Acknowledgments

The record would be incomplete if I did not express my humble thanks to these greatly talented people, all of whom helped me immensely:

Mr. William S. Baring-Gould, author, of *Sherlock Holmes of Baker Street*, (Clarkson N. Potter, 1962), *The Annotated Sherlock Holmes* (Clarkson N. Potter, 1967), whom I'm sorry I never met.

Dr. Julian Wolff, Commissionaire, The Baker Street Irregulars, editor, *The Baker Street Journal*, who has always been very kind to me even though I live in Los Angeles.

Mr. & Mrs. DeForeest B. Wright, for cooking instructions, Mr. & Mrs. DeForeest B. Wright, Jr., for recipes, Miss Helen L. Wright, for research, Mr. William T. Wright, for not playing his saxophone too often, who all contributed to this book; who all added to my too limited knowledge of cooking; who have all been long-suffering since the beginning of my Sherlockian studies in 1965; who will now be left in peace until I write my next book.

Mrs. Marina Worden, Miss Ardis Merola, Miss Michele Condrey, Miss Kim Bradford, sources of inspiration, who have always believed in me and whose friendship and love I value highly.

Mr. John Francis Farrell, Jr., my co-author and friend, who allowed me to re-type my entire manuscript two weeks before deadline after I stole his typewriter for eight days, and he still had 125 pages to do. Mr. Frank Shunto, who drew Sherlock's tie under a turnover collar, at my most earnest behest. This is as it should be according to Sidney Paget, who from 1891-1908, illustrated the Holmes stories for the *Strand* magazine and always drew Sherlock's tie that way (unless Holmes was in disguise); he must have known something about it.

INDEX OF RECIPES

CASSEROLES AND STEWS

CEREAL

CHEESE DISHES

CROQUETTES AND
FRITTERS

CUSTARDS, PUDDINGS,
AND GELATINS

DESSERTS

EGGS

FISH AND SEAFOOD

PANCAKES, WAFFLES, AND CREPES

SAUCES

SOUFFLES

SOUPS

TEA FOODS AND CANAPES

VEGETABLES